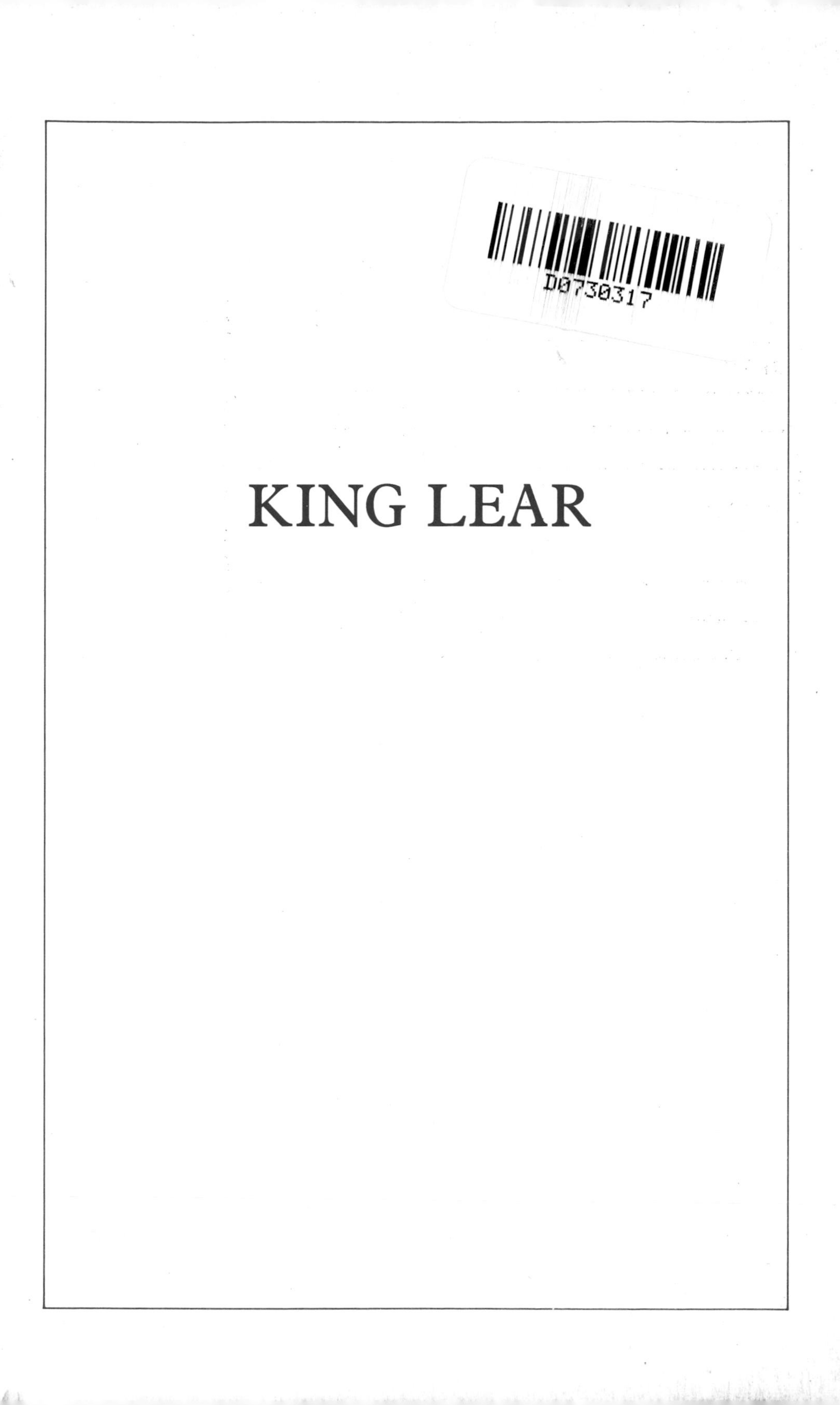

KING LEAR

HBJ SHAKESPEARE

KING LEAR

edited by

Ken Roy

Harcourt Brace Jovanovich, Canada

Toronto Orlando San Diego London Sydney

55 Horner Avenue, Toronto, Ontario M8Z 4X6

HBJ Shakespeare: Series Editor, Ken Roy

Canadian Cataloguing in Publication Data

Shakespeare, William, 1564–1616
King Lear

(HBJ Shakespeare)
For use in high schools.
ISBN 0-7747-1365-8

I. Roy, Ken. II. Title. III. Series.

PR2819.A2R6 1990 822.3′3 C90-093251-1

92 93 94 5 4 3 2

Illustrators: Marika and Laszlo Gal
Cover Illustrators: Marika and Laszlo Gal

Printed in Canada

Acknowledgments

The editor and publisher acknowledge the consultants listed below for their contributions to the development of this program:

G. John Terpstra
English Department Head, City Adult Learning Centre, Toronto Board of Education, Toronto, Ontario

James Welwood
English Teacher, Humberside Collegiate, Toronto Board of Education, Toronto, Ontario

To the Reader

The story of King Lear and his three daughters is a very old one that was related by many writers before Shakespeare used it as the basis for his play. Shakespeare's version of the story, however is a very complex one. It communicates on many levels, appealing both to feelings and to intellect. As you read the play, you will probably notice that you relate in many different ways to the situations and the characters, and to the tensions created by the interplay of the two. You may want to examine parts of the play again to discover what Shakespeare has done with a relatively simple plot.

King Lear is the only Shakespearean tragedy to contain a fully developed sub-plot which runs parallel to, and frequently merges with, the main plot. The sub-plot highlights the play's major themes and underscores a violence and ruthlessness that rivals anything contemporary. As you read, you will encounter motivations of fear, guilt, pride, revenge, greed, and ambition that will bring to mind situations current in television soap operas and the more sensational newspapers. And you will probably find that the issues and questions that the play raises are as relevant to you as they were to Shakespeare's audiences.

Before reading each scene, you will have the opportunity to explore ideas and themes. Your personal experiences may also contribute to your understanding of the play's characters and events. You will be encouraged to discuss and share your opinions co-operatively in small groups. As well, you will have the opportunity to write personal responses in a journal.

Each scene is followed by activities related specifically to that scene. You may choose to pause after each individual scene, a group of scenes, or the end of each act before responding to them. Most of the activities, like the questions before each scene, invite both group and personal responses.

Now that you have some idea about how the play is presented, and about the many ways you might experience it, the overview of major themes of the play that follows will help you get started.

Getting Started

Everyone is familiar with stories in which a situation that initially seems uneventful quickly turns sour: things simply don't turn out the way they are supposed to. Suddenly wrong answers are given to straightforward questions, unreasonable demands are made, loyalties are misinterpreted, actions are directed by greed, and people are falsely accused. In short, the world is turned upside down and the lives of the people caught in these situations are changed forever.

The following activities will help you explore what causes the upheaval of the world in *King Lear*. Discuss some of them in groups before you start reading the play. Use your journal to respond to any you find particularly interesting, thought provoking, or personal. You may wish to refer to these entries and to alter or expand them once you begin reading and discussing the play.

1. You are all probably familiar with the story of Cinderella. Briefly summarize the main points of this story in your journal or notebook. Discuss your version with your group. Revise it if necessary, and keep for future reference.

2. We have all seen, on television news and documentaries, examples of ways in which countries have suffered after political upheaval. With a partner or in a group, discuss some of the details and opinions that you have found in the media. Make a list of your observations and share them with the class. Keep this list for future reference.

3. What do you believe is the state of the traditional family today? What factors do you think caused this condition?

Note your observations in your journal and share some of your less personal ideas with a group. Complete your journal notes by explaining what you think creates a strong family unit.

4. In Shakespeare's time, women did not have the same rights as they do today. With a partner (of the opposite sex) discuss what rights you think women *do* have as opposed to what rights they *ought* to have. Share some of these ideas with the class.

5. When you think you have been unfairly treated, how do you usually respond? Record your thoughts in a journal entry.

6. When you see an adult behave in what you believe to be an unreasonable manner, what course of action do you usually take? What course of action do you think you *should* take in such a situation? In your opinion, if you did take action, would you make any difference in the person's behaviour?

7. Describe a man and a woman who best fulfill your idea of "manliness" and "womanliness." Are the two in any way similar? Discuss your views with a partner.

8. Write a note explaining the difference between taking action to support a decision you have made and seeking revenge on a person who doesn't do what you expect of them.

9. When two people are competing for a job or a position and one is chosen out of favouritism, what is your reaction to: a) the person chosen, and b) the person who does the choosing? How often do you think this situation happens in real life? When it happens, how do you deal with it?

10. Have you ever tried to persuade a person you know that he or she has made a wrong decision? What were the results? Would you do the same thing again?

11. We tend to assume, rightly or wrongly, that adults always make rational decisions. Recall a situation, either real

or from a story, in which this was not the case. What were the results? What advice would you have given the adult(s)? If a similar circumstance occurred in your experience, how would you respond?

12. What is your definition of an egomaniac? What person do you know, either real or from a movie or television, who fits this description? What might you say to the person to help correct his or her behaviour?
13. Have you ever been insulted, or been present when someone was insulted in front of friends? How did you (or the insulted person) feel? What might you say to people who insult others?
14. Do people always get what they deserve? Relate a situation in which someone got more, or less, than he or she deserved. How did you feel about the outcome? Could you have done anything to change it?

Dramatis Personae

(Characters in the Play)

Lear, King of Britain
Goneril, **Regan**, **Cordelia** — Lear's daughters
King of France
Duke of Albany, Goneril's husband
Duke of Cornwall, Regan's husband
Duke of Burgundy
Earl of Kent
Earl of Gloucester
Edgar, Gloucester's son
Edmund, Gloucester's bastard son
Curan, a courtier
An old man, Gloucester's tenant
Doctor
The Fool
Oswald, Goneril's steward
A Captain in Edmund's employ
Gentlemen, a Herald, Servants of Cornwall
Knights in Lear's service, Officers, Messengers, Soldiers, Attendants
Scene: Britain

Act 1, Scene 1

In this scene . . .

The scene begins with Gloucester and Kent discussing King Lear's decision to divide his kingdom. Gloucester introduces his illegitimate son, Edmund, who has been out of the country for nine years.

King Lear, Cornwall, Albany, Goneril, Regan, and Cordelia enter and the division process begins. Lear asks each of his daughters how much they love him. It is on the basis of their answers that he will apportion his lands. The elder daughters, Goneril and Regan, flatter Lear, professing to love him more than anything else in the world. When Cordelia is asked what she can say to receive the largest share of Lear's kingdom, she replies, "Nothing." Her response enrages Lear who immediately disowns and disinherits her. When Kent attempts to intervene on Cordelia's behalf, he is banished.

At this point, the Duke of Burgundy and the King of France enter. Both have been seeking Cordelia's hand in marriage. Once the Duke of Burgundy discovers that Cordelia will not have a dowry, he withdraws his offer of marriage. The King of France, however, accepts her as she is and prepares to take her to his kingdom. In a parting speech, Cordelia condemns her sisters for their hypocrisy.

Left alone, Goneril and Regan discuss what has happened. They have agreed to take turns in accommodating their father and his one hundred knights. Now they are afraid that Lear is mentally unstable and worry that they may suffer from his irrationality as Cordelia has. In order to protect themselves from their father's whims, they agree to work together.

1	*affected:* favoured, preferred, i.e., showed more affection for
2	*Albany:* a part of Scotland that, according to Holinshed's *Chronicles*, extended from "the river Humber to the point of Caithness"
5-7	*qualities:* The mental and moral qualities of the dukes are so evenly balanced that one deserves no more than the other; i.e., each will receive equal shares of the kingdom; *curiosity:* careful examination; *moiety:* share, though not necessarily half
9	*His breeding . . . charge:* I am responsible for his birth.
10	*acknowledge him:* recognize him as my son
11	*brazed:* hardened, accustomed (literally, plated with brass, as in the word "brazen")
12	*conceive:* understand; pun on the word "conception"
16	*smell:* detect; also a sexual pun
17	*issue:* outcome, offspring or children
18	*proper:* handsome, excellent
19-20	*by order of law:* legitimate; *some year/elder:* about a year older (than Edmund)
21	*knave:* boy. Here, the word is used in an affectionate sense rather than a derogatory one.
22	*fair:* beautiful
23	*whoreson:* literally, son of a whore. Here, it is likely used in a good-natured manner.

Act 1, Scene 1

Inside Lear's palace.

Enter Kent, Gloucester, and Edmund, in rear.

Kent: I thought the King had more affected the Duke of Albany than Cornwall.

Gloucester: It did always seem so to us; but now, in the division of the kingdom, it appears not which of the Dukes he values most, for qualities are so weighed 5 that curiosity in neither can make choice of either's moiety.

Kent: Is not this your son, my lord?

Gloucester: His breeding, sir, hath been at my charge. I have so often blushed to acknowledge him that now I am 10 brazed to it.

Kent: I cannot conceive you.

Gloucester: Sir, this young fellow's mother could, whereupon she grew round-wombed, and had indeed, sir, a son for her cradle ere she had a husband for her bed. Do 15 you smell a fault?

Kent: I cannot wish the fault undone, the issue of it being so proper.

Gloucester: But I have a son, sir, by order of law, some year elder than this, who yet is no dearer in my account. 20 Though this knave came something saucily to the world before he was sent for, yet was his mother fair, there was good sport at his making, and the whoreson must be acknowledged.—Do you know this noble gentleman, Edmund? 25

Edmund: [*Advancing.*] No, my lord.

Gloucester: My Lord of Kent: remember him hereafter as my honourable friend.

29 *My services to your lordship:* I am at your service, sir. A polite way of acknowledging an introduction.

30 *sue:* beg, would like

32 *out:* away, out of the country

Stage Direction – *sennet:* a trumpet call; *coronet:* a small crown

35 *Attend:* here, a royal command: wait upon; be of assistance to

37 *we:* the "royal" plural. As king, Lear embodies, or represents, the kingdom as a whole. He stands for "king and country"; therefore, he refers to himself in the plural.

38 *Know:* be informed that

39 *fast intent:* firm intention

42 *crawl:* move slowly

44 *constant will:* fixed purpose or unwavering intention; *publish:* make public, make known to everyone

45 *several dowers:* separate gifts; separate portions of Lear's kingdom

46 *prevented:* stopped (before any strife starts)

47 *rivals:* contestants

48 *amorous sojourn:* amorous visit; time spent at Lear's court for the purpose of wooing Cordelia

50 *divest:* give away

51 *Interest:* legal ownership

53 *largest bounty:* biggest share, greatest reward

54 *Where nature . . . challenge:* to the daughter whose worth will match my natural affection as a father, and will entitle her to the largest portion of my kingdom

56 *than word . . . matter:* than words can ever express

57 *space:* freedom to go where I choose; *liberty:* freedom to think and speak as I please

58 *what:* whatever

59 *grace:* popularity, favour

60 *found:* i.e., in a child

61 *A love . . . unable:* a love that is beyond speech or expression

62 *Beyond all . . . much:* more than all of these comparisons

Edmund: My services to your lordship.
Kent: I must love you, and sue to know you better. 30
Edmund: Sir, I shall study deserving.
Gloucester: He hath been out nine years, and away he shall again. [*Sound a sennet.*]
The King is coming.
[*Enter one bearing a coronet, King Lear, Cornwall, Albany, Goneril, Regan, Cordelia, and Attendants.*]
Lear: Attend the lords of France and Burgundy, Gloucester. 35
Gloucester: I shall, my lord.
[*Exeunt Gloucester and Edmund.*]
Lear: Meantime we shall express our darker purpose.
Give me the map there. Know that we have divided
In three our kingdom, and 'tis our fast intent
To shake all cares and business from our age, 40
Conferring them on younger strengths while we
Unburdened crawl toward death. Our son of Cornwall,
And you, our no less loving son of Albany,
We have this hour a constant will to publish
Our daughters' several dowers, that future strife 45
May be prevented now. The princes, France and Burgundy,
Great rivals in our youngest daughter's love,
Long in our court have made their amorous sojourn,
And here are to be answered. Tell me, my daughters
(Since now we will divest us both of rule, 50
Interest of territory, cares of state),
Which of you shall we say doth love us most?
That we our largest bounty may extend
Where nature doth with merit challenge. Goneril,
Our eldest-born, speak first. 55
Goneril: Sir, I love you more than word can wield the matter;
Dearer than eyesight, space, and liberty;
Beyond what can be valued, rich or rare;
No less than life, with grace, health, beauty, honour;
As much as child e'er loved, or father found; 60
A love that makes breath poor, and speech unable.
Beyond all manner of so much I love you.
Cordelia: [*Aside.*] What shall Cordelia speak? Love, and be silent.

64 *Of all . . . this:* Lear points to areas on a map. Evidently, he has decided on these areas beforehand, and his actions are mere ceremony.

65 *champaigns riched:* fertile fields

66 *wide-skirted meads:* abundant pastures

67 *issues:* children

68 *perpetual:* in absolute possession forever

71 *self metal:* same material or substance

72 *And prize . . . worth:* value myself the same as my sister

73 *my very deed of love:* my love exactly; my love is exactly the same as hers.

74-76 *Only she . . . possesses:* She falls short of expressing my love; the joys that I experience with the most sensitive part of my nature cannot compare with the joy of loving you.

77 *felicitate:* made happy

78 *In your dear Highness' love:* in the love I have for you

80 *More ponderous than my tongue:* My love is heavier than my words.

83 *validity:* value, worth; *pleasure:* ability to give pleasure

85 *least:* smallest

86 *vines . . . milk:* references to the main industries of the two regions

87 *interessed:* interested, closely concerned with

88 *more opulent:* richer, more valuable

92 *Nothing will come of nothing:* a Latin proverb *Ex nihilo nihil fit* – Out of nothing comes nothing

93-94 *I cannot . . . mouth:* I cannot pretend to love you more than I do. (Cordelia's metaphor is better contemplated than explained.)

95 *According to my bond:* according to the duty of a child to a father and a subject to a king

99 *right fit:* as they properly should be

Lear: Of all these bounds, even from this line to this,
With shadowy forests and with champaigns riched, 65
With plenteous rivers and wide-skirted meads,
We make thee lady. To thine and Albany's issues
Be this perpetual.—What says our second daughter,
Our dearest Regan, wife of Cornwall? Speak.
Regan: I am made 70
Of that self metal as my sister,
And prize me at her worth. In my true heart
I find she names my very deed of love,
Only she comes too short, that I profess
Myself an enemy to all other joys 75
Which the most precious square of sense possesses,
And find I am alone felicitate
In your dear Highness' love.
Cordelia: [*Aside.*] Then poor Cordelia!
And yet not so, since I am sure my love's
More ponderous than my tongue. 80
Lear: To thee and thine hereditary ever
Remain this ample third of our fair kingdom,
No less in space, validity, and pleasure
Than that conferred on Goneril.—Now, our joy,
Although our last and least; to whose young love 85
The vines of France and milk of Burgundy
Strive to be interessed; what can you say to draw
A third more opulent than your sisters? Speak.
Cordelia: Nothing, my lord.
Lear: Nothing? 90
Cordelia: Nothing.
Lear: Nothing will come of nothing. Speak again.
Cordelia: Unhappy that I am, I cannot heave
My heart into my mouth. I love your Majesty
According to my bond, no more nor less. 95
Lear: How, how, Cordelia? Mend your speech a little,
Lest you may mar your fortunes.
Cordelia: Good my lord,
You have begot me, bred me, loved me; I
Return those duties back as are right fit,
Obey you, love you, and most honour you. 100
Why have my sisters husbands, if they say

103 *plight:* promise of marriage

106 *To love my father all:* to love my father only

110 *dower:* dowry, the property you take with you when you marry

112 *Hecate:* queen of witches and goddess of darkness

115 *disclaim:* give up, renounce

116 *Propinquity:* closeness of relationship, filial ties – here, father to daughter

118 *this:* my heart; *Scythian:* an ancient tribe of southern Russia, supposed to be particularly brutal

119 *makes his generation messes:* eats his children

122 *Good my liege:* My good lord. Said, likely, in astonishment.

124 *Come not . . . wrath:* Do not step between the fiercest beast and its anger. The dragon was probably Lear's own heraldic device.

125-126 *to set . . . nursery:* to risk everything on the strength of receiving loving care from Cordelia. "To set my rest" was a phrase used in a card game called primero; *Hence and . . . sight:* It is not at all clear to whom Lear directs this command.

128 *Who stirs?:* probably directed at someone who makes a noise and distracts Lear when he is demanding the court's attention

130 *digest:* combine, absorb

131 *Let pride . . . her:* Let her own pride, which she calls frankness or plain speech, be her dowry to attract a husband.

132 *invest you jointly with:* bestow upon you

133 *Preëminence:* authority

133-134 *effects/That troop with majesty:* all the things that go along with kingship

135 *reservation:* a right to; a group of knights especially reserved for Lear

137 *by due turn:* The two daughters, in turn, will have Lear as a guest.

138 *additions:* honours, titles; *sway:* power

139 *Revenue:* income; *execution of the rest:* the carrying out of the remaining royal duties and responsibilities

They love you all? Happily, when I shall wed,
That lord whose hand must take my plight shall carry
Half my love with him, half my care and duty.
Sure I shall never marry like my sisters, 105
To love my father all.
Lear: But goes thy heart with this?
Cordelia: Ay, good my lord.
Lear: So young, and so untender?
Cordelia: So young, my lord, and true.
Lear: Let it be so! Thy truth then be thy dower! 110
For, by the sacred radiance of the sun,
The mysteries of Hecate and the night;
By all the operation of the orbs
From whom we do exist and cease to be;
Here I disclaim all my paternal care, 115
Propinquity and property of blood,
And as a stranger to my heart and me
Hold thee from this for ever. The barbarous Scythian,
Or he that makes his generation messes
To gorge his appetite, shall to my bosom 120
Be as well neighboured, pitied, and relieved,
As thou may sometime daughter.
Kent: Good my liege—
Lear: Peace, Kent!
Come not between the dragon and his wrath.
I loved her most, and thought to set my rest 125
On her kind nursery.—Hence and avoid my sight!—
So be my grave my peace as here I give
Her father's heart from her! Call France! Who stirs?
Call Burgundy! Cornwall and Albany,
With my two daughters' dowers digest the third; 130
Let pride, which she calls plainness, marry her.
I do invest you jointly with my power,
Preëminence, and all the large effects
That troop with majesty. Ourself, by monthly course,
With reservation of an hundred knights 135
By you to be sustained, shall our abode
Make with you by due turn. Only we shall retain
The name, and all th' additions to a king. The sway,
Revenue, execution of the rest,

141 *part:* share

145 *make from the shaft:* avoid the arrow; i.e., do not try to stand in the way of my decision

146 *fork:* double-pointed arrow head which inflicted a more painful wound than a single point

147-148 *Be Kent . . . mad:* Kent may be unmannerly when you behave like a madman; *old man?:* Kent is obviously upset and speaks exceptionally bluntly.

149-151 *Thinkest thou . . . folly:* Do you think that my sense of loyalty to you will make me afraid to speak out when you give up your royal power to those who flatter you? My honour forces me to speak plainly when a king begins to act foolishly. These lines contain six examples of metonymy: *duty, power, flattery, plainness, honour, majesty*. Metonymy is the use of a characteristic or attribute to denote a particular subject. For example, "duty" could be used as a metonym for "loyal subject."

153 *Answer my life my judgement:* I stake my life on my judgement.

156 *Reverb:* reverberate, echo; *hollowness:* both insincerity and loudness

157 *pawn:* in chess, the least important piece. The pawn can be used to protect the most important piece, the king. Here, it is an expression of Kent's total loyalty to Lear.

161 *blank:* white spot in the centre of the target. Kent implies that Lear should listen to his wisest advisor.

162 *Apollo:* Greek god of the sun and the god of order

163 *vassal:* the lowest of servants miscreant: literally, unbeliever; i.e., in the god Apollo because Kent uses the reference "thy gods"

164 *forbear:* be merciful, or understanding

165-166 *Kill thy . . . disease:* Kill your doctor and pay the disease instead. Kent implies that Lear's rash judgement is a symptom of a sickness that the king does not even want to cure.

168 *recreant:* traitor

170 *That:* since

171 *durst:* dared; *strained:* excessive

Beloved sons, be yours; which to confirm, 140
This coronet part between you.
Kent: Royal Lear,
Whom I have ever honoured as my king,
Loved as my father, as my master followed,
As my great patron thought on in my prayers—
Lear: The bow is bent and drawn, make from the shaft. 145
Kent: Let it fall rather, though the fork invade
The region of my heart! Be Kent unmannerly
When Lear is mad. What wouldst thou do, old man?
Thinkest thou that duty shall have dread to speak
When power to flattery bows? To plainness honour's
bound 150
When majesty falls to folly. Reserve thy state
And in thy best consideration check
This hideous rashness. Answer my life my judgement,
Thy youngest daughter does not love thee least,
Nor are those empty-hearted whose low sounds 155
Reverb no hollowness.
Lear: Kent, on thy life, no more!
Kent: My life I never held but as a pawn
To wage against thine enemies, nor fear to lose it,
Thy safety being motive.
Lear: Out of my sight!
Kent: See better, Lear, and let me still remain 160
The true blank of thine eye.
Lear: Now by Apollo—
Kent: Now by Apollo, King,
Thou swearest thy gods in vain.
Lear: O vassal! Miscreant!
[*Reaches for his sword.*]
Albany, Cornwall: Dear sir, forbear!
Kent: Kill thy physician and thy fee bestow 165
Upon the foul disease. Revoke thy gift,
Or, whilst I can vent clamour from my throat,
I'll tell thee thou dost evil.
Lear: Hear me, recreant!
On thine allegiance, hear me!
That thou hast sought to make us break our vows, 170
Which we durst never yet, and with strained pride

172 *sentence:* decree, decision

173 *nor . . . nor:* neither . . . nor; *nature:* temperament; *place:* status as king

174 *potency made good:* royal power asserted; *reward:* punishment

176 *disasters:* accidents or misfortunes

179 *trunk:* body

180 *Jupiter:* used here as one of the gods of wrath

182 *Since thus:* in this manner

183 *Freedom lives . . . here:* To keep my freedom, I must leave Britain. Since banishment means the loss of my freedom, my true banishment is here in Britain where there is no freedom.

186 *large:* noble-sounding; *approve:* confirm

189 *shape his old course:* carry his old ways of speaking plainly; also, direct his life

Stage direction – *Flourish:* a fanfare of trumpets to mark the entry of important people – in this case, an earl, a duke, and a king. The fanfare is sounded by Lear's musicians.

193 *rivalled:* competed for Cordelia's hand in marriage

194 *require:* ask; *present:* immediate; *dower:* dowry

196 *crave:* desire

198 *dear:* both beloved and valuable; *hold:* consider, regard

200 *aught:* anything; *that little seeming substance:* that little creature who seems so genuine but is so false

201 *pieced:* added

202 *fitly like:* be to your complete liking

To come betwixt our sentence and our power,
Which nor our nature nor our place can bear,
Our potency made good, take thy reward.
Five days we do allot thee for provision 175
To shield thee from disasters of the world,
And on the sixth to turn thy hated back
Upon our kingdom. If, on the tenth day following,
Thy banished trunk be found in our dominions,
The moment is thy death. Away! By Jupiter, 180
This shall not be revoked.

Kent: Fare thee well, King. Since thus thou wilt appear,
Freedom lives hence, and banishment is here.
[*To Cordelia.*] The gods to their dear shelter take thee, maid,
That justly thinkest and hast most rightly said! 185
[*To Regan and Goneril.*] And your large speeches may your deeds approve,
That good effects may spring from words of love.
Thus Kent, O princes, bids you all adieu;
He'll shape his old course in a country new. [*Exit.*]
[*Flourish. Enter Gloucester, with France and Burgundy; Attendants.*]

Gloucester: Here's France and Burgundy, my noble lord. 190

Lear: My Lord of Burgundy,
We first address toward you, who with this king
Hath rivalled for our daughter. What in the least
Will you require in present dower with her,
Or cease your quest of love?

Burgundy: Most royal Majesty, 195
I crave no more than hath your Highness offered,
Nor will you tender less.

Lear: Right noble Burgundy,
When she was dear to us, we did hold her so,
But now her price is fallen. Sir, there she stands.
If aught within that little seeming substance, 200
Or all of it, with our displeasure pieced,
And nothing more, may fitly like your Grace,
She's there, and she is yours.

Burgundy: I know no answer.

204	*infirmities:* weaknesses, defects; *owes:* has, suffers from
205	*Unfriended:* without a friend; *adopted to our hate:* accepted only as an object of my hatred
206	*Dowered with our curse:* with only my curse on her as her dowry; *strangered:* made a stranger, or disowned, by my oath
208	*Election makes . . . conditions:* No one can choose under such conditions. Burgundy is withdrawing his offer of marriage.
209	*by the . . . me:* I swear by whatever god made me
210	*For:* as for; *King:* the King of France
211	*I would . . . stray:* I would not stray so far from your friendship.
212	*To:* as to; *match you where I hate:* to have you married to one I hate; *beseech:* beg
213	*To avert . . . way:* to turn your affection to a more worthy woman
214	*wretch:* an outcast; *nature:* a human nature
216	*best object:* favourite
217	*argument:* theme, constant subject; *balm:* comfort
218	*trice:* amount
219-220	*dismantle/So . . . favour:* strip away so many layers of affection; *Sure:* certainly
221	*unnatural:* contrary to what is natural in human behaviour
222	*monsters it:* makes it a monster, or something ugly and abnormal; *fore-vouched:* previously stated
223	*Fall into taint:* become bad, corrupted, or spoiled
223-225	*which to . . . me:* which goes so much against reason that only a miracle could make me believe it
226	*glib and oily art:* the art of using words easily and smoothly
227	*and purpose not:* without meaning what I say
228-235	*that you . . . liking:* I beg you to make it clear that you have not deprived me of your affection because of some crime, but because, I lack the cunning to seek favours constantly and I lack a flattering tongue.
237	*a tardiness in nature:* natural reluctance or slowness
238	*unspoke:* unspoken

Lear: Will you, with those infirmities she owes,
Unfriended, new adopted to our hate, 205
Dowered with our curse, and strangered with our oath,
Take her, or leave her?
Burgundy: Pardon me, royal sir.
Election makes not up in such conditions.
Lear: Then leave her, sir; for by the power that made me,
I tell you all her wealth. [*To France.*] For you, great King, 210
I would not from your love make such a stray
To match you where I hate; therefore beseech you
To avert your liking a more worthier way
Than on a wretch whom nature is ashamed
Almost to acknowledge hers.
France: This is most strange, 215
That she whom even but now was your best object,
The argument of your praise, balm of your age,
The best, the dearest, should in this trice of time
Commit a thing so monstrous to dismantle
So many folds of favour. Sure her offence 220
Must be of such unnatural degree
That monsters it, or your fore-vouched affection
Fall into taint; which to believe of her
Must be a faith that reason without miracle
Should never plant in me.
Cordelia: I yet beseech your Majesty 225
(If for I want that glib and oily art
To speak and purpose not, since what I well intend,
I'll do it before I speak), that you make known
It is no vicious blot, murder, or foulness,
No unchaste action or dishonoured step, 230
That hath deprived me of your grace and favour;
But even for want of that for which I am richer,
A still-soliciting eye, and such a tongue
As I am glad I have not, though not to have it
Hath lost me in your liking.
Lear: Better thou 235
Hadst not been born than not to have pleased me better.
France: Is it but this—a tardiness in nature
Which often leaves the history unspoke

241-242 *mingled with . . . point:* mixed with other motives (the dowry), not connected with the main object (love)

243 *dowry:* gift (of nature or fortune)

244 *but:* just, only; *that portion which yourself proposed:* the original share to be given to Cordelia

249 *Peace be with Burgundy:* a formal dismissal or farewell

250 *respect and fortunes:* calculating desire for wealth

255 *Be:* may it be

257 *inflamed:* passionate; *respect:* a word used in a different sense by Cordelia in the previous speech; here, it means affection

258 *dowerless:* another reference to Cordelia's inheritance, now lost

260 *waterish:* both having many rivers (waters) and weak (morally diluated)

261 *unprized precious:* unappreciated by Lear and Burgundy, but precious to me; *of:* from

262 *though unkind:* though Lear and Burgundy are unkind

263 *here, a better where:* these words are used as nouns. "Where" means a better place or a better station in life (than "here").

270 *jewels:* an ironic reference to Goneril and Regan as Lear's precious possessions; *washed:* both tearful and clear-sighted, in the sense of "washed clear of illusion"

272 *loath:* unwilling, hesitant

274 *professed:* which have professed

That it intends to do? My Lord of Burgundy,
What say you to the lady? Love's not love 240
When it is mingled with regards that stand
Aloof from th' entire point. Will you have her?
She is herself a dowry.
Burgundy: Royal King,
Give but that portion which yourself proposed,
And here I take Cordelia by the hand, 245
Duchess of Burgundy.
Lear: Nothing! I have sworn; I am firm.
Burgundy: I am sorry then you have so lost a father
That you must lose a husband.
Cordelia: Peace be with Burgundy!
Since that respect and fortunes are his love, 250
I shall not be his wife.
France: Fairest Cordelia, that art most rich, being poor;
Most choice, forsaken; and most loved, despised!
Thee and thy virtues here I seize upon.
Be it lawful I take up what's cast away. 255
Gods, gods! 'tis strange that from their coldest neglect
My love should kindle to inflamed respect.
Thy dowerless daughter, King, thrown to my chance,
Is queen of us, of ours, and our fair France.
Not all the dukes of waterish Burgundy 260
Can buy this unprized precious maid of me.
Bid them farewell, Cordelia, though unkind.
Thou losest here, a better where to find.
Lear: Thou hast her, France; let her be thine; for we
Have no such daughter, nor shall ever see 265
That face of hers again. Therefore be gone
Without our grace, our love, our benison.
Come, noble Burgundy.
[*Flourish. Exeunt Lear, Burgundy, Cornwall, Albany, Gloucester, and Attendants.*]
France: Bid farewell to your sisters.
Cordelia: The jewels of our father, with washed eyes 270
Cordelia leaves you. I know you what you are;
And, like a sister, am most loath to call
Your faults as they are named. Love well our father.
To your professed bosoms I commit him;

275 *stood I:* if I stood; *grace:* favour, blessing

276 *prefer:* recommend

278 *Prescribe not us:* Do not dictate to us; *study:* purpose, intention, endeavour

280 *At fortune's alms:* as an act of charity; *You have obedience scanted:* You have neglected obedience (to your father)

281 *And well . . . wanted:* and deserve the lack of affection from your husband that you have shown your father.

282 *unfold:* reveal; *plighted cunning:* cunning that has been concealed by pledges of love

286-287 *appertains to:* concerns; *will/hence:* will leave this place

290 *changes:* whims, quirks

293 *grossly:* too obviously

294-295 *he hath . . . himself:* He has always been impulsive; i.e., he has seldom known his own mind. Goneril expands on this observation in her reply to Regan.

298 *imperfections of long-engraffed condition:* faults arising from long habit

299 *therewithal:* together with the imperfections; *infirm:* senile

300 *choleric:* irritable

301 *unconstant starts:* sudden impulses

304 *hit together:* agree, act together

305 *carry authority:* wields power; *disposition:* attitude of mind

306 *last surrender:* giving up of the throne; *offend:* is simply a nuisance

308 *i' the heat:* immediately. Similar to our expression "strike while the iron is hot."

But yet, alas, stood I within his grace, 275
I would prefer him to a better place!
So farewell to you both.

Goneril: Prescribe not us our duty.

Regan: Let your study
Be to content your lord, who hath received you
At fortune's alms. You have obedience scanted, 280
And well are worth the want that you have wanted.

Cordelia: Time shall unfold what plighted cunning hides,
Who covers faults, at last with shame derides,
Well may you prosper!

France: Come, my fair Cordelia.
[*Exeunt France and Cordelia.*]

Goneril: Sister, it is not little I have to say of what most 285
nearly appertains to us both. I think our father will hence tonight.

Regan: That's most certain, and with you; next month with us.

Goneril: You see how full of changes his age is. The obser- 290
vation we have made of it hath not been little. He always loved our sister most, and with what poor judgement he hath now cast her off appears too grossly.

Regan: 'Tis the infirmity of his age; yet he hath ever but slenderly known himself. 295

Goneril: The best and soundest of his time hath been but rash; then must we look from his age to receive, not alone the imperfections of long-engraffed condition, but therewithal the unruly waywardness that infirm and choleric years bring with them. 300

Regan: Such unconstant starts are we like to have from him as this of Kent's banishment.

Goneril: There is further compliment of leave-taking between France and him. Pray you let's hit together. If our father carry authority with such disposition as he bears, 305
this last surrender of his will but offend us.

Regan: We shall further think of it.

Goneril: We must do something, and i' the heat. [*Exeunt.*]

Act 1, Scene 1: Activities

1. You are preparing a video report on Lear's division of his kingdom for national television news. You must edit your video for a one-minute time slot. Make an outline of segments of the scene, indicating what you will include and also what you will exclude. After careful editing, decide what kind of slant you have given your story. Encourage classmates to help you make your decisions.

2. Discuss with your group or with a partner the advantages of being an older, middle, or younger child – or an only child – in terms of parental favour or support. Use newspaper and magazine articles as back-up for your argument. Alternatively, conduct a survey among your peers to investigate who, if anyone, enjoys preferred treatment. Now see whether your findings are consistent with King Lear's treatment of his daughters.

   If you could have written or spoken to King Lear before he considered the division of his kingdon (lines 37–122), what might you have said to prevent him from making the decisions he did?

3. King Lear states that he has decided to "set" his "rest" on Cordelia's "kind nursery" (lines 125–126). With a partner, discuss what it is, exactly, that Lear means. Decide whether or not it is particularly wise to "set" your "rest" on anyone. If you were Kent, would you, too, have interceded in the proceedings at this point? How could you have done it differently? Is Kent's interjection particularly significant?

4. You are a newspaper reporter based at the court. You are gathering material for a book on King Lear's rule. Write an unofficial account of the banishments of Kent and Cordelia for your own notebook, commenting in particular on Lear's behaviour and on that of the nobles

who witness it. You may even wish to record the general court reaction. Add to your "reporter's notebook" as the play progresses.

5. In groups of three, role-play an interview with Goneril and Regan. The interviewer should try to get the sisters to reveal their true feelings toward their father, their youngest sister, and each other. A list of ten carefully prepared questions should achieve the desired results.

   Write a newspaper or magazine gossip column, using the information you have gleaned from your interview, or present the rehearsed interview to the class.

6. Soliloquies are speeches in which actors talk to the audience about themselves and their intentions. The other characters in the play are either not present or do not hear what is said. Write a soliloquy for Kent in which he reveals his feelings about his banishment. You may wish to write it in modern English. The speech should fit logically into the play and develop from actual events in it. Perform a brief dramatic reading of your soliloquy for your group or for the rest of the class.

7. Create a "map" of Act 1, Scene 1. To do this, first select a quote that you think is particularly significant to the action of the scene, to the setting, or to the revelation of a character or a theme. Now brainstorm with your group for important words, phrases, or impressions that are linked to the quote. Write your responses in clusters or groups that help to show the connections and relationships that are important to the topic you have chosen.

   Post your maps for the rest of the class to see and discuss with the whole class the insights that the maps have given you into the aspect of the play you chose to explore.

8. A playbill is a poster advertising a play. It should contain the title of the play, the names of the better known

members of the cast, the name of the director, dates of performance, the theatre, some pertinent critical quotes, and perhaps an illustration. As a group, create a playbill for a performance of *King Lear* as it might appear in the early 1600s. Remember, the object is to entice people to see the play.

9. In groups, prepare five controversial issue statements about Scene 1, such as "Children must always obey their parents" or "It is always better to say nothing than to say what you believe." Write all your statements on cards and place them in a central box in the class.

   Each student should then select one at random and, in groups, argue either for or against it. All arguments must be based on issues represented in the scene. At the end of each presentation, discuss whether the speaker relied more on emotion than reason to persuade the audience. Were you convinced by the speaker's argument? You may wish to repeat this activity after you have read the whole play.

10. Cordelia seems to be the sincere daughter that every father would hope for. In your journal, give an account of your impressions of Cordelia and the special characteristics that she possesses. As Cordelia, write a letter of explanation to Kent outlining why you behaved as you did in the division scene, lines 37–122.

11. List all the characters you have met in this scene, and note in your journal your impressions of them. You may wish to add to your list as the play progresses. So far, with which character(s) do you most identify and with which do you least identify?

12. The first scene of a play is important for many reasons. Brainstorm, in groups, to decide what you think an effective opening scene should accomplish. Has Shakespeare lived up to your expectations in *King Lear?* What has he done that you didn't expect? What did you expect him to do that he didn't?

13. In his division speech (lines 37–55), King Lear insists on making choices based on favouritism and flattery. In groups, make a list of the possible reasons why Lear would use this method to arrive at such a major decision as the division of his kingdom. Test the items on your list as the play progresses, eliminating those that do not hold up and adding any new ideas that may occur.

For the next scene . . .

We have all at one time or another felt deprived of certain rights. In your journal, list the rights you believe you should be able to take for granted. Of which rights, if any, have you been deprived?

Act 1, Scene 2

In this scene . . .

Edmund, Gloucester's illegitimate son, reveals in a soliloquy that he is intent on removing everything that stands in the way of possessing his father's earldom. Edmund determines that he must win his father's affections and cast suspicion on the character of his half-brother, Edgar. By means of a forged letter, he convinces his father that Edgar is plotting Gloucester's death so that he can claim his inheritance. Gloucester rashly believes Edmund's story, feeling that the world is turning upside down. Gloucester then leaves to await Edgar, who arrives at his father's castle moments later. Edmund convinces Edgar that Gloucester is angry with him and that Edgar should flee the household.

3 *Stand in . . . custom:* be dependent on hateful conventions, put up with conventional laws

4 *curiosity:* nice distinctions (in the sense of false delicacy), squeamishness; *deprive me:* keep me from my rights.

5 *For that:* because; *moonshines:* months

6 *Lag of:* short of; *Why bastard? Wherefore base?:* Why is the term "bastard" attached to me?

7 *dimensions:* proportions; *compact:* put together

8 *generous:* noble; *shape:* figure; *as true:* as true a resemblance to my father

9 *honest:* virtuous; presumably, with the secondary sense of married; *madam's:* woman's; *issue:* child

10 *base? . . . Bastardy?:* Edmund protests against the assumption that because he is illegitimate, he is low and disgusting.

11 *lusty stealth of nature:* the enjoyment of a natural and vigorous sexual life

12 *composition:* completeness, stronger constitution; *fierce:* energetic

13 *within a . . . bed:* a reference to the marriage bed and what goes on there

14 *fops:* fools

15-16 *Well then, . . . land:* Edmund feels that he has justified a claim to what Edgar, Gloucester's legitimate son, will inherit.

17-18 *Our father's . . . legitimate:* Our father loves me as much as he loves Edmund; *Fine word:* but, after all, only a word

19 *speed:* should succeed, bring about the expected results

20 *invention:* plan; *thrive:* prove successful

22 *stand up for bastards:* take the side of, but also (possibly) a sexual pun

24 *Prescribed:* limited, restricted

25 *Confined to exhibition?:* limited to an allowance of money (from Goneril and Regan)

26 *Upon the gad?:* on the spur of the moment

Scene 2

Inside Gloucester's castle.

Enter Edmund the Bastard, a letter in his hand.

Edmund: Thou, Nature, art my goddess; to thy law
My services are bound. Wherefore should I
Stand in the plague of custom and permit
The curiosity of nations to deprive me,
For that I am some twelve or fourteen moonshines 5
Lag of a brother? Why bastard? Wherefore base?
When my dimensions are as well compact,
My mind as generous, and my shape as true,
As honest madam's issue? Why brand they us
With base? With baseness? Bastardy? Base, base? 10
Who, in the lusty stealth of nature, take
More composition and fierce quality
Than doth, within a dull, stale, tired bed,
Go to the creating a whole tribe of fops
Got 'tween asleep and wake? Well then, 15
Legitimate Edgar, I must have your land.
Our father's love is to the bastard Edmund
As to the legitimate. Fine word, "legitimate"!
Well, my legitimate, if this letter speed
And my invention thrive, Edmund the base 20
Shall top the legitimate; I grow; I prosper.
Now, gods, stand up for bastards!
[*Enter Gloucester.*]
Gloucester: Kent banished thus? And France in choler parted?
And the King gone tonight? Prescribed his power?
Confined to exhibition? All this done 25
Upon the gad? Edmund, how now? What news?
Edmund: So please your lordship, none.
[*Puts away the letter.*]

32 *terrible dispatch:* desperate putting away

34 *Come:* Gloucester expects to be given the letter.

35 *spectacles:* Elizabethan gentlemen, but not those of Lear's time, wore spectacles.

37 *o'er-read:* read over

39 *o'erlooking:* looking over

41 *detain:* keep

42 *blame:* blameworthy

45 *essay or taste:* test

46-48 *This policy . . . them:* This custom of revering and respecting the elderly makes life miserable for us when we should be enjoying it most; it denies us our fortune (what we are entitled to; inheritance) until we are too old to appreciate it.

49 *idle and fond:* useless and foolish; *bondage:* oppression, slavery

50-51 *aged tyranny:* tyranny of an older person (Gloucester); *sways:* rules; *not as . . . suffered:* not because he has power so much as because we allow him to

52-53 *If our . . . him:* a thinly veiled suggestion of murder

53 *revenue:* estate, wealth

56-57 *Had he . . . this?:* Could he possibly have written this?

60 *casement:* a French window (a window that opens like a door)

61 *closet:* room

62 *character:* handwriting

63 *matter:* content of the letter; *durst:* would dare

64 *fain:* gladly, willingly

Gloucester: Why so earnestly seek you to put up that letter?
Edmund: I know no news, my lord.
Gloucester: What paper were you reading? 30
Edmund: Nothing, my lord.
Gloucester: No? What needed then that terrible dispatch of it into your pocket? The quality of nothing hath not such need to hide itself. Let's see. Come, if it be nothing, I shall not need spectacles. 35
Edmund: I beseech you, sir, pardon me. It is a letter from my brother that I have not all o'er-read; and for so much as I have perused, I find it not fit for your o'erlooking.
Gloucester: Give me the letter, sir. 40
Edmund: I shall offend, either to detain or give it. The contents, as in part I understand them, are to blame.
Gloucester: Let's see, let's see!
Edmund: I hope, for my brother's justification, he wrote this but as an essay or taste of my virtue. 45
Gloucester: [*Reads.*] "This policy and reverence of age makes the world bitter to the best of our times; keeps our fortunes from us till our oldness cannot relish them. I begin to find an idle and fond bondage in the oppression of aged tyranny, who sways, not as it hath 50 power, but as it is suffered. Come to me, that of this I may speak more. If our father would sleep till I waked him, you should enjoy half his revenue for ever, and live the beloved of your brother."

EDGAR.

Hum! Conspiracy? "Sleep till I waked him, you should 55 enjoy half his revenue." My son Edgar! Had he a hand to write this? a heart and brain to breed it in? When came you to this? Who brought it?
Edmund: It was not brought me, my lord; there's the cunning of it. I found it thrown in at the casement of my 60 closet.
Gloucester: You know the character to be your brother's?
Edmund: If the matter were good, my lord, I durst swear it were his; but in respect of that, I would fain think it were not. 65
Gloucester: It is his.

69 *sounded:* sounded you out, tested your feelings

72-73 *at perfect age:* when fully mature; *declined:* past their best years; *ward:* a person under the care of a guardian

76 *brutish:* animal-like

77-78 *sirrah:* an old term for "fellow" or "sir" which expresses annoyance or impatience; usually addressed to a servant; *appre-/hend:* arrest

78 *Abominable:* hated, unnatural

80 *suspend your indignation:* Control your anger.

82 *you should . . . course:* You would be following a well-designed and safe plan of action; *where:* whereas

84 *make a great gap:* create a breach, undermine

85 *shake in pieces:* destroy; *heart:* spirit; *obedience:* duty as a son; *pawn:* stake, bet

86 *writ:* written; *feel:* test

87-88 *pretence/of danger:* dangerous intention

90 *judge it meet:* think it fit

91-92 *auricular/assurance:* assurance of your own hearing

97-100 *wind/me into him:* Worm your way into his confidence for me; *frame the . . . wisdom:* Carry out the plan according to your own common sense; *unstate:* disinherit, give up my estate; *to be in a/due resolution:* to be sure whether he is innocent or guilty

103 *late:* recent; *eclipses in the sun and moon:* An eclipse of the sun occurred in October 1605, and an eclipse of the moon in September. Scholars use this information in dating the play; *portend:* give warning of

104 *wisdom of nature:* our reasoning powers

105 *reason:* explain; *nature:* our world; *scourged:* punished, afflicted

106 *sequent effects:* results that follow

106-109 *Love cools . . . father:* these are some of the "sequent effects"

Edmund: It is his hand, my lord, but I hope his heart is not in the contents.
Gloucester: Hath he never before sounded you in this business? 70
Edmund: Never, my lord. But I have heard him oft maintain it to be fit that, sons at perfect age, and fathers declined, the father should be as ward to the son, and the son manage his revenue.
Gloucester: O villain, villain! His very opinion in the letter! 75 Abhorred villain! Unnatural, detested, brutish villain! Worse than brutish! Go, sirrah, seek him. I'll apprehend him. Abominable villain! Where is he?
Edmund: I do not well know, my lord. If it shall please you to suspend your indignation against my brother till 80 you can derive from him better testimony of his intent, you should run a certain course; where, if you violently proceed against him, mistaking his purpose, it would make a great gap in your own honour and shake in pieces the heart of his obedience. I dare pawn 85 down my life for him that he hath writ this to feel my affection to your honour, and to no other pretence of danger.
Gloucester: Think you so?
Edmund: If your honour judge it meet, I will place you where 90 you shall hear us confer of this and by an auricular assurance have your satisfaction, and that without any further delay than this very evening.
Gloucester: He cannot be such a monster.
Edmund: Nor is not, sure. 95
Gloucester: To his father, that so tenderly and entirely loves him. Heaven and earth! Edmund, seek him out; wind me into him, I pray you; frame the business after your own wisdom. I would unstate myself to be in a due resolution. 100
Edmund: I will seek him, sir, presently, convey the business as I shall find means, and acquaint you withal.
Gloucester: These late eclipses in the sun and moon portend no good to us. Though the wisdom of nature can reason it thus and thus, yet nature finds itself scourged 105 by the sequent effects. Love cools, friendship falls off,

108 *bond:* obligation of son to father and father to son

109-110 *This villain . . . prediction:* Edgar's actions are consistent with the portent or omen of the eclipse

110-111 *the King . . . nature:* The King (Lear) departs from his own natural tendencies – the love of his child; *bias* refers to the natural curve followed by a bowling ball.

112-113 *best of our time:* best example of our times; *hollowness:* deceit

115 *it shall lose thee nothing:* You have nothing to lose.

118 *foppery:* foolishness, stupidity

119 *surfeits:* results of excesses

120-121 *make guilty . . . stars:* make the sun, moon, and stars guilty of our misfortunes

121-122 *villains on/necessity:* as if we had no choice but to be villains

123 *spherical predominance:* power of the planets

126 *divine thrusting on:* supernatural influence

127 *whoremaster:* a term of contempt suggesting the coarseness of human sexual nature; *goatish:* lustful, lecherous

128 *charge:* responsibility, liability

128-129 *compounded with my/mother:* coupled with my mother (to produce me)

129 *under the Dragon's Tail:* a reference to the position of the moon and the constellation Draco, the Dragon.

131 *that:* what;

132 *maidenliest:* most innocent; *firmament:* starry heavens

134 *Pat:* On the dot, exactly as needed; *catastrophe:* contrived incident completing the plot of a play

135-136 *Tom/o' Bedlam:* name given to those who had been in Bedlam Hospital, the insane asylum of St. Mary of Bethlehem, in London; *divisions:* between brothers

143 *he:* Edmund is thinking of the author of the predictions he mentions.

144 *unnaturalness:* an end of the natural affection between parent and child

145-146 *dearth:* shortage, famine; *dissolutions of ancient ami-/ties:* breaking up of old friendships

brothers divide. In cities, mutinies; in countries, discord; in palaces, treason; and the bond cracked 'twixt son and father. This villain of mine comes under the prediction; there's son against father: the King falls 110 from bias of nature; there's father against child. We have seen the best of our time. Machinations, hollowness, treachery, and all ruinous disorders follow us disquietly to our graves. Find out this villain, Edmund; it shall lose thee nothing; do it carefully. 115 And the noble and true-hearted Kent banished! His offence, honesty! 'Tis strange. [*Exit.*]

Edmund: This is the excellent foppery of the world, that, when we are sick in fortune, often the surfeits of our own behaviour, we make guilty of our disasters the 120 sun, the moon, and stars; as if we were villains on necessity: fools by heavenly compulsion; knaves, thieves, and treachers by spherical predominance; drunkards, liars, and adulterers by an enforced obedience of planetary influence; and all that we are evil 125 in, by a divine thrusting on. An admirable evasion of whoremaster man, to lay his goatish disposition to the charge of a star! My father compounded with my mother under the Dragon's Tail, and my nativity was under Ursa Major, so that it follows I am rough and 130 lecherous. Fut! I should have been that I am, had the maidenliest star in the firmament twinkled on my bastardizing.

[*Enter Edgar.*]

Pat! he comes, like the catastrophe of the old comedy. My cue is villainous melancholy, with a sigh like Tom 135 o' Bedlam. O, these eclipses do portend these divisions! Fa, sol, la, mi.

Edgar: How now, brother Edmund? What serious contemplation are you in?

Edmund: I am thinking, brother, of a prediction I read this 140 other day, what should follow these eclipses.

Edgar: Do you busy yourself with that?

Edmund: I promise you, the effects he writes of succeed unhappily: as of unnaturalness between the child and the parent; death, dearth, dissolutions of ancient ami- 145

146 *divisions in state:* differences of opinion within the country; *maledictions:* curses, false rumours

147-148 *diffidences:* instances of mistrust; *banishment of/friends:* probably a reference to Kent

148 *dissipation of cohorts:* disbanding of soldiers; *nuptial breaches:* breaking up of marriages

150 *a sectary astronomical?:* a follower of astrology

151 *When saw . . . last?:* Edmund answers Edgar's question, but not in a way that Edgar can understand.

158 *Bethink yourself:* think carefully, consider

159 *at my entreaty:* with my strong urging; *forbear his presence:* give up seeing him

160-161 *qualified the . . . displea-/sure:* has softened his anger

161-162 *with/the . . . allay:* that his anger would scarcely be satisfied, even if you were physically harmed

164-165 *That's my fear:* the quick, insincere reply of an easy liar; *continent for-/bearance:* controlled restraint

167 *fitly:* at a suitable time

170 *to the best:* to the best of my ability and knowledge

171 *meaning:* intention

172 *faintly:* only partly, inadequately

173 *the image and horror:* the horrible reality. This is an example of a device called hendiadys, which is the use of two words joined by a conjunction. The phrase ordinarily would be "the horrible image" or "the image of horror."

174 *anon?:* soon, in due time

176 *noble:* honourable

179 *practices:* intrigues; *ride easy:* go easily (as the experienced rider fits the horse's back and rides smoothly and comfortably); *I see the business:* I see the way I must go (to achieve my objectives).

181 *All with . . . fit:* To me everything is fitting and justifiable if I can use it to achieve my purposes.

ties; divisions in state, menaces and maledictions against king and nobles; needless diffidences, banishment of friends, dissipation of cohorts, nuptial breaches, and I know not what.

Edgar: How long have you been a sectary astronomical? 150

Edmund: When saw you my father last?

Edgar: The night gone by.

Edmund: Spake you with him?

Edgar: Ay, two hours together.

Edmund: Parted you in good terms? Found you no displea- 155 sure in him by word nor countenance?

Edgar: None at all.

Edmund: Bethink yourself wherein you may have offended him; and at my entreaty forbear his presence until some little time hath qualified the heat of his displea- 160 sure, which at this instant so rageth in him that with the mischief of your person it would scarcely allay.

Edgar: Some villain hath done me wrong.

Edmund: That's my fear. I pray you have a continent forbearance till the speed of his rage goes slower; and, as 165 I say, retire with me to my lodging, from whence I will fitly bring you to hear my lord speak. Pray ye, go! There's my key. If you do stir abroad, go armed.

Edgar: Armed, brother?

Edmund: Brother, I advise you to the best. I am no honest 170 man if there be any good meaning toward you. I have told you what I have seen and heard; but faintly, nothing like the image and horror of it. Pray you, away!

Edgar: Shall I hear from you anon?

Edmund: I do serve you in this business. [*Exit Edgar.*] 175

A credulous father! And a brother noble,
Whose nature is so far from doing harms
That he suspects none; on whose foolish honesty
My practices ride easy! I see the business.
Let me, if not by birth, have lands by wit; 180
All with me's meet that I can fashion fit. [*Exit.*]

Act 1, Scene 2: Activities

1. In your journal, paraphrase Edmund's theory of nature (lines 1–22). Respond to this soliloquy and discuss your ideas with a group. Decide what the consequences would be if everyone had the same theory. Predict what you think might happen when Edmund puts his theory into action.

2. As a group, decide why Gloucester is so ready to accept that Edgar is conspiring against him. What advice would you give Gloucester at this point in the play? What will you tell him about his perceptions and his role as a father? Present your advice to the class.

3. Gloucester makes a series of predictions in lines 103 to 114. With a partner, make a list of these and determine how many of them have actually occurred. Does this convince you of the validity of Gloucester's philosophy? Write a response to him in which you either agree or disagree with what he believes.

For the next scene . . .

In your journal, recount a situation in which one or more of your acquaintances wished to make someone else in your group of friends feel truly unwanted and outcast. What was done to accomplish this? How effective was it? How did you feel about the tactics used and the outcome? What advice might you give people who employ such measures?

Act 1, Scene 3

In this scene . . .

Goneril is discussing with Oswald, her steward, the difficulties she is having as she plays host to her father and his knights. Because she wants to be rid of Lear as soon as possible, she instructs Oswald to provoke Lear so that his actions will give her a reason to evict him.

1 *chiding:* scolding; finding fault with

4 *By day and night:* constantly; (possibly an oath)

5 *flashes into . . . other:* has outbreaks of impulsive behaviour; *gross:* large, significant; *crime:* offence

7 *riotous:* boisterous and unrestrained. Probably a lie Goneril will use for her own purposes; *upbraids:* complains about, finds fault with

8 *trifle:* matter of slight importance

10 *If you . . . services:* if you serve (Lear) with less attention than before

11 *the fault . . . answer:* I will take the responsibility for your actions.

Stage Direction – *Horns:* The calls sounded on hunting horns were important in keeping the hunt properly organized. Here, the horns are used by Lear to announce his return. He evidently expects to be received royally. Lear, though eighty years of age, is still vigorous enough to hunt.

13 *Put on:* pretend; *what:* whatever; *weary negligence:* neglect (of Lear) because of fatigue

14 *I'd have . . . question:* I want it (this neglect) to be discussed.

15 *distaste:* dislike

16 *Whose mind . . . one:* whose views are the same as mine in this matter

17 *Not to be overruled:* not to be changed by any authority that Lear may attempt to use; *Idle:* foolish

20-21 *Old fools . . . flatteries:* Goneril suggests that Lear is in his second childhood and, like a child, must be treated with restrictions and rebukes as well as flatteries in order to make him behave.

24 *grows:* comes as a result

25 *I would . . . occasions:* I wish to create opportunities (for complaint against Lear) from these contrived grievances.

27 *my very course:* the same course of action that I am taking

Scene 3

Inside the Duke of Albany's palace.

Enter Goneril and Oswald,
her Steward.

Goneril: Did my father strike my gentleman for chiding of
his fool?
Oswald: Ay, madam.
Goneril: By day and night, he wrongs me! Every hour
He flashes into one gross crime or other 5
That sets us all at odds. I'll not endure it.
His knights grow riotous, and himself upbraids us
On every trifle. When he returns from hunting,
I will not speak with him. Say I am sick.
If you come slack of former services, 10
You shall do well; the fault of it I'll answer.
[*Horns within.*]
Oswald: He's coming, madam; I hear him.
Goneril: Put on what weary negligence you please,
You and your fellows. I'd have it come to question.
If he distaste it, let him to my sister, 15
Whose mind and mine I know in that are one,
Not to be overruled. Idle old man,
That still would manage those authorities
That he hath given away! Now, by my life,
Old fools are babes again, and must be used 20
With checks as flatteries, when they are seen abused.
Remember what I have said.
Oswald: Very well, madam.
Goneril: And let his knights have colder looks among you.
What grows of it, no matter. Advise your fellows so.
I would breed from hence occasions, and I shall, 25
That I may speak. I'll write straight to my sister
To hold my very course. Prepare for dinner. [*Exeunt.*]

Act 1, Scene 3: Activities

1. You are a set designer. Design or describe the set you would create for this scene. As a costume designer, how would you dress Goneril and Oswald?

2. It seems that Goneril and Regan have had a recent conversation about their father. Create a dialogue for this conversation. Rehearse your dialogue and present it to the class either as a drama or as reader's theatre – an oral presentation in which the reader's interpretation of the words enables the audience to imagine what happened.

3. As an actor, you have been given the part of Oswald. Decide how you would play this character, based on the information provided in this scene. With a partner as Goneril, role-play the scene for your group or for the class.

4. As Goneril, write the letter that you send to Regan. Have a partner in the role as Regan respond verbally to the contents of the letter.

For the next scene . . .

What do you think a medieval court fool or jester might look like? What sort of costume might the character wear? What role would the person play in a royal court?

Who might be a contemporary version of the court fool? Name as many people as you like, describe what you think their chief function is, and try to identify the source of their popularity.

If you were the fool in Lear's court, and knowing all that has transpired, what kinds of things might you say to him? How do you think he would respond? Write a note in your journal, as a fool, on the nature of your job.

Act 1, Scene 4

In this scene . . .

We discover that Kent has not left England as Lear ordered, but has decided to disguise himself in order to serve the old king. Lear meets Kent, decides that he would make a good servant, and instructs Kent to follow him.

A knight enters and tells Lear about the poor treatment he is receiving at the Duke of Albany's palace. Lear decides to discuss the matter with Goneril. Before he is able to do so, he engages in an angry exchange with Oswald. Kent takes Lear's side by threatening to beat Oswald. At this point, the Fool enters and proceeds to point out to Lear the stupidity of his previous decision to divide his kingdom.

Goneril comes in search of Lear and informs him that, if he is to remain in her household, he must reduce the number of his knights. This enrages Lear who then determines to go with his retinue to Regan. Albany, who seems unaware of what has been going on, enters and hears his wife instruct Oswald to inform Regan of Lear's intended arrival. Although Albany does not approve of Goneril's actions, he does nothing to prevent them.

2 *diffuse:* disguise, cause to be indistinct

2-4 *my good . . . likeness:* I may be able to perform the good purpose for which I disguised myself in the first place.

4 *razed my likeness:* destroyed my appearance. Literally, "razed" means shaved, and is likely a pun on razor as Kent may, in fact, have shaved off his beard.

6 *So may it come:* it may happen that

7 *full of labours:* ready to do any work that needs to be done

Stage Direction – *Horns within:* hunting horns announcing Lear's return

8 *jot:* instant, moment; *Let me . . . ready:* Lear wants instant service and commands as he has always done.

15 *judgement:* the eternal judgement of the soul

16 *to eat no fish:* a phrase with several possible meanings. Kent will ignore fast days. This would indicate that he is not a Roman Catholic but a loyal Protestant (a reference to Elizabethan politics). Kent may also be pointing out that he is not a weakling because he is a meat eater. He may also be making a bawdy, sexual pun.

25 *countenance:* bearing, demeanour

26 *fain:* willingly

28 *Authority:* the attitude of a true ruler. This is not flattery on Kent's part.

Scene 4

Inside the Duke of Albany's palace.

Enter Kent, disguised.

Kent: If but as well I other accents borrow,
That can my speech diffuse, my good intent
May carry through itself to that full issue
For which I razed my likeness. Now, banished Kent,
If thou canst serve where thou dost stand condemned, 5
So may it come, thy master, whom thou lovest,
Shall find thee full of labours.

[*Horns within. Enter Lear, Knights, and Attendants.*]

Lear: Let me not stay a jot for dinner; go get it ready. [*Exit an Attendant.*] How now? What art thou?
Kent: A man, sir. 10
Lear: What dost thou profess? What wouldst thou with us?
Kent: I do profess to be no less than I seem, to serve him truly that will put me in trust, to love him that is honest, to converse with him that is wise and says little, to fear judgement, to fight when I cannot choose, and 15 to eat no fish.
Lear: What art thou?
Kent: A very honest-hearted fellow, and as poor as the King.
Lear: If thou be'st as poor for a subject as he is for a king, thou art poor enough. What wouldst thou? 20
Kent: Service.
Lear: Who wouldst thou serve?
Kent: You.
Lear: Dost thou know me, fellow?
Kent: No, sir, but you have that in your countenance which 25 I would fain call master.
Lear: What's that?
Kent: Authority.

30 *keep honest counsel:* hold my tongue when necessary

30-31 *mar a . . . it:* botch an elaborate story in telling it (by not using fancy words); that is, I'm a blunt sort of fellow.

35-36 *Not so . . . anything:* Kent answers indirectly and indelicately that since he is young enough to be interested in sex, he is not old enough to be foolishly affectionate for other reasons. His answer evidently pleases Lear, who engages him on the spot.

43 *So please you:* Oswald, following Goneril's instructions, ignores Lear's question.

44 *clotpoll:* blockhead, nitwit

45-46 *Where's my . . . asleep:* Lear is impatient. This is the second time he has called for his fool, and there is no response (probably one of Goneril's tactics).

47 *mongrel?:* Oswald

51 *roundest:* bluntest, surliest

55 *entertained:* treated

56 *as you were wont:* as you used to be

57 *abatement:* lessening, decrease

57-58 *general/dependants:* most of the servants

62-63 *for my duty . . . wronged:* because of my loyalty, I cannot be silent in the face of the wrong done to you.

64 *rememberest:* remind or recall

65 *faint neglect:* hardly noticeable neglect, or the weary negligence suggested by Goneril

Lear: What services canst thou do?
Kent: I can keep honest counsel, ride, run, mar a curious tale in telling it, and deliver a plain message bluntly. That which ordinary men are fit for, I am qualified in, and the best of me is diligence. 30
Lear: How old art thou?
Kent: Not so young, sir, to love a woman for singing, nor so old to dote on her for anything. I have years on my back forty-eight. 35
Lear: Follow me; thou shalt serve me. If I like thee no worse after dinner, I will not part from thee yet. Dinner, ho, dinner! Where's my knave? My fool? Go you and call my fool hither. 40 [*Exit an Attendant.*]
[*Enter Oswald the Steward.*]
You, you, sirrah, where's my daughter?
Oswald: So please you— [*Exit.*]
Lear: What says the fellow there? Call the clotpoll back. [*Exit a Knight.*] Where's my fool, ho? I think the world's asleep. 45
[*Enter Knight.*]
How now? Where's that mongrel?
Knight: He says, my lord, your daughter is not well.
Lear: Why came not the slave back to me when I called him? 50
Knight: Sir, he answered me in the roundest manner, he would not.
Lear: He would not?
Knight: My lord, I know not what the matter is, but to my judgement your Highness is not entertained with that ceremonious affection as you were wont. There's a great abatement of kindness appears as well in the general dependants as in the Duke himself also and your daughter. 55
Lear: Ha! sayest thou so? 60
Knight: I beseech you pardon me, my lord, if I be mistaken, for my duty cannot be silent when I think your Highness wronged.
Lear: Thou but rememberest me of mine own conception. I have perceived a most faint neglect of late, which 65

66-67 *mine own jealous curiosity:* my own watchful suspicion; *pretence:* deliberate showing

75 *Who am I, sir?:* Lear expects the reply "The King."

77 *My lord's knave:* Albany's boy or villain. Lear does not refer to Goneril again until she enters (line 184); *whoreson:* This word was used frequently in the rather generalized sense of base or low.

81 *Do you . . . rascal?:* Do you dare to look me in the eye as an equal?

83 *football player?:* Football, an early form of soccer, played by boys in the street in Elizabeth's day, was regarded as a low game and the players were looked on as nuisances. Tripping was perhaps acceptable, as well as tackling, in this rough sport.

86 *differences:* in rank (between king and servant)

87-88 *If you . . . tarry:* Roughly, if you want to be knocked flat again, stay.

88 *Go to:* exclamation of impatience

88-89 *Have you/wisdom?:* Have you sense enough to go (before you are flattened again)?

89 *So:* You have the sense to go (likely said as Oswald retreats).

91 *earnest:* sum paid in advance to make a bargain binding

92 *coxcomb:* the hat worn by professional jesters, red in colour and designed in the general shape of a cock's comb

94 *you were best:* It would be best for you (to take my hat).

96 *For . . . favour:* because you are a fool to support someone who is out of favour

97-98 *Nay, an . . . shortly:* If you cannot go along with prevailing opinion, you are sure to be in difficulty soon.

99 *banished:* Lear has made Goneril and Regan independent by dividing his Kingdom and has therefore "banished" them from his former realm; *on's:* of his

100 *a blessing:* Cordelia is Queen of France, though Lear meant to punish her by banishment.

I have rather blamed as mine own jealous curiosity than as a very pretence and purpose of unkindness. I will look further into it. But where's my fool? I have not seen him this two days.

Knight: Since my young lady's going into France, sir, the fool hath much pined away. 70

Lear: No more of that; I have noted it well. Go you and tell my daughter I would speak with her. [*Exit Knight.*] Go you, call hither my fool. [*Exit an Attendant.*]

[*Re-enter Steward.*]

O, you, sir, you! Come you hither, sir. Who am I, sir? 75

Oswald: My lady's father.

Lear: "My lady's father"? My lord's knave! You whoreson dog! You slave! You cur!

Oswald: I am none of these, my lord! I beseech your pardon. 80

Lear: Do you bandy looks with me, you rascal? [*Strikes him.*]

Oswald: I'll not be strucken, my lord.

Kent: Nor tripped neither, you base football player? [*Trips him.*]

Lear: I thank thee, fellow. Thou servest me, and I'll love thee. 85

Kent: Come, sir, arise, away! I'll teach you differences. Away, away! If you will measure your lubber's length again, tarry; but away! Go to! Have you wisdom? So. [*Exit Oswald.*]

Lear: Now, my friendly knave, I thank thee. 90

[*Enter Fool.*]

There's earnest of thy service. [*Gives Kent money.*]

Fool: Let me hire him too. Here's my coxcomb.

[*Offers Kent his cap.*]

Lear: How now, my pretty knave? How dost thou?

Fool: Sirrah, you were best take my coxcomb.

Kent: Why, fool? 95

Fool: Why? For taking one's part that's out of favour. Nay, an thou canst not smile as the wind sits, thou'lt catch cold shortly. There, take my coxcomb! Why, this fellow has banished two on's daughters, and did the third a blessing against his will. If thou follow 100

101 *thou must needs:* you absolutely must. "Needs" is emphatic.

105-106 *If I . . . myself:* If I gave my daughters all I owned, I'd be a fool (like you); *mine:* my coxcomb; *Beg:* Lear is now in the position of a beggar, totally dependent upon his daughters.

107 *the whip:* The Fool has gone far enough.

108 *must to kennel:* must go outside to the dog-house

109-110 *Lady Brach may . . . stink:* "Lady" was a common name for a hound bitch; "Brach" was a polite term for all hound bitches. Here Lady Brach seems to symbolize flattery or lies. In other words, truth (what the Fool has said) is rejected but flattery and lies are welcomed.

111 *A pestilent gall:* literally, a bothersome or irritating sore (caused by rubbing). However, gall also refers to the secretion of the liver (bile) which is extremely bitter. The comment is likely a reference to Oswald's insolence as well as to the Fool's comments and, perhaps, even to Lear's own deeds.

114 *nuncle:* a contraction of mine uncle, my uncle – perhaps as a child would say it or perhaps a familiar term used by a fool to his master

117 *owest:* ownest (own)

115-124 *Have more . . . score:* a string of wise sayings stressing the importance of common sense over impulsiveness

126-127 *Then 'tis . . . it:* You get no advice from a lawyer without paying him a proper fee. You got nothing because you gave me nothing.

131-132 *so much . . . to:* Since Lear has given away all his land, he can no longer expect to collect rent on it.

140 *for him stand:* stand in his place

137-144 *That lord . . . there:* The Fool suggests that Lear is responsible for his own foolish action. He indicates that he is the "sweet" fool and that Lear is the "bitter" fool.

him, thou must needs wear my coxcomb.—How now, nuncle? Would I had two coxcombs and two daughters!

Lear: Why, my boy?

Fool: If I gave them all my living, I'd keep my coxcombs myself. There's mine! Beg another of thy daughters. 105

Lear: Take heed, sirrah—the whip.

Fool: Truth's a dog must to kennel; he must be whipped out, when the Lady Brach may stand by the fire and stink. 110

Lear: A pestilent gall to me!

Fool: Sirrah, I'll teach thee a speech.

Lear: Do.

Fool: Mark it, nuncle.

Have more than thou showest, 115
Speak less than thou knowest,
Lend less than thou owest,
Ride more than thou goest,
Learn more than thou trowest,
Set less than thou throwest; 120
Leave thy drink and thy whore,
And keep in-a-door,
And thou shalt have more
Than two tens to a score.

Kent: This is nothing, fool. 125

Fool: Then 'tis like the breath of an unfeed lawyer—you gave me nothing for it. Can you make no use of nothing, nuncle?

Lear: Why, no, boy. Nothing can be made out of nothing. 130

Fool: [*To Kent.*] Prithee tell him, so much the rent of his land comes to. He will not believe a fool.

Lear: A bitter fool!

Fool: Dost thou know the difference, my boy, between a bitter fool and a sweet one? 135

Lear: No, lad; teach me.

Fool: That lord that counselled thee
To give away thy land,
Come place him here by me—
Do thou for him stand. 140

146 *that:* the title of fool; i.e., you are a born fool, in the sense of being innocent or naive

148 *fool:* foolish, meaningless

149 *will not let me:* will not let me keep all my foolishness for myself

150 *monopoly:* sole right to deal in foolishness; *they:* the lords and great men; *have part on't:* share in it

152 *snatching:* demanding their share

150-152 *And/ladies . . . snatching:* One of the common court corruptions in Elizabethan times was the granting of monopolies to favoured persons.

152-153 *Nuncle, give . . . crowns:* a riddle

157 *clovest:* split

158 *thou borest . . . dirt:* You acted like a man who carries his donkey instead of riding it.

159 *crown:* top of the head

165 *apish:* imitative; like apes, which imitate

162-165 *Fools had . . . apish:* Fools are never in more disfavour than now, when even wise men have become foolish (foppish); and fools do not know how to behave, since the wise men have so closely imitated them.

167 *sirrah:* used when speaking to servants or social inferiors, or as a term of insult to an equal

168-169 *madest thy/daughters thy mother:* when you put yourself into the charge of your daughters, expecting them to care for you

169-170 *when thou . . . breeches:* when you gave them the stick with which to punish you and took down your own trousers to be whipped

173 *play bo-peep:* play hide-and-seek. The implication is that Lear has covered his eyes as if playing the childhood game, and has put himself among the fools because of his foolish abdication.

176 *fain:* gladly, willingly

177 *An:* if

The sweet and bitter fool
Will presently appear;
The one in motley here,
The other found out there.

Lear: Dost thou call me fool, boy? 145

Fool: All thy other titles thou hast given away; that thou wast born with.

Kent: This is not altogether fool, my lord.

Fool: No, faith; lords and great men will not let me. If I had a monopoly out, they would have part on't. And 150 ladies too, they will not let me have all the fool to myself; they'll be snatching. Nuncle, give me an egg, and I'll give thee two crowns.

Lear: What two crowns shall they be?

Fool: Why, after I have cut the egg i' the middle and eat 155 up the meat, the two crowns of the egg. When thou clovest thy crown i' the middle and gavest away both parts, thou borest thine ass on thy back o'er the dirt. Thou hadst little wit in thy bald crown when thou gavest thy golden one away. If I speak like myself in 160 this, let him be whipped that first finds it so.

[*Sings.*] *Fools had ne'er less grace in a year,*
For wise men are grown foppish;
And know not how their wits to wear,
Their manners are so apish. 165

Lear: When were you wont to be so full of songs, sirrah?

Fool: I have used it, nuncle, ever since thou madest thy daughters thy mother; for when thou gavest them the rod, and puttest down thine own breeches, 170

[*Sings.*] *Then they for sudden joy did weep,*
And I for sorrow sung,
That such a king should play bo-peep
And go the fools among.

Prithee, nuncle, keep a schoolmaster that can teach 175 thy fool to lie. I would fain learn to lie.

Lear: An you lie, sirrah, we'll have you whipped.

Fool: I marvel what kin thou and thy daughters are. They'll have me whipped for speaking true; thou'lt have me whipped for lying; and sometimes I am whipped for 180

181 *holding my peace:* keeping quiet

183 *pared:* cut away, peeled

184 *parings:* cuttings, peelings. The Fool refers to Goneril as one of the "cuttings" of Lear's mind; Regan is the other. Nothing remains of his mind according to the Fool.

185 *frontlet:* frown (a "frontlet" was a band worn around the head)

188-189 *an O without/a figure:* the mathematical symbol (0) that denotes zero or nothing

194 *nor . . . nor:* neither . . . nor; *crum:* crumb. The couplet applies, as usual, to Lear.

196 *a shealed peascod:* a shelled or empty peapod – a quite useless thing, emptied of all value

199 *carp:* complain

200 *rank:* gross, excessive, brutal; *riots:* fights

202 *redress:* correction, satisfaction

204 *protect:* permit; *course:* action; *put it on:* encourage it

205 *allowance:* permission

206 *scape censure:* escape sharp criticism; *nor the redresses sleep:* nor would the remedies fail to be applied

207 *tender:* desire (for); *wholesome weal:* healthy state

208 *working:* working out, outcome

209 *else:* otherwise; *were:* would be

205-210 *which if . . . proceeding:* Goneril implies if you permit riotousness among your knights, I will place the blame squarely on you. My measures to control your men stem from my desire for a healthy state.

211-213 *For you . . . young:* The cuckoo lays its eggs in other birds' nests. Once hatched, the cuckoo outgrows the other young birds by taking most of the food brought by its foster-parents.

213 *it:* its

216-219 *I would . . . are:* Goneril suggests that Lear's moods are more violent than usual.

217 *Whereof I . . . fraught:* which I know you possess

218 *dispositions:* moods

holding my peace. I had rather be any kind o' thing
than a fool! And yet I would not be thee, nuncle.
Thou hast pared thy wit o' both sides and left nothing
i' the middle. Here comes one o' the parings.

[*Enter Goneril.*]

Lear: How now, daughter? What makes that frontlet on? 185
You are too much o' late i' the frown.

Fool: Thou wast a pretty fellow when thou hadst no need
to care for her frowning. Now thou art an O without
a figure. I am better than thou art now: I am a fool,
thou art nothing. [*To Goneril.*] Yes, forsooth, I will 190
hold my tongue. So your face bids me, though you say
nothing.

Mum, mum!
He that keeps nor crust nor crum,
Weary of all, shall want some.— 195

[*Pointing at Lear.*] That's a shealed peascod.

Goneril: Not only, sir, this your all-licensed fool,
But other of your insolent retinue
Do hourly carp and quarrel, breaking forth
In rank and not-to-be-endured riots. Sir, 200
I had thought, by making this well known unto you,
To have found a safe redress; but now grow fearful,
By what yourself too late have spoke and done,
That you protect this course, and put it on
By your allowance: which if you should, the fault 205
Would not scape censure, nor the redresses sleep,
Which, in the tender of a wholesome weal,
Might in their working do you that offence
Which else were shame, that then necessity
Must call discreet proceeding. 210

Fool: For you know, nuncle,
The hedge-sparrow fed the cuckoo so long
That it had it head bit off by it young.
So out went the candle, and we were left darkling.

Lear: Are you our daughter? 215

Goneril: I would you would make use of your good wisdom,
Whereof I know you are fraught, and put away
These dispositions which of late transport you
From what you rightly are.

220 *May not . . . horse?:* Even a fool may see that things are not right when a daughter instructs her father, a king

221 *Whoop, Jug, I love thee:* possibly an allusion to an old song. Jug, in this context, could mean "whore." Jug, in some Elizabethan poems is used to denote the sexual act.

224 *notion:* intellect, understanding; *discernings:* perception

225 *lethargied:* without life or energy, paralyzed; *Sleeping or waking?:* Am I asleep or awake?

228 *marks of sovereignty:* signs by which I know I am a king

229 *false:* falsely

231 *Which:* whom

233-234 *admiration:* pretence of amazement (pretence that he does not know who Goneril is); *the savour/Of:* the same as

240 *Shows like:* looks like; *riotous:* immoral; *Epicurism:* self-indulgence; *lust:* sexual desire

242 *graced:* honourable, gracious, noble

243 *Be then desired:* be requested

244 *else will . . . begs:* otherwise will take into her own hands what she is now requesting

245 *A little . . . train:* to reduce your retinue of knights somewhat

246 *remainders:* those that remain; *depend:* stay on as dependants

247 *besort:* be fitting for, suit

248 *Darkness and devils:* an explosion of rage

249 *train:* followers

250 *Degenerate bastard:* Lear means that Goneril has not only become base, but cannot be his lawful daughter.

252 *strike:* hit; *people:* household servants; *disordered rabble:* disorderly knights

253 *betters:* those who are better than they themselves are. The reference is to Goneril's servants.

254 *Woe that too late repents:* woe to whoever repents (of his action) too late

Fool: May not an ass know when the cart draws the horse? 220
Whoop, Jug, I love thee!
Lear: Does any here know me? This is not Lear.
Does Lear walk thus? Speak thus? Where are his eyes?
Either his notion weakens, or his discernings
Are lethargied—Sleeping or waking? Ha! Sure 'tis not
so! 225
Who is it that can tell me who I am?
Fool: Lear's shadow.
Lear: I would learn that; for, by the marks of sovereignty,
Knowledge, and reason, I should be false persuaded
I had daughters. 230
Fool: Which they will make an obedient father.
Lear: Your name, fair gentlewoman?
Goneril: This admiration, sir, is much o' the savour
Of other your new pranks. I do beseech you
To understand my purposes aright. 235
As you are old and reverend, you should be wise.
Here do you keep a hundred knights and squires;
Men so disordered, so debauched, and bold
That this our court, infected with their manners,
Shows like a riotous inn. Epicurism and lust 240
Make it more like a tavern or a brothel
Than a graced palace. The shame itself doth speak
For instant remedy. Be then desired
By her that else will take the thing she begs
A little to disquantity your train, 245
And the remainders that shall still depend
To be such men as may besort your age,
Which know themselves and you.
Lear: Darkness and devils!
Saddle my horses! Call my train together!
Degenerate bastard, I'll not trouble thee; 250
Yet have I left a daughter.
Goneril: You strike my people, and your disordered rabble
Make servants of their betters.
[*Enter Albany*.]
Lear: Woe that too late repents!—O, sir, are you come?
Is it your will? Speak, sir!—Prepare my horses. 255
Ingratitude, thou marble-hearted fiend,

258 *sea-monster:* probably a reference to the various fearsome monsters that appear in Greek mythology

259 *kite:* bird of prey of the hawk family. Some species are scavengers, hence, the reference to Goneril.

260 *of choice and rarest parts:* of the best and most unusual accomplishments

261 *particulars:* details

262-263 *in the . . . name:* are most conscientious in living up to the reputation that they have established

263 *most small fault:* What Lear had considered Cordelia's fault now seems petty and unimportant.

265 *an engine:* a crowbar or lever; *wrenched my frame of nature:* twisted or tore my real nature

267 *gall:* bitterness

272 *Nature:* in this context, goddess of fruitfulness

276 *increase:* birth

277 *derogate:* debased, corrupt

278 *teem:* become pregnant

279 *spleen:* malice

280 *thwart disnatured torment:* perverse unnatural ordeal

282 *cadent:* falling; *fret channels:* wear marks

283 *pains and benefits:* cares for her child

286 *Away, away:* addressed to all who are near

288 *afflict:* trouble

289 *disposition:* mood; *scope:* freedom

290 *dotage:* senility, second childhood

291 *at a clap?:* all at once, at one blow

More hideous when thou showest thee in a child
Than the sea-monster!
Albany: Pray, sir, be patient.
Lear: [*To Goneril*] Detested kite, thou liest!
My train are men of choice and rarest parts, 260
That all particulars of duty know
And in the most exact regard support
The worships of their name.—O most small fault,
How ugly didst thou in Cordelia show!
Which, like an engine, wrenched my frame of nature 265
From the fixed place; drew from my heart all love
And added to the gall. O Lear, Lear, Lear!
Beat at this gate that let thy folly in
[*Beats his forehead with his fist.*]
And thy dear judgement out! Go, go, my people.
Albany: My lord, I am guiltless, as I am ignorant 270
Of what hath moved you.
Lear: It may be so, my lord.
Hear, Nature, hear! Dear goddess, hear!
Suspend thy purpose, if thou didst intend
To make this creature fruitful.
Into her womb convey sterility; 275
Dry up in her the organs of increase;
And from her derogate body never spring
A babe to honour her! If she must teem,
Create her child of spleen, that it may live
And be a thwart disnatured torment to her. 280
Let it stamp wrinkles in her brow of youth,
With cadent tears fret channels in her cheeks,
Turn all her mother's pains and benefits
To laughter and contempt, that she may feel
How sharper than a serpent's tooth it is 285
To have a thankless child! Away, away! [*Exit.*]
Albany: Now, gods that we adore, whereof comes this?
Goneril: Never afflict yourself to know more of it,
But let his disposition have that scope
As dotage gives it. 290
[*Re-enter Lear.*]
Lear: What, fifty of my followers at a clap?
Within a fortnight?

294 *shake my manhood thus:* so disturb my manly dignity

295 *perforce:* forcibly, whether I will them or not

293-296 *I am/ . . . them:* Lear is anguished at the thought that Goneril can make him weep.

296 *Blasts and fogs:* Wind and fog, apart from their discomfort, were thought to carry illness with them; hence, the curse.

297 *Th' untented woundings:* raw, open wounds. If a wound were "untented," foreign matter would be left in the flesh, and the wound would fester.

298 *fond:* foolish

299 *Beweep this cause:* if you (the eyes) should weep again because of Goneril's treatment

300 *cast:* throw away; *waters that you loose:* tears that you release

301 *temper:* moisten for mixing

303 *comfortable:* willing to give me comfort

305 *flay:* tear away the skin

306 *the shape:* the former stature or rank

309-310 *I cannot . . . you:* Albany feels he must protest, despite his love for Goneril.

311 *content:* be quiet

314-315 *Take the fool with/thee:* Take the Fool and your folly or foolishness.

316-320 *A fox . . . after:* Even a fool would buy a rope to hang a fox, or a daughter like Goneril, if she were caught. Thus the Fool follows the old master rather than remaining where such creatures are; *halter:* hangman's noose

321 *This man . . . counsel:* Lear has been well-advised.

322 *politic:* good policy

322-326 *'Tis politic . . . mercy:* Goneril's ironical words seem to be directed towards the more tolerant attitude of her husband.

323-324 *At point:* fully armed and ready for action; *buzz:* whisper; *that on . . . dislike:* that on any possible pretext Lear may use their strength to permit him to do as he pleases

325 *enguard:* protect; *dotage:* senility

327 *Well, you . . . far:* Albany protests mildly against Goneril's anger.

Albany: What's the matter, sir?
Lear: I'll tell thee. [*To Goneril.*] Life and death! I am ashamed
That thou hast power to shake my manhood thus;
That these hot tears, which break from me perforce, 295
Should make thee worth them. Blasts and fogs upon thee!
Th' untented woundings of a father's curse
Pierce every sense about thee!—Old fond eyes,
Beweep this cause again, I'll pluck ye out,
And cast you, with the waters that you loose, 300
To temper clay. Yea, is it come to this?
Ha! Let it be so. I have another daughter,
Who I am sure is kind and comfortable.
When she shall hear this of thee, with her nails
She'll flay thy wolvish visage. Thou shalt find 305
That I'll resume the shape which thou dost think
I have cast off for ever.
[*Exeunt Lear, Kent, and Attendants.*]
Goneril: Do you mark that, my lord?
Albany: I cannot be so partial, Goneril,
To the great love I bear you— 310
Goneril: Pray you, content.—What, Oswald, ho!
[*To the Fool.*] You, sir, more knave than fool, after your master!
Fool: Nuncle Lear, nuncle Lear, tarry! Take the fool with thee. 315
A fox, when one has caught her,
And such a daughter,
Should sure to the slaughter,
If my cap would buy a halter.
So the fool follows after. [*Exit.*] 320
Goneril: This man hath had good counsel! A hundred knights?
'Tis politic and safe to let him keep
At point a hundred knights; yes, that on every dream,
Each buzz, each fancy, each complaint, dislike,
He may enguard his dotage with their powers 325
And hold our lives in mercy.—Oswald, I say!
Albany: Well, you may fear too far.

328 *still:* always; *harms:* dangers

331 *sustain him:* keeps him as a guest

332 *unfitness:* unsuitability (of doing so) or unfitness of Lear as a house guest; *How now:* a common salutation or greeting.

336 *full:* fully

338 *compact:* complete or make (it) more convincing; add to its substance

340 *This milky gentleness and course:* this mild and gentle approach

341 *under pardon:* pardon me for saying so

342 *more at task for:* more likely to be taken to task for; *want:* lack

343 *Than praised for harmful mildness:* than you are likely to be praised for dangerous mildness.

344 *How far . . . tell:* What particular insight you may have, I do not know.

345 *Striving to . . . well:* better to leave well enough alone

347 *event:* outcome, in the sense of "we shall see what will happen"

Goneril: Safer than trust too far.
Let me still take away the harms I fear,
Not fear still to be taken. I know his heart.
What he hath uttered I have writ my sister. 330
If she sustain him and his hundred knights,
When I have showed the unfitness—
[*Enter Steward.*] How now, Oswald?
What, have you writ that letter to my sister?
Oswald: Yes, madam.
Goneril: Take you some company, and away to horse! 335
Inform her full of my particular fear,
And thereto add such reasons of your own
As may compact it more. Get you gone,
And hasten your return. [*Exit Oswald.*] No, no, my lord!
This milky gentleness and course of yours, 340
Though I condemn not, yet, under pardon,
You are much more at task for want of wisdom
Than praised for harmful mildness.
Albany: How far your eyes may pierce I cannot tell.
Striving to better, oft we mar what's well. 345
Goneril: Nay then—
Albany: Well, well; the event. [*Exeunt.*]

Act 1, Scene 4: Activities

1. You are King Lear. Write a letter to your daughter Regan explaining why you think it is time for you to move to her castle. Explain the ways in which you are being mistreated by Goneril and her husband, and what your feelings are about this situation. State clearly why you believe that Regan's behaviour towards you will be much better than Goneril's. You may find it helpful to refer to Act 1, Scene 1.

2. You are Goneril. Suddenly your father and one hundred of his knights arrive at your palace. How do you entertain them? How do you house them and feed them? What concerns do you have? What anxieties do you experience? Create a conversation with your household steward, Oswald, incorporating the questions above. Insert the conversation at a logical place in the act to this point.

3. As Goneril you have been entertaining your father and his knights for some time. Although your father is dependent on your hospitality, he treats your household as his own. Write a letter to your sister Regan providing her with information about recent occurrences at your house. Give her some specific advice for dealing with your father who, you warn her, is on his way to reside at her household.

4. You are Kent. Write a letter to Cordelia, explaining the following:
   - how you will continue to serve the king
   - that you have disguised yourself
   - that you have changed your personality and your speech, and
   - when you might reveal your identity.

   As Kent, read this letter or role-play its contents to a group.

5. As Kent, prepare a speech that would explain to a friend why you would want to serve a man who just banished

you from his kingdom. Outline the risks you are taking, should you be discovered.

6. In a group, prepare a dramatic presentation of the scene segment in which Lear questions Kent about his allegiance (lines 11–34). The object is to make the action underscore the themes you want to emphasize, as well as to reveal the differences in character.

7. In this scene, we are given no indication of what the Duke of Albany's palace is like, or even where it is. With a partner or in a group, discuss what the setting might look like for a stage production of this scene. Remember to use whatever details you can from the scene. Consider what the castle might look like and how the surroundings might appear. What would the weather be like? How would you convey this through the use of lighting? The illustration on page 46 may give you some ideas. Create a sketch of your set and display it for others in the class to comment upon.

8. Select one character from this scene and follow him or her throughout the play. As you read, make a note of key words, phrases, or lines that reveal key information about your character. Make sure that you include the act, scene, and line so that you can easily trace character development. Use many strategies such as the following to help you organize: columns, a map, a character sunburst, or a chart. At the end of the play, prepare a two-minute monologue that reveals the important aspects of your character and present it to a group or to the class.

For the next scene . . .

In your journal, write about a time when friends were unjust to you but you realized that, perhaps, the injustice was brought about by something you had done to one of them. How did you feel? What did you do?

Act 1, Scene 5

In this scene . . .

Lear's retinue has been reduced to only his most loyal followers. The old king instructs Kent to deliver a letter he has written to his daughter Regan in the town of Gloucester, informing her of Lear's imminent arrival. He cautions Kent to tell Regan no more than what is contained in the letter. The Fool continues to remind Lear of his mistakes, and, as he realizes what has happened to him, Lear begins to feel the approach of madness. At the end of the scene, Lear departs for Regan's household.

1 *before:* ahead; *Gloucester:* the town; *these letters:* this letter

2-3 *Acquaint my . . . letter:* Tell my daughter no more than she asks (her demand) as a result of my letter

3-5 *If/your . . . you:* If you do not hurry, I shall be there before you.

8 *in's:* in his

9 *kibes:* sores caused by rubbing, or chilblains (inflamations of the hands and feet caused by exposure to cold and moisture)

11 *I prithee:* I beg you (literally, I pray you)

12 *slipshod:* wearing slippers or slip shoes. The Fool probably means: You will never have to wear slippers because of chilblains since you have no intelligence, even in your heels, as your journey to Regan shows.

14 *kindly:* a pun, both in an affectionate way and after her kind (according to her nature)

15 *she's as . . . apple:* She's as much like her sister as a crabapple is like an apple. (Both are apples but the crabapple is sour and wild.)

16 *I can . . . tell:* I know a thing or two about what will happen.

18 *She'll taste . . . crab:* She (Regan) will treat you in the same way as Goneril did.

Scene 5

A courtyard of the Duke of Albany's palace.

Enter Lear, Kent, and Fool.

Lear: Go you before to Gloucester with these letters. Acquaint my daughter no further with anything you know than comes from her demand out of the letter. If your diligence be not speedy, I shall be there afore you. 5

Kent: I will not sleep, my lord, till I have delivered your letter. [*Exit.*]

Fool: If a man's brains were in's heels, were it not in danger of kibes?

Lear: Ay, boy. 10

Fool: Then I prithee be merry. Thy wit shall not go slipshod.

Lear: Ha, ha, ha!

Fool: Shalt see thy other daughter will use thee kindly; for though she's as like this as a crab's like an apple, 15 yet I can tell what I can tell.

Lear: What canst tell, boy?

Fool: She'll taste as like this as a crab does to a crab. Thou canst tell why one's nose stands i' the middle on's face? 20

Lear: No.

Fool: Why, to keep one's eyes of either side's nose, that what a man cannot smell out, he may spy into.

Lear: I did her wrong.

Fool: Canst tell how an oyster makes his shell? 25

Lear: No.

Fool: Nor I neither; but I can tell why a snail has a house.

Lear: Why?

31 *horns:* sign of a cuckolded husband (a husband deceived by his wife) – a favourite Elizabethan butt of humour. Here, the horns seem to suggest the condition of men in general, in that they are made fools of or tricked by women.

32 *forget my nature:* cease to be a kind father

35 *seven stars:* the Pleiades, a cluster of stars in the constellation Taurus; *mo:* more; *pretty:* apt, appropriate

38 *To take it again perforce:* Lear may be thinking about resuming his royalty with the help of Cornwall and Regan. Alternatively, he is thinking about Goneril's ingratitude for taking away the privileges she had earlier agreed to give him.

42-43 *Though shouldst . . . wise:* Lear is old enough to be wise but is, instead, a great fool.

44-45 *O, let . . . mad:* the first sense of the onset of madness; *in temper:* sane

49-50 *She that's . . . shorter:* The Fool, turning to the audience, and perhaps imitating Lear, says in effect: Any young girl who cannot see that the King's departure is a sad one, and merely laughs at his unhappy state, is too stupid to retain her virginity for long, unless men are incapable of seduction.

Fool: Why, to put's head in; not to give it away to his daughters, and leave his horns without a case. 30

Lear: I will forget my nature. So kind a father!—Be my horses ready?

Fool: Thy asses are gone about 'em. The reason why the seven stars are no mo than seven is a pretty reason. 35

Lear: Because they are not eight?

Fool: Yes indeed. Thou wouldst make a good fool.

Lear: To take it again perforce! Monster ingratitude!

Fool: If thou wert my fool, nuncle, I'd have thee beaten for being old before thy time. 40

Lear: How's that?

Fool: Thou shouldst not have been old till thou hadst been wise.

Lear: O, let me not be mad, not mad, sweet heaven! Keep me in temper; I would not be mad! 45

[*Enter a Gentleman.*]

How now? Are the horses ready?

Gentleman: Ready, my lord.

Lear: Come, boy.

Fool: She that's a maid now, and laughs at my departure,
Shall not be a maid long, unless things be cut shorter. 50

[*Exeunt.*]

Act 1, Scene 5: Activities

1. Brainstorm with your group and write the letter that Lear has Kent deliver to Regan. Share your letter with other groups. How do the letters differ in content?

2. Extract the Fool's speeches from this scene and, with a partner, summarize what he says. Does the Fool make any sense to you? In your opinion, does he make any sense to Lear?

   As the host of a talk show, arrange to interview the Fool. Prepare a list of questions to ask him, the answers to which should reveal his true feelings about Lear and his own role in the play.

3. With a partner, discuss why, all of a sudden, Lear fears the approaching of madness. Decide what you think might be some of the symptoms of madness. As Lear's doctor, analyse his mental state according to your list of symptoms and write a report for your files.

4. If, as a character, you could intervene in this scene, what might you say to Lear? With a partner, role-play the conversations you might have, alternating the roles of Lear and the intervener.

5. Create an alternative rhyming couplet of your own to end this scene. Remember to keep the context of the scene. Share your couplet with the rest of the class.

6. In groups, discuss whether or not it would be possible to cut this scene from the play. Prepare as strong an argument as possible and share it with the rest of the class.

Act 1: Consider the Whole Act

1. You are a servant in Goneril's household. Prepare a profile of yourself and the kind of job you perform. Your answers to some of the following questions might be included in the profile:
   - How long have you been living there?
   - Why is your job important to this establishment?
   - Do you need any special training to do this job?
   - Do you get along with others in the household?
   - What are your hours?
   - What, exactly, are your duties?
   - What changes have you noticed in the general routine since the arrival of King Lear and his knights?
   - What is your reaction to the behaviour of King Lear's knights?
   - What is your assessment of the way Goneril treats her father?
   - How has the extra company affected your job?
   - If you were Goneril, what would you do to make the situation more tolerable?

   Share your profile with a partner or, with a partner, role-play an interview, taking turns as interviewer and servant.

2. The Fool often speaks in riddles, many of which are very puzzling. Make a list of some of your favourite riddles in this act and explain how they fit into the segments of the play in which they appear.

   Create a riddle of your own and place it in an appropriate place in one of the scenes from this act. Have a partner attempt to answer your riddle, and be prepared to explain why you think your riddle is appropriate for the play and for the place you have chosen to insert it.

   Share some of your riddles with the rest of the class.

3. When Lear feels he has been wronged by his daughters, he flies into uncontrollable rages and curses them vehemently. As Lear, write a letter to Ann Landers explaining your anger with your daughters and why you feel you are justified in feeling this way. Give your letter to a partner who, acting as Ann Landers, will reply to your letter.

   Alternatively, write your account of Lear's outbursts as an observer at the court. Remember, you are trying to convey your impressions as objectively as you can.

4. It is obvious that the characters in this play have some basic family problems. Imagine you are a social worker who might offer advice to Lear or to Gloucester about ways to keep families together. Select one of these two characters and, in your journal, consider what you think went wrong in his family life and what some possible solutions might be.

5. Some of the Fool's responses are in the form of songs – pop songs of his own time. Select two or three of the Fool's songs and substitute some modern lyrics that would be appropriate. Would music enhance or detract from the mood of the play?

   Prepare a narrative version or reading of a segment of the play in which you insert one of your pop songs in place of one used by the Fool. You may wish to make a video of the segment and have the class comment on the success of your production.

6. Some directors have argued that the character of the Fool adds nothing to the essence of the play and could easily be cut without damaging the overall impact. From what you have experienced so far, to what extent could you justify such an argument? If you agree, how would you make the transitions in order to exclude the Fool? If you disagree, what would be your argument for leaving the play as it is? Share these observations with your group or with the rest of the class.

7. You have been transported into Lear's world and have been given the opportunity to interview one character from this act. You are permitted to ask only ten questions of that character in order to find out whatever information you wish to know. Remember, the more carefully worded the questions, the more revealing the response.
8. The first act of this play is fairly static. As a director, how would you ensure that your audience did not lose interest before the act was over? With your group or with a partner, prepare a written sketch or story board in which you show what you would do to maintain audience interest and keep the play moving. Could you prepare a short video presentation to illustrate your approach?
9. Create a landscape in a painting or a collage that conveys the mood of Act 1 of *King Lear*, and give it a title. What will you choose as the focus of your landscape or collage to convey your sense of the atmosphere? Remember that the landscape need not be realistic.
10. There are many references to mythological gods in this act. Find out as much as you can about these figures. What significance do they have to Lear in this act? To which ones does he refer? Why do you think he invokes them on a fairly regular basis? Do these figures mean anything at all to us today? Explain your response.
11. Have each member of your group select one of the major characters in this scene and create a mask for that character. As a group, create a mime in which you act out a portion of the scene in which your characters appear. Your aim is to convey the action and theme of the sequence to the audience.

For the next scene . . .

How do you respond to the idea that the end justifies the means – that is, any action is justifiable as long as it achieves the desired goal? What do you think of deception as a means of achieving an end?

Act 2, Scene 1

In this scene . . .

This scene takes place at Gloucester's castle. Edmund proceeds with his plan to trick Gloucester into believing that Edgar is seeking his life. He first convinces Edgar to flee for his safety since the arrival of Regan and Cornwall is eminent. While he is alone Edmund stabs himself, planning to say that Edgar attacked him when Edmund refused to help in Gloucester's murder. When Gloucester enters and hears Edmund's accusations, he promises to give Edmund an inheritance which should have been Edgar's.

Regan and the Duke of Cornwall arrive, seeking Gloucester's support in a dispute that has arisen between Albany and Cornwall over their rights to the kingdom. In addition, Regan claims to have left her palace as a means of avoiding Lear.

Regan suggests that Edgar's actions can be blamed on the influence of Lear's "riotous knights." Edmund supports her suggestion and then wins Cornwall's favour when Gloucester describes his apparent loyalty. Regan tells Gloucester that she needs his advice to deal with the conflict that has occurred between Goneril and King Lear.

1 *Save thee:* God save you – a common greeting

8 *ear-bussing:* literally, ear kissing, as in "whispered"; *arguments?:* subjects of conversation, here likely in the sense of opinions

10 *toward:* imminent, about to occur; *'twixt:* betwixt, between

15 *weaves itself perforce:* joins in naturally and inevitably; *business:* plot

17 *of a queasy question:* that needs to be handled delicately. Queasy means nauseous and is intended to suggest the delicacy with which such a condition must be treated.

18 *act:* accomplish; *Briefness:* speed or quick action; *Briefness and fortune, work:* May swift action and good luck help to bring me success.

19 *Brother, a . . . say:* Edmund calls out to his brother.

20 *watches:* keeps watch; *fly:* escape from

21 *Intelligence:* information (the military sense of "intelligence")

24 *i' the haste:* in a great hurry

26 *Upon his party:* criticizing his dispute

27 *Advise yourself:* consider, try to recall; *on't:* of it

Act 2, Scene 1

A courtyard inside Gloucester's castle.

Enter Edmund the Bastard and Curan, severally.

Edmund: Save thee, Curan.
Curan: And you, sir. I have been with your father, and given him notice that the Duke of Cornwall and Regan his Duchess will be here with him this night.
Edmund: How comes that? 5
Curan: Nay, I know not. You have heard of the news abroad—I mean the whispered ones, for they are yet but ear-bussing arguments?
Edmund: Not I. Pray you, what are they?
Curan: Have you heard of no likely wars toward 'twixt the Dukes of Cornwall and Albany? 10
Edmund: Not a word.
Curan: You may do, then, in time. Fare you well, sir.
[*Exit.*]
Edmund: The Duke be here tonight? The better! Best!
This weaves itself perforce into my business. 15
My father hath set guard to take my brother;
And I have one thing, of a queasy question,
Which I must act. Briefness and fortune, work!
Brother, a word! Descend! Brother, I say!
[*Enter Edgar.*]
My father watches. O sir, fly this place! 20
Intelligence is given where you are hid.
You have now the good advantage of the night.
Have you not spoken 'gainst the Duke of Cornwall?
He's coming hither; now, i' the night, i' the haste,
And Regan with him. Have you nothing said 25
Upon his party 'gainst the Duke of Albany?
Advise yourself.

29 *In cunning:* as a clever trick, so that we don't appear to be working together; thus, a trick to fool Gloucester

31 *Yield:* surrender; *before:* in front of

32 *So farewell:* likely an expression of satisfaction

33-34 *would beget . . . endeavour:* would make people believe that I have had a terrible fight

34-35 *I have . . . sport:* Young men under the influence of alcohol, in order to prove their worthiness and commitment, would frequently wound themselves and then drink to the health of their mistresses in a mixture of their own blood and whatever it was they were drinking.

39-40 *Mumbling of . . . mistress:* The crescent moon was associated with the horned goddess (*auspicious*, favourable) of witchcraft. Edmund is playing on Gloucester's superstitious beliefs.

41 *Look, sir, I bleed:* a ploy to get Gloucester's attention and to allow Edgar to escape.

42 *Fled this way, sir:* Edmund points in the wrong direction.

45 *that:* when

46 *parricides:* sons who murder their fathers; *bend:* direct

47 *manifold and strong:* Both words have the same meaning.

48 *in fine:* finally

49 *loathly opposite:* hatefully opposed

50 *unnatural:* It is not natural for son to murder father; *in fell motion:* with a deadly thrust (a fencing term)

51-52 *prepared:* already drawn; *charges home/my unprovided body:* thrust his sword straight at my defenceless body; *launched:* lanced, pierced

53 *best alarumed spirits:* my spirit, aroused to its highest pitch

54 *Bold in the quarrel's right:* made bold by the justice of my cause

55 *gasted:* terrified, panic-stricken

56 *Full:* quite

58 *And found-dispatch:* And when he's found, kill him.

59 *arch and patron:* chief protector

Edgar: I am sure on't, not a word.
Edmund: I hear my father coming. Pardon me!
In cunning I must draw my sword upon you.
Draw, seem to defend yourself; now quit you well.— 30
Yield! Come before my father. Light, ho, here!
Fly, brother.—Torches, torches!—So farewell.
[*Exit Edgar.*]
Some blood drawn on me would beget opinion
Of my more fierce endeavour. [*Stabs his arm.*] I have seen drunkards
Do more than this in sport.—Father, father!— 35
Stop, stop! No help?
[*Enter Gloucester, and Servants with torches.*]
Gloucester: Now, Edmund, where's the villain?
Edmund: Here stood he in the dark, his sharp sword out,
Mumbling of wicked charms, conjuring the moon
To stand auspicious mistress.
Gloucester: But where is he? 40
Edmund: Look, sir, I bleed.
Gloucester: Where is the villain, Edmund?
Edmund: Fled this way, sir. When by no means he could—
Gloucester: Pursue him, ho! Go after. [*Exeunt some Servants.*] By no means what?
Edmund: Persuade me to the murder of your lordship;
But that I told him the revenging gods 45
'Gainst parricides did all the thunder bend;
Spoke with how manifold and strong a bond
The child was bound to the father—sir, in fine,
Seeing how loathly opposite I stood
To his unnatural purpose, in fell motion 50
With his prepared sword he charges home
My unprovided body, launched mine arm;
And when he saw my best alarumed spirits,
Bold in the quarrel's right, roused to the encounter,
Or whether gasted by the noise I made, 55
Full suddenly he fled.
Gloucester: Let him fly far.
Not in this land shall he remain uncaught;
And found—dispatch. The noble Duke my master,
My worthy arch and patron, comes tonight.

61 *thanks:* gratitude – and reward

62 *to the stake:* to the place of his execution or to death

65 *pight:* determined; *curst:* strong, angry

66 *discover:* denounce, reveal his intentions

67 *unpossessing:* landless, without property

68-70 *If I . . . faithed?:* Do you think if I denied your accusations, that any trust, virtue, or value in your character would cause your words to be believed instead of mine?

70 *faithed?:* believed

72-73 *My very character:* my own handwriting; *turn it all/To:* twist matters so that the blame for what happened would rest upon

73 *suggestion:* evil instigation; *damned practice:* treachery

74-77 *thou must . . . it:* you must assume that people are stupid indeed if they do not think you would benefit from my death.

76 *pregnant:* obvious; *potential:* powerful, compelling

77 *strange:* unnatural; *fastened:* hardened

78 *letter:* Gloucester refers to the letter in Act 1, Scene 2; *I never got him:* I never begot him; i.e., I could not be the father of such a son.

Stage direction – *Tucket:* a special trumpet call identifying a particular party (here, Cornwall)

80 *ports:* seaports; *villain:* Edmund

81 *picture:* drawing, with a description

84 *natural boy:* Illegitimate children were called this because they were conceived by natural desire.

85 *capable:* able to inherit (his father's property)

87 *I have heard strange news:* i.e., of Edgar's alleged plot

88 *all vengeance comes too short:* Total revenge is not enough.

91 *godson:* Regan seems to suggest that Lear has had some influence on Edgar's character.

92 *He whom my father named?:* the son, whom Lear named Edgar

93 *it:* that Edgar is Lear's godson

By his authority I will proclaim it, 60
That he which finds him shall deserve our thanks,
Bringing the murderous coward to the stake;
He that conceals him, death.

Edmund: When I dissuaded him from his intent
And found him pight to do it, with curst speech 65
I threatened to discover him. He replied,
"Thou unpossessing bastard, dost thou think,
If I would stand against thee, would the reposal
Of any trust, virtue, or worth in thee
Make thy words faithed? No. What I should deny 70
(As this I would; ay, though thou didst produce
My very character), I'd turn it all
To thy suggestion, plot, and damned practice;
And thou must make a dullard of the world,
If they not thought the profits of my death 75
Were very pregnant and potential spirits
To make thee seek it."

Gloucester: O strange and fastened villain!
Would he deny his letter, said he? I never got him.
[*Tucket within.*]
Hark, the Duke's trumpets! I know not why he comes.
All ports I'll bar; the villain shall not scape; 80
The Duke must grant me that. Besides, his picture
I will send far and near, that all the kingdom
May have due note of him, and of my land,
Loyal and natural boy, I'll work the means
To make thee capable. 85
[*Enter Cornwall, Regan, and Attendants.*]

Cornwall: How now, my noble friend? Since I came hither
(Which I can call but now) I have heard strange news.

Regan: If it be true, all vengeance comes too short
Which can pursue the offender. How dost, my lord?

Gloucester: O madam, my old heart is cracked, it's cracked! 90

Regan: What, did my father's godson seek your life?
He whom my father named? Your Edgar?

Gloucester: O lady, lady, shame would have it hid!

Regan: Was he not companion with the riotous knights
That tended upon my father? 95

Gloucester: I know not, madam. 'Tis too bad, too bad!

97 *consort:* company. The word is often used as a term of contempt.

98 *though he were ill affected:* that he would be made disloyal

99 *'Tis they . . . death:* They (Lear's riotous knights) have incited him to seek Gloucester's life.

100 *the expense and waste:* the privilege of spending and squandering; *revenues:* income

101 *present:* same

102 *them:* the riotous knights

106 *A childlike office:* a filial duty, obligation of a son

107 *bewray his practice:* reveal his evil schemes (i.e., Edgar's plot)

111-112 *Make your . . . please:* Carry out your plans for his capture and use my authority any way you please for that purpose.

113 *virtue and obedience:* virtuous obedience

113-114 *doth this . . . itself:* is to be so greatly commended or praised; *ours:* under our protection and patronage.

116 *seize on:* engage in our service

117 *however else:* however inadequate I might be in other respects

119 *threading dark-eyed night:* making our way through the darkness as though it were the eye of a needle

120 *Occasions:* situations; *prize:* importance

123 *differences:* disputes, quarrels

124 *answer from our home:* give my answer away from home

125 *From hence:* from here; *attend dispatch:* are waiting to be sent

126-127 *Lay comforts to your bosom:* Be comforted; *bestow/Your . . . businesses:* Give your essential advice to us for our (political) affairs.

128 *Which craves the instant use:* which must be put into effect immediately

Stage direction – *Flourish:* fanfare of trumpets to mark and honour the exit of important people

Edmund: Yes, madam, he was of that consort.
Regan: No marvel then though he were ill affected.
'Tis they have put him on the old man's death,
To have the expense and waste of his revenues. 100
I have this present evening from my sister
Been well informed of them, and with such cautions
That, if they come to sojourn at my house,
I'll not be there.
Cornwall: Nor I, assure thee, Regan.
Edmund, I hear that you have shown your father 105
A childlike office.
Edmund: 'Twas my duty, sir.
Gloucester: He did bewray his practice, and received
This hurt you see, striving to apprehend him.
Cornwall: Is he pursued?
Gloucester: Ay, my good lord.
Cornwall: If he be taken, he shall never more 110
Be feared of doing harm. Make your own purpose,
How in my strength you please. For you, Edmund,
Whose virtue and obedience doth this instant
So much commend itself, you shall be ours.
Natures of such deep trust we shall much need; 115
You we first seize on.
Edmund: I shall serve you, sir,
Truly, however else.
Gloucester: For him I thank your Grace.
Cornwall: You know not why we came to visit you—
Regan: Thus out of season, threading dark-eyed night.
Occasions, noble Gloucester, of some prize, 120
Wherein we must have use of your advice.
Our father he hath writ, so hath our sister,
Of differences, which I best thought it fit
To answer from our home. The several messengers
From hence attend dispatch. Our good old friend, 125
Lay comforts to your bosom, and bestow
Your needful counsel to our businesses,
Which craves the instant use.
Gloucester: I serve you, madam.
Your Graces are right welcome. [*Exeunt. Flourish.*]

Act 2, Scene 1: Activities

1. You are an investigative reporter for a newspaper or a television station. Report for your reading or viewing audience the "news abroad" that Curan talks about.

2. Create a soliloquy for Edmund in which he reviews the plans he has made to trick his father and his brother in order to gain Cornwall's favour. Where would you insert the soliloquy in this scene?

3. From what you have seen of Gloucester so far, what kind of father do you think he is? In your journal, first as Edgar and then as Edmund, tell Gloucester what you think of his attitude towards you.

4. Regan blames Lear's knights for Edgar's strange behaviour. Why do you suppose she does? Write a short speech in which you respond to Regan.

5. Cornwall begins to explain to Gloucester the reasons for his visit (line 118), but it is Regan who finishes the speech. In your journal, write your observations about the relationship between Cornwall and Regan.

   If this was the only segment of the scene between Gloucester, Cornwall, and Regan that you were to observe, what conclusions would you draw about the events that have transpired in the play so far? If you had one comment to make to Regan at this point, what would it be?

For the next scene . . .

In your journal describe an experience in which you thought that being frank and honest was the correct approach to solving a problem. What happened?

Act 2, Scene 2

In this scene . . .

Outside Gloucester's castle Oswald and Kent meet again, although Oswald does not appear to recognize Kent. Kent is still angry with Oswald for his wretched behaviour to King Lear and attacks him both verbally and physically. The resulting skirmish and Oswald's cries for help bring Cornwall, Regan, Gloucester, and a host of servants to see what is the matter. For his abuse of Oswald and also for his insolence to Cornwall, Kent is placed in the stocks, despite Gloucester's pleas against humiliating a servant of the King. When the others leave, Gloucester remains to offer Kent his sympathy. Although he offers to intercede on Kent's behalf, Kent begs him not to. Left alone, Kent produces a letter that is from Cordelia. Cordelia knows of the role he has assumed and he feels confident she will take action to put things right again. Kent falls asleep, asking fortune to turn her wheel and "smile once more."

Stage direction – *Without:* outside; *severally:* separately

1 *Good dawning:* equivalent to good morning, but indicative of the fact that it is still dark; *Art of this house?:* Are you a member of this household?

2 *Ay:* Yes

3 *set:* stable

4 *mire:* mud

5 *Prithee:* literally, I pray thee; *if thou . . . me:* If you have any courtesy, please tell me.

8 *Lipsbury Pinfold:* an involved pun. "Lipsbury," equivalent to Liptown, means the mouth. A "pinfold" is a corral or pen in which stray cattle are kept. The expression therefore means: If I had you in my mouth (or jaws), or if I had you in my power.

10 *use:* treat

13 *an eater of broken meats:* an eater of scraps

13-22 *A knave . . . addition:* Kent is much better at gratuitous insult than at sarcastic humour.

14-17 *three-suited:* Three suits per year were allowed a servant by custom; *hundred-/pound:* with small property; *worsted-stocking:* cheap stocking scorned by gentlemen, who wore silk; *lily-livered:* cowardly, white-livered; *action-taking:* going to law instead of meeting an enemy in a duel, cowardly; *glass-gazing:* vain, always gazing into the mirror; *superservicea-/ble:* going beyond the normal limits of a servant's duty in order to gain favour with the master

17 *finical:* fussy; *one-trunk-inheriting slave:* a servant whose total belongings would fit into one trunk

18 *bawd:* pimp or procurer

19-20 *the composition:* the composite of, the combination; *pander:* pimp

21 *clamorous whining:* noisy wailing, loud crying

22 *addition:* title (all the titles Kent has given him)

24 *rail on:* abuse verbally

25 *brazen-faced:* bold, "nervy"; *varlet:* scoundrel

Scene 2

Without the gates of Gloucester's castle.

Enter Kent and Oswald the Steward, severally.

Oswald: Good dawning to thee, friend. Art of this house?
Kent: Ay.
Oswald: Where may we set our horses?
Kent: I' the mire.
Oswald: Prithee, if thou lovest me, tell me. 5
Kent: I love thee not.
Oswald: Why then, I care not for thee.
Kent: If I had thee in Lipsbury Pinfold, I would make thee care for me.
Oswald: Why dost thou use me thus? I know thee not. 10
Kent: Fellow, I know thee.
Oswald: What dost thou know me for?
Kent: A knave, a rascal, an eater of broken meats; a base, proud, shallow, beggarly, three-suited, hundred-pound, filthy, worsted-stocking knave; a lily-livered, 15 action-taking, whoreson, glass-gazing, superserviceable, finical rogue; one-trunk-inheriting slave; one that wouldst be a bawd in way of good service, and art nothing but the composition of a knave, beggar, coward, pander, and the son and heir of a mongrel bitch; 20 one whom I will beat into clamorous whining if thou deny'st the least syllable of thy addition.
Oswald: Why, what a monstrous fellow art thou, thus to rail on one that's neither known of thee nor knows thee!
Kent: What a brazen-faced varlet art thou, to deny thou 25 knowest me! Is it two days ago since I tripped up thy heels and beat thee before the King? [*Draws his sword.*] Draw, you rogue! for, though it be night, yet

29-30 *I'll make . . . you:* I'll put so many holes in you that you will soak up the moonlight as a piece of bread (sop) soaks up liquid

30 *cullionly:* villainous, base; *barbermonger:* one who is always at the barber's.

33 *Vanity the puppet's part:* Goneril's part. Kent insults Goneril as a vain woman and a mere puppet compared to her father.

34-36 *so car-/bonado:* slash, carve up; *Come your/ways:* Come on!

38 *neat:* dressed

Stage direction – *Beats him:* strikes him (humiliatingly) with the flat side of his sword blade

Stage direction – *Parts them:* separates Kent and Oswald

42 *With you:* I'll fight with you (Edmund) then; *goodman:* a mocking expression implying that Edmund the boy is presumptuous to try to stop Kent the man.

43 *flesh ye:* give you your first lesson

48 *difference?:* dispute, quarrel

49 *scarce in breath:* can scarcely get my breath.

50 *No marvel . . . valour:* No wonder, you have upset your courage so much with the thought that you may have to use it.

51-52 *disclaims in thee:* denies any part of your making

54-56 *A tailor . . . trade:* implies that no stonecutter, or painter – however incompetent – could have produced Oswald

58 *ancient:* old (Kent is disguised)

59 *At suit . . . beard:* because of his age

60 *whoreson zed! Thou, unnecessary letter:* The letter "z" is unnecessary in English since *s* can usually serve.

61 *unbolted:* Unbolted mortar was unsifted and lumpy, and had to be trodden with wooden shoes before it could be used.

62 *daub:* to coat or cover; *jakes:* backhouse, latrine, outdoor toilet

63 *Spare my . . . wagtail?* Oswald, is bowing obediently, bobbing up and down like a type of bird which moves its tail up and down.

65 *beastly:* disgusting, offensive; *reverence?:* respect for superiors

66 *anger hath a privilege:* You must make allowance for a man who is extremely angry.

the moon shines. I'll make a sop o' the moonshine of
you. You whoreson cullionly barbermonger, draw! 30

Oswald: Away! I have nothing to do with thee.

Kent: Draw, you rascal! You come with letters against the
King, and take Vanity the puppet's part against the
royalty of her father. Draw, you rogue, or I'll so car-
bonado your shanks! Draw, you rascal! Come your 35
ways!

Oswald: Help, ho! Murder! Help!

Kent: Strike, you slave! Stand, rogue! Stand, you neat slave!
Strike! [*Beats him.*]

Oswald: Help, ho! murder! murder! 40

[*Enter Edmund, with his rapier drawn.*]

Edmund: How now? What's the matter? [*Parts them.*]

Kent: With you, goodman boy, if you please! Come, I'll
flesh ye! Come on, young master!

[*Enter Gloucester, Cornwall, Regan, Servants.*]

Gloucester: Weapons? Arms? What's the matter here?

Cornwall: Keep peace, upon your lives! 45
He dies that strikes again. What is the matter?

Regan: The messengers from our sister and the King.

Cornwall: What is your difference? Speak.

Oswald: I am scarce in breath, my lord.

Kent: No marvel, you have so bestirred your valour. You 50
cowardly rascal, nature disclaims in thee; a tailor
made thee.

Cornwall: Thou art a strange fellow. A tailor make a man?

Kent: A tailor, sir: a stonecutter or a painter could not have
made him so ill, though they had been but two hours 55
at the trade.

Cornwall: Speak yet, how grew your quarrel?

Oswald: This ancient ruffian, sir, whose life I have spared
At suit of his grey beard—

Kent: Thou whoreson zed! Thou unnecessary letter! My 60
lord, if you'll give me leave, I will tread this unbolted
villain into mortar and daub the wall of a jakes with
him. "Spare my grey beard," you wagtail?

Cornwall: Peace, sirrah!
You beastly knave, know you no reverence? 65

Kent: Yes, sir, but anger hath a privilege.

68 *sword:* the mark of a man

70-71 *oft bite . . . unloose:* who often bite through the bonds of natural affection or, which should be too tight to be untied

71 *smooth:* flatter; *passion:* outburst

72 *That in . . . rebel:* that break out in their masters

73 *Being oil to fire:* stimulate anger, as oil feeds a fire; *snow to the colder moods:* encourage feelings of indifference

74 *Renege:* deny; *affirm:* assert

74-75 *and turn . . . masters:* The body of the halcyon (kingfisher) was thought to be an accurate weather-vane, turning its beak into the wind. Oswald, and those like him, would obey their masters, just as the kingfisher would obey the wind.

76 *Knowing naught . . . following:* understanding nothing, but following their master like obedient dogs

77 *epileptic:* Oswald's face is twisted into a sort of smile, which fails to hide his fear. He appears about to have a fit.

79 *Goose:* a symbol of stupidity; *Sarum Plain:* Salisbury Plain

80 *Camelot:* site of King Arthur's Court. Kent is saying that he would glady chase Oswald about, beating him with the flat of his sword, while Oswald utters goose-like shrieks.

83 *contraries:* opponents

86 *His countenance likes me not:* I just don't like his face.

93 *saucy roughness:* rough insolence

93-94 *constrains the . . . nature:* forces himself to put on this act or manner of insolence that is contrary to his own nature

98 *Harbour:* have within themselves, conceal; *craft:* cunning; *more corrupter ends:* more wicked purposes

99 *silly-ducking:* constantly bowing; *observants:* self-seeking servants

100 *That stretch their duties nicely:* that exert themselves with great conscientiousness

102 *Under the . . . aspect:* begging the indulgence of your great power.

104 *Phœbus' front:* forehead of the sun

Cornwall: Why art thou angry?
Kent: That such a slave as this should wear a sword,
Who wears no honesty. Such smiling rogues as these,
Like rats, oft bite the holy cords atwain 70
Which are too intrinse to unloose; smooth every passion
That in the natures of their lords rebel,
Being oil to fire, snow to the colder moods;
Renege, affirm, and turn their halcyon beaks
With every gale and vary of their masters, 75
Knowing naught (like dogs) but following.
A plague upon your epileptic visage!
Smile you my speeches, as I were a fool?
Goose, if I had you upon Sarum Plain,
I'd drive ye cackling home to Camelot. 80
Cornwall: What, art thou mad, old fellow?
Gloucester: How fell you out? Say that.
Kent: No contraries hold more antipathy
Than I and such a knave.
Cornwall: Why dost thou call him knave? What is his fault? 85
Kent: His countenance likes me not.
Cornwall: No more perchance does mine, nor his, nor hers.
Kent: Sir, 'tis my occupation to be plain:
I have seen better faces in my time
Than stands on any shoulder that I see 90
Before me at this instant.
Cornwall: This is some fellow
Who, having been praised for bluntness, doth affect
A saucy roughness, and constrains the garb
Quite from his nature. He cannot flatter, he,
An honest mind and plain, he must speak truth: 95
An they will take it, so; if not, he's plain.
These kind of knaves I know which in this plainness
Harbour more craft and more corrupter ends
Than twenty silly-ducking observants
That stretch their duties nicely. 100
Kent: Sir, in good faith, in sincere verity,
Under the allowance of your great aspect,
Whose influence, like the wreath of radiant fire
On flickering Phœbus' front—
Cornwall: What meanest by this?

106-109 *He that . . . it:* Kent means: I assume that someone fooled you in the past with plain words, and therefore made himself a liar, which I would not be, even if I should make you so angry with my bluntness that you would prefer me to flatter you.

112 *late:* recently

113 *upon his misconstruction:* following his (Lear's) misinterpretation of something I said

114 *compact:* in compact with, or in agreement with Lear; *flattering his displeasure:* encouraging Lear's annoyance

116-117 *And put . . . worthied him:* and made such a hero of himself in Lear's eyes

118 *attempting:* attacking, "taking on"; *who:* Oswald; *self-subdued:* self-controlled

119 *fleshment:* excitement aroused by "fleshing," or first success

120-121 *None of . . . fool:* Dishonest people like this always make fools of the mighty or powerful. (Ajax was known as a mighty warrior, with a somewhat slow perception.) Kent's comment enrages Cornwall who assumes, perhaps rightly, that Kent is referring to him.

121 *stocks:* instrument of punishment for minor offences, consisting of a wooden form with holes for hands and feet, and sometimes the head

122 *stubborn:* rough, ungovernable; *ancient:* old; *reverend:* aged

127 *grace and . . . master:* both the office and person of the King

133 *being:* since you are; *knave:* servant (hence a menial; one of low status or condition)

135 *away:* out

138 *low:* demeaning, humiliating; *correction:* punishment

Kent: To go out of my dialect, which you discommend so much. I know, sir, I am no flatterer. He that beguiled you in a plain accent was a plain knave, which, for my part, I will not be, though I should win your displeasure to entreat me to it. 105

Cornwall: What was the offence you gave him? 110

Oswald: I never gave him any.
It pleased the King his master very late
To strike at me, upon his misconstruction;
When he, compact, and flattering his displeasure,
Tripped me behind; being down, insulted, railed 115
And put upon him such a deal of man
That worthied him, got praises of the King
For him attempting who was self-subdued;
And, in the fleshment of this dread exploit,
Drew on me here again.

Kent: None of these rogues and cowards 120
But Ajax is their fool.

Cornwall: Fetch forth the stocks!
You stubborn ancient knave, you reverend braggart,
We'll teach you—

Kent: Sir, I am too old to learn.
Call not your stocks for me. I serve the King,
On whose employment I was sent to you. 125
You shall do small respect, show too bold malice
Against the grace and person of my master,
Stocking his messenger.

Cornwall: Fetch forth the stocks! As I have life and honour,
There shall he sit till noon. 130

Regan: Till noon? Till night, my lord, and all night too!

Kent: Why, madam, if I were your father's dog,
You should not use me so.

Regan: Sir, being his knave, I will.

Cornwall: This is a fellow of the selfsame colour
Our sister speaks of. Come, bring away the stocks! 135
[*Stocks brought out.*]

Gloucester: Let me beseech your Grace not to do so.
His fault is much, and the good King his master
Will check him for it. Your purposed low correction

139 *contemnedest:* most despised, most despicable

141 *take it ill:* take it as an insult

142 *so lightly . . . messenger:* given so little respect through the humiliation of his servant

143 *answer:* be responsible for

148 *pleasure:* will, desire

150 *rubbed nor stopped:* opposed, resisted. A "rub" in the game of bowls is an obstacle which diverts a ball from its proper course; *entreat:* to plead for

153 *grow out at heels:* become worn out (like the heel of a sock or stocking), may come to an end

154 *Give you good morrow:* a salutation: God give you a good tomorrow; equivalent to our expression, "See you in the morning."

156 *that must . . . saw:* that must prove the truth of the common saying

157-158 *Thou out . . . sun:* a proverb: out of God's blessing into the warm sun, or from good to bad (the sun's heat was thought of as harsh)

159 *beacon:* sun; *globe:* earth

160 *comfortable:* comforting

161-162 *Nothing almost . . . misery:* When we are discouraged, any relief seems a miracle. (Kent thinks it a miracle that Cordelia's letter has reached him.)

164 *obscured:* disguised

165-166 *this enormous state:* this unnatural condition; *to give/Losses their remedies:* to make up or repair losses; *o'erwatched:* worn out

167-168 *Take vantage . . . lodging:* take advantage of sleep in order not to see these shameful stocks

169 *Fortune, good . . . wheel:* According to legend, the goddess Fortune sits by a wheel from which people are hung, and occasionally turns it. The most fortunate are those at the top; some, less so, are ascending; and the unlucky remainder are descending or at the very bottom of the wheel.

Is such as basest and contemnedest wretches
For pilferings and most common trespasses 140
Are punished with. The King must take it ill
That he, so slightly valued in his messenger,
Should have him thus restrained.

Cornwall: I'll answer that.

Regan: My sister may receive it much more worse,
To have her gentleman abused, assaulted, 145
For following her affairs. Put in his legs.
[*Kent is put in the stocks.*]
Come, my good lord, away.
[*Exeunt all but Gloucester and Kent.*]

Gloucester: I am sorry for thee, friend. 'Tis the Duke's pleasure,
Whose disposition, all the world well knows,
Will not be rubbed nor stopped. I'll entreat for thee. 150

Kent: Pray do not, sir. I have watched and travelled hard.
Some time I shall sleep out, the rest I'll whistle.
A good man's fortune may grow out at heels.
Give you good morrow!

Gloucester: The Duke's to blame in this; 'twill be ill taken. 155
[*Exit.*]

Kent: Good King, that must approve the common saw,
Thou out of heaven's benediction comest
To the warm sun!
Approach, thou beacon to this under globe,
That by thy comfortable beams I may 160
Peruse this letter. Nothing almost sees miracles
But misery. I know 'tis from Cordelia,
Who hath most fortunately been informed
Of my obscured course—and [*Reads.*] "shall find time
From this enormous state, seeking to give 165
Losses their remedies"—All weary and o'erwatched,
Take vantage, heavy eyes, not to behold
This shameful lodging.
Fortune, good night; smile once more, turn thy wheel.
[*Sleeps.*]

Act 2, Scene 2: Activities

1. As Kent, write a soliloquy for the beginning of this scene. It should reveal to the audience why you feel that plain speech and bluntness are important characteristics for a person to maintain, even though the consequences may be unpleasant. Present your soliloquy to your group and ask them to respond to the ideas you have suggested.

2. As Oswald, you have clearly defined duties in Regan's household. In a letter to a friend in a similar position, give your version of the encounter between yourself and Kent. Include your impressions of Kent and your responses to what you consider to be an unprovoked attack. Were you pleased with Cornwall's swift justice? How do you respond to Kent's accusation that "a tailor/ made thee" (lines 51–52)?

3. With a partner, prepare a dialogue that might take place between Cornwall and Regan after they have left Kent in the stocks. As Cornwall, what are your concerns about what is happening in your part of the kingdom? As Regan, what course of action have you chosen to keep things in control? Who is the dominant figure in your dialogue? Rehearse your dialogue and present it to your group, to another group, or to the whole class for their responses.

4. Write the letter that Cordelia has sent to Kent. Remember to be consistent with her character as you perceived it in Act 1. Be sure to explain why you have written to Kent and why the letter was not sent to Gloucester. Indicate also what course of action you intend to take and what Kent's role in this action will be.

   Do you see any connection between Kent's behaviour and the contents of Cordelia's letter?

5. Kent hurls many insults at Oswald (lines 4–22 and 25–30). Without being overtly crude, rewrite these speeches in current English as you might deliver them to someone you perceived as being a modern-day Oswald. Consider whether you believe Kent's perception of Oswald to be accurate before you write your speech. Could you ever imagine yourself saying these things to anyone? How would you feel if these things were said to you?

6. Kent asks "fortune" to help him (line 169). Edmund also talks about "fortune" (Act 1, Scene 2, lines 118–133). In your group, discuss the difference between the two views of fortune. What are your own views? Do you think "fortune" plays any role at all in human lives? Which view of fortune do you think is most appropriate to the outcome of the play? Record your personal feelings in your journal.

7. Have one member of your group assume the role of Kent in this scene. Have this person write the speech that Kent, who cannot reveal his identity, might have delivered to Oswald. Have another member of the group assume the role of Oswald and respond to Kent's speech, indicating what course of action he might take.

   As a group, listen to the "new" versions and compare them with what actually happened in the play. Which version is more effective? As you make your decision, be sure to consider the entire action of the play so far.

For the next scene . . .

Has your true identity ever been an obstacle to your safety? If you had to disguise yourself, even from friends and family, how would you do it?

Act 2, Scene 3

In this scene . . .

Edgar has heard of the death warrant issued by Gloucester. He decides to disguise himself as a Bedlam beggar in order to escape detection. The beggars, also called Tom O'Bedlams, were patients with mental disabilities who were turned out of Bedman hospitals to beg for food. Their wanderings about the countryside were commonplace. Edgar will cease to exist; he will now call himself Poor Tom and act like one of the Tom O'Bedlams.

1 *proclaimed:* denounced as a criminal. Proclamations were read publicly.

2 *happy:* lucky, fortunate

3 *port:* seaport. Gloucester alerted all the ports to watch for Edgar.

5 *attend:* await; *taking:* capture

6 *am bethought:* have decided

8 *penury:* poverty; *in contempt of man:* to show how worthless man is

10 *elf:* tangle; matted locks of hair that resulted from infrequent use of a comb were often said to be the work of elves.

11 *presented:* bold; *outface:* defy

12 *persecutions of the sky:* distresses caused by the changes in weather

13 *proof and precedent:* example

14 *Bedlam beggars:* vagrants of the late sixteenth and early seventeenth centuries who were, or pretended to be, discharged inmates of Bedlam Hospital, the insane asylum of St. Mary of Bethlehem.

15 *numbed and mortified:* lifeless and deadened

17 *object:* sight

18 *pelting:* paltry, insignificant, worthless; *sheepcotes:* buildings for sheltering sheep

19 *bans:* curses

20 *Enforce their charity:* extort the charity of others; *"Poor Turlygod! Poor Tom!":* Edgar is practising the beggar's cries.

21 *That's something . . . am:* As Poor Tom, I may live; as Edgar, I'm dead.

Scene 3

Open country in the neighbourhood of Gloucester's castle.

Enter Edgar.

Edgar: I heard myself proclaimed,
And by the happy hollow of a tree
Escaped the hunt. No port is free, no place
That guard and most unusual vigilance
Does not attend my taking. Whiles I may scape, 5
I will preserve myself; and am bethought
To take the basest and most poorest shape
That ever penury, in contempt of man,
Brought near to beast. My face I'll grime with filth,
Blanket my loins, elf all my hair in knots, 10
And with presented nakedness outface
The winds and persecutions of the sky.
The country gives me proof and precedent
Of Bedlam beggars, who, with roaring voices,
Strike in their numbed and mortified bare arms 15
Pins, wooden pricks, nails, sprigs of rosemary;
And with this horrible object, from low farms,
Poor pelting villages, sheepcotes, and mills,
Sometime with lunatic bans, sometime with prayers,
Enforce their charity. "Poor Turlygod! Poor Tom!" 20
That's something yet! Edgar I nothing am. [*Exit.*]

Act 2, Scene 3: Activities

1. Create a segment for "Crime Stoppers" or "The Ten Most Wanted Men" on television, describing Edgar as a dangerous criminal. Show a video of him and give a physical description (including details of what he was wearing when last seen), the crime of which he is accused, and any other information that might help to identify and apprehend him.

   Alternatively, design a "Wanted" poster that includes the same information. In addition, prepare the proclamation that would be read to the public.

2. In groups, discuss why you think Edgar chose the disguise of a Bedlam beggar. Given Edgar's background, how would he know how to act? If Edgar were suddenly transported to this century, what disguise might he adopt?

3. You are a psychiatrist and believe you can help Poor Tom regain his sanity. Write a report outlining what steps you might take to achieve this goal. Remember that Tom is not likely to be a violent beggar and would not likely wish attention drawn to himself.

4. You are a director of a modern production of *King Lear*. The actor who is playing Edgar has complained to you that modern-day audiences simply would not understand this speech because it is very artificial. The actor believes that the speech must be cut and modified if it is to be believable. In a director's log, write your responses to his objections.

For the next scene . . .

In your journal record your thoughts about how you might feel if you were suddenly deserted by those you love and left on your own. How do you think you might respond?

Act 2, Scene 4

In this scene . . .

Having found Regan absent from her palace, Lear arrives at Gloucester's castle and is immediately confronted by the sight of Kent in the stocks. When Kent explains how he came to be imprisoned, Lear is outraged.

Lear looks for Regan, only to discover that she refuses to see him. When Cornwall and Regan arrive, Kent is set free by Gloucester's intervention. Lear explains that Goneril has cut his retinue in half. He has come to stay with Regan instead, believing that she will be more kind and dutiful than her sister. However, Regan defends Goneril and advises Lear to return to her.

When Goneril arrives, the two sisters attempt to reduce Lear's status to that of a mere dependant. They insist that he can stay with them only if he dismisses all of his knights. Lear, inarticulate with rage and indignation, fears he will go mad. As a fierce storm breaks, Lear rushes out, determined not to give in to his daughters' demands. Regan and Cornwall shut the castle gates to lock him out.

1 *they:* Regan and Cornwall

4 *remove:* departure

6 *Makest thou . . . pastime?:* Is this shamefulness something you make a habit of doing to pass the time?

7 *cruel:* a pun, "cruel" being a word for "worsted," a cloth from which garters were made

9 *loins:* waist

10-11 *over-lusty:* too lively, vigorous; also implies "full of sexual desire"; *netherstocks:* stockings. "Wooden netherstocks" is a reference to the stocks themselves.

12 *place:* position, rank

21 *Jupiter:* the supreme diety of the ancient Romans, ruler of gods and humans, and the god of the heavens

22 *Juno:* the wife of Jupiter, the goddess of marriage and childbirth; *durst:* would not dare to

24 *To do . . . outrage:* to commit such an offence upon one who is entitled to respect

Scene 4

Without the gates of Gloucester's castle; Kent in the stocks.

Enter Lear, Fool, and Gentleman.

Lear: 'Tis strange that they should so depart from home,
And not send back my messenger.
Gentleman: As I learned,
The night before there was no purpose in them
Of this remove.
Kent: Hail to thee, noble master!
Lear: Ha! 5
Makest thou this shame thy pastime?
Kent: No, my lord.
Fool: Ha, ha! He wears cruel garters.
Horses are tied by the head, dogs and bears by the neck, monkeys by the loins, and men by the legs. When a man's over-lusty at legs, then he wears wooden 10 netherstocks.
Lear: What's he that hath so much thy place mistook
To set thee here?
Kent: It is both he and she—
Your son and daughter.
Lear: No. 15
Kent: Yes.
Lear: No, I say.
Kent: I say yea.
Lear: No, no, they would not!
Kent: Yes, they have. 20
Lear: By Jupiter, I swear no!
Kent: By Juno, I swear ay!
Lear: They durst not do it;
They could not, would not do it. 'Tis worse than murder
To do upon respect such violent outrage.

25 *Resolve:* tell; *modest:* reasonable; *which way:* why

26 *usage:* treatment

27 *Coming from us:* inasmuch as you come from us (the royal "we"), the King

28 *commend:* deliver; *letters:* letter

30 *duty:* respect; *reeking post:* sweaty messenger

31 *stewed:* very hot, excited

33 *spite of intermission:* in spite of interrupting my business

34 *presently:* immediately

35 *meinie:* retinue, followers, household; *straight:* immediately

36-37 *attend/The . . . answer:* wait until they were ready to answer

39 *poisoned:* spoiled, made impossible

41 *Displayed so saucily:* behaved so churlishly or insolently

42 *more man than wit:* more courage than judgement

44 *trespass:* the attack on Oswald

46-47 *Winter's not . . . way:* Your troubles are not over yet.

48-55 *Fathers that . . . year:* Roughly fathers who have no money have blind (uncaring) children. Fathers who are rich have very caring children. Fortune, like a whore, opens her door only when there is someone willing to pay money. But you (Lear) will have more dollars – a pun on the word "dolours," meaning griefs or sadnesses – than you can count in a year.

49 *blind:* to their duties as sons and daughters

50 *bear:* possess; *bags:* bags of money

51 *kind:* only because of the money

52 *arrant:* notorious

53 *turns the key:* opens the door

56-57 *mother swells . . . passio:* hysterical suffering that begins as a physical sensation below the heart and rises towards it. The word "mother" is used to indicate emotion — a female trait.

58 *Thy element's:* your proper place is

Resolve me with all modest haste which way 25
Thou mightst deserve or they impose this usage,
Coming from us.

Kent: My lord, when at their home
I did commend your Highness' letters to them,
Ere I was risen from the place that showed
My duty kneeling, came there a reeking post, 30
Stewed in his haste, half breathless, panting forth
From Goneril his mistress salutations;
Delivered letters, spite of intermission,
Which presently they read; on whose contents,
They summoned up their meinie, straight took horse, 35
Commanded me to follow and attend
The leisure of their answer, gave me cold looks,
And meeting here the other messenger,
Whose welcome I perceived had poisoned mine—
Being the very fellow which of late 40
Displayed so saucily against your Highness—
Having more man than wit about me, drew.
He raised the house with loud and coward cries.
Your son and daughter found this trespass worth
The shame which here it suffers. 45

Fool: Winter's not gone yet, if the wild geese fly that way.

Fathers that wear rags
Do make their children blind;
But fathers that bear bags 50
Shall see their children kind.
Fortune, that arrant whore,
Ne'er turns the key to the poor.

But for all this, thou shalt have as many dolours for thy daughters as thou canst tell in a year. 55

Lear: O, how this mother swells up toward my heart!
Hysterica passio! Down, thou climbing sorrow,
Thy element's below! Where is this daughter?

Kent: With the Earl, sir, here within.

Lear: Follow me not;
Stay here. [*Exit.*] 60

Gentleman: Made you no more offence but what you speak of?

Kent: None.

63 *How chance:* why does

67-68 *We'll set . . . winter:* The Fool seems to mean that Lear's fortunes have come to an end as do the ant's when winter arrives; *follow their noses:* go straight forward; but: except; *All that . . . stinking:* All those who possess judgement accept the testimony given by their own eyes, except the blind, who use their sense of smell only, and even a blind man in this way could see the truth of the situation (that Lear's plight is wretched). This wise saying, and those that follow, are meant by the Fool to indicate that he understands not only that Lear is abandoned, but also, that some, like Kent, do not seem to realize how low Lear's fortunes have fallen.

77-84 *That sir . . . perdy:* A rather convoluted argument about loyalty. The sense is that the man who serves for personal gain serves only for show. He has no inner sense of loyalty and serves only because of what he will gain from his master's position or rank. Such a person will abandon you when things become difficult and leave you to suffer by yourself. But I will remain. Let the "wise man" run away, but the servant (knave) who runs away turns out in the end to have been a fool who is seen by everyone to be contemptible. In other words, the faithless man is the true fool.

84 *perdy:* a form of oath from the French "par Dieu" meaning "by God"

88 *fetches:* pretexts, pretences (from sailing: a "fetch" or a "tack")

89 *images:* very pictures or clearest indications; *revolt and flying off:* synonymous words meaning "disloyalty."

91 *quality:* temperament

92 *unremovable and fixed:* synonymous words meaning "unyielding" or "inflexible"

94 *Confusion:* ruination

95 *What quality?:* What has his disposition to do with it?

96 *I'd speak:* I simply wish to speak.

98 *Dost thou understand me, man?:* Lear simply cannot grasp the idea that he has been deliberately snubbed.

How chance the King comes with so small a number?
Fool: An thou hadst been set i' the stocks for that question,
thou'dst well deserved it. 65
Kent: Why, fool?
Fool: We'll set thee to school to an ant, to teach thee there's
no labouring i' the winter. All that follow their noses
are led by their eyes but blind men, and there's not
a nose among twenty but can smell him that's stinking. 70
Let go thy hold when a great wheel runs down a hill,
lest it break thy neck with following it; but the great
one that goes upward, let him draw thee after. When
a wise man gives thee better counsel, give me mine
again: I would have none but knaves follow it, since 75
a fool gives it.

That sir which serves and seeks for gain,
And follows but for form,
Will pack when it begins to rain
And leave thee in the storm. 80
But I will tarry; the fool will stay,
And let the wise man fly.
The knave turns fool that runs away;
The fool no knave, perdy.

Kent: Where learned you this, fool? 85
Fool: Not i' the stocks, fool.
[*Enter Lear and Gloucester.*]
Lear: Deny to speak with me? They are sick! they are
weary!
They have travelled all the night! Mere fetches—
The images of revolt and flying off!
Fetch me a better answer.
Gloucester: My dear lord, 90
You know the fiery quality of the Duke,
How unremovable and fixed he is
In his own course.
Lear: Vengeance! Plague! Death! Confusion!
Fiery? What quality? Why, Gloucester, Gloucester, 95
I'd speak with the Duke of Cornwall and his wife.
Gloucester: Well, my good lord, I have informed them so.
Lear: Informed them? Dost thou understand me, man?
Gloucester: Ay, my good lord.

101 *commands, tends service:* Lear commands his daughter's service, and offers his own.

103 *hot:* hot-tempered

104 *May be . . . well:* Lear makes excuses for the Duke's snub. He cannot believe that such a thing could happen to a king.

105 *Infirmity:* illness; *neglect all office:* overlook duty

106 *Whereto our health is bound:* that we are bound to carry out when in good health.

108 *forbear:* be tolerant, be patient

109 *am fallen out with:* am annoyed with; *more headier:* too headstrong; *will:* impulse

110 *To take:* because I have mistaken

111 *sound:* healthy; *Death on my state:* A curse on my royal power; *Wherefore:* Why? For what reason?

113 *remotion:* avoidance (of me), remoteness from me

114 *practice:* trickery, deceit, a scheme

115 *and's:* and his

118 *cry sleep to death:* make sleep impossible

121-124 *Cry to . . . down:* The Fool's comment means that Lear is as naive about Regan and Cornwall as a cockney (a city woman) was about making an eel pie. She did not know enough to kill the eels before cooking them, and as they squirmed abut, making the pie a mess, she rapped them over the head – when it was too late.

124-125 *'Twas her . . . hay:* Her brother was evidently no more intelligent or practical than his sister

126 *Good morrow:* Since it is evening, the greeting is ironical; *Grace:* Majesty

129-131 *If thou . . . adultress:* If you are not glad to see me, you can be no daughter of mine.

132 *that:* the matter of the stocks

133 *naught:* wicked (naughty)

Lear: The King would speak with Cornwall; the dear father 100
Would with his daughter speak, commands, tends
service.
Are they informed of this? My breath and blood!
Fiery? the fiery Duke? Tell the hot Duke that—
No, but not yet! May be he is not well.
Infirmity doth still neglect all office 105
Whereto our health is bound. We are not ourselves
When nature, being oppressed, commands the mind
To suffer with the body. I'll forbear;
And am fallen out with my more headier will,
To take the indisposed and sickly fit 110
For the sound man. [*Looks at Kent.*] Death on my state!
Wherefore
Should he sit here? This act persuades me
That this remotion of the Duke and her
Is practice only. Give me my servant forth.
Go tell the Duke and's wife I'd speak with them— 115
Now, presently. Bid them come forth and hear me,
Or at their chamber door I'll beat the drum
Till it cry sleep to death.

Gloucester: I would have all well betwixt you. [*Exit.*]

Lear: O me, my heart, my rising heart! But down! 120

Fool: Cry to it, nuncle, as the cockney did to the eels when she put 'em i' the paste alive. She knapped 'em o' the coxcombs with a stick and cried "Down, wantons, down!" 'Twas her brother that, in pure kindness to his horse, buttered his hay. 125

[*Enter Cornwall, Regan, Gloucester, Servants.*]

Lear: Good morrow to you both.

Cornwall: Hail to your Grace!
[*Kent here set at liberty.*]

Regan: I am glad to see your Highness.

Lear: Regan, I think you are; I know what reason
I have to think so. If thou shouldst not be glad,
I would divorce me from thy mother's tomb, 130
Sepulchring an adultress. [*To Kent.*] O, are you free?
Some other time for that.—Beloved Regan,
Thy sister's naught. O Regan, she hath tied

134 *like a vulture:* an allusion to the eternal punishment of Prometheus. In the Greek myth he was chained to a rock where, each day, a vulture would tear out his liver and eat it while, each night, it would be restored.

136 *depraved:* wicked. Lear refers to Goneril's character or "quality."

137 *take patience:* have patience

139 *scant:* neglect

141 *obligation:* filial obligation, obligation of a son or a daughter to parents

143 *wholesome:* proper

146-147 *Nature in . . . confine:* You are on the threshold of death.

148 *discretion:* some discrete person; *discerns:* understands, perceives; *state:* your mental condition or your dependent condition

150 *make return:* go back

152 *this:* the action Lear immediately performs; *becomes the house:* suits the royal house; i.e., suits my dignity (as a king)

154 *Age is unnecessary:* Old people are useless; i.e., a person has no right to become old (probably spoken ironically).

155 *vouchsafe:* grant; *raiment:* clothing

156 *unsightly tricks:* undignified actions (falling to his knees and whining for charity)

158 *abated me . . . train:* reduced my retinue to half

159 *Looked black:* glared; *struck me with her tongue:* abused me with words

160 *Most serpent-like:* like a snake with its flickering tongue (which was thought to be a weapon for stinging)

162 *top:* head; *young bones:* possibly a reference to her unborn children

163 *taking:* infectious

166 *fen-sucked:* sucked up from marshes (by the sun)

167 *fall and blister:* fall upon Goneril and raise blisters on her

Sharp-toothed unkindness, like a vulture, here!
[*Points to his heart.*]
I can scarce speak to thee. Thou'lt not believe 135
With how depraved a quality—O Regan!
Regan: I pray you, sir, take patience. I have hope
You less know how to value her desert
Than she to scant her duty.
Lear: Say, how is that?
Regan: I cannot think my sister in the least 140
Would fail her obligation. If, sir, perchance
She have restrained the riots of your followers,
'Tis on such ground, and to such wholesome end,
As clears her from all blame.
Lear: My curses on her!
Regan: O, sir, you are old! 145
Nature in you stands on the very verge
Of her confine. You should be ruled, and led
By some discretion that discerns your state
Better than you yourself. Therefore I pray you
That to our sister you do make return; 150
Say you have wronged her.
Lear: Ask her forgiveness?
Do you but mark how this becomes the house:
[*Kneeling.*] "Dear daughter, I confess that I am old.
Age is unnecessary. On my knees I beg
That you'll vouchsafe me raiment, bed, and food." 155
Regan: Good sir, no more! These are unsightly tricks.
Return you to my sister.
Lear: [*Stands up.*] Never, Regan!
She hath abated me of half my train;
Looked black upon me; struck me with her tongue,
Most serpent-like, upon the very heart. 160
All the stored vengeances of heaven fall
On her ingrateful top! Strike her young bones,
You taking airs, with lameness!
Cornwall: Fie, sir, fie!
Lear: You nimble lightnings, dart your blinding flames
Into her scornful eyes! Infect her beauty, 165
You fen-sucked fogs, drawn by the powerful sun,
To fall and blister!

169 *the rash mood:* the mood of compulsive anger

171 *tender-hefted nature:* disposition governed by tenderness, gentle disposition

175 *bandy:* exchange; literally, bat back and forth (like a tennis ball); *scant my sizes:* reduce my allowances

176 *oppose the bolt:* to close the bolt (or lock) of the door

178 *offices of nature:* duties of a daughter; *bond of childhood:* obligation formed in childhood, a child's duty to her parents

179 *Effects:* actions; *dues of gratitude:* what gratitude is owing to a father

181 *to the purpose:* Come to the point, say what you mean.

183 *approves:* confirms

185-186 *easy, borrowed . . . follows:* confident pride, borrowed from his mistress Goneril who protects him

187 *varlet:* scoundrel

189 *on't:* of it

190 *sweet sway:* loving authority, gentle rule

191 *Allow:* permit, approve of; *obedience:* your obedience to my wish; *if you yourselves are old:* if you can sympathize with one who is old; if you can understand what it is to be old

192 *Make it your cause:* defend its privileges

196-197 *All's not . . . so:* Not everything is an offence just because your lack of judgement and your senility (dotage) make you think it so.

197 *sides:* breast, heart. Lear feels he is bursting with distress.

199 *disorders:* misbehaviour, misconduct

200 *advancement:* promotion, honour

Regan: O the blest gods! So will you wish on me
When the rash mood is on.
Lear: No, Regan, thou shalt never have my curse. 170
Thy tender-hefted nature shall not give
Thee o'er to harshness. Her eyes are fierce, but thine
Do comfort and not burn. 'Tis not in thee
To grudge my pleasures, to cut off my train,
To bandy hasty words, to scant my sizes, 175
And, in conclusion, to oppose the bolt
Against my coming in. Thou better knowest
The offices of nature, bond of childhood,
Effects of courtesy, dues of gratitude.
Thy half of the kingdom hast thou not forgot, 180
Wherein I thee endowed.
Regan: Good sir, to the purpose.
Lear: Who put my man in the stocks? [*Tucket within.*]
Cornwall: What trumpet's that?
Regan: I know it—my sister's. This approves her letter
That she would soon be here.
[*Enter Oswald the Steward.*]
Is your lady come?
Lear: This is a slave, whose easy, borrowed pride 185
Dwells in the fickle grace of her he follows.
Out, varlet, from my sight!
Cornwall: What means your Grace?
Lear: Who stocked my servant? Regan, I have good hope
Thou didst not know on't.
[*Enter Goneril.*] Who comes here? O heavens,
If you do love old men, if your sweet sway 190
Allow obedience, if you yourselves are old,
Make it your cause! Send down, and take my part!
[*To Goneril.*] Art not ashamed to look upon this beard?—
O Regan, will you take her by the hand?
Goneril: Why not by the hand, sir? How have I offended? 195
All's not offence that indiscretion finds
And dotage terms so.
Lear: O sides, you are too tough!
Will you yet hold? How came my man i' the stocks?
Cornwall: I set him there, sir, but his own disorders
Deserved much less advancement.

201 *being weak, seem so:* Since you are powerless, behave as if you are.

204 *train:* retinue

205-206 *I am . . . entertainment:* I am not now at home and am unable, therefore, to provide what you require for your comfort.

208 *abjure:* abandon, give up; *roofs:* shelter, to which Lear is entitled

209 *wage:* struggle, fight

211 *Necessity's sharp pinch:* a summary of the choice he has just announced; i.e., it is inevitable that poverty should bring exposure to the cold, the wind, and the rain.

212 *hot-blooded:* passionate; *France:* the King of France

213 *brought:* forced. Since no one has forced Lear to do anything for a long time, he finds the thought of such coercion intolerable.

214 *knee:* bow before; *squire-like:* like a servant

215 *To keep base life afoot:* to keep body and soul together, to keep from starvation

216 *sumpter:* pack-animal, beast of burden

218 *mad:* insane (not angry)

223 *must needs:* am compelled to; *boil:* pus-filled sore

224 *plague sore:* external sign or mark of bubonic plague; *embossed carbuncle:* particularly large boil forming a distinct lump on the surface of the body.

225 *corrupted:* diseased, infected

226 *shame:* Goneril's disgrace as a cruel daughter

227 *Thunder-bearer:* Jupiter

228 *Jove:* Zeus, judge of all humans

229 *Mend:* make amends; *be better:* be a better daughter

233 *give ear, sir, to:* pay attention, listen to

234 *those that . . . passion:* who consider reasonably your violent emotion

235 *and so:* Regan breaks off, implying: You are old, and that explains your irrational actions.

Lear: You? Did you? 200
Regan: I pray you, father, being weak, seem so.
If, till the expiration of your month,
You will return and sojourn with my sister,
Dismissing half your train, come then to me.
I am now from home, and out of that provision 205
Which shall be needful for your entertainment.
Lear: Return to her, and fifty men dismissed?
No, rather I abjure all roofs, and choose
To wage against the enmity o' the air,
To be a comrade with the wolf and owl— 210
Necessity's sharp pinch! Return with her?
Why, the hot-blooded France, that dowerless took
Our youngest born, I could as well be brought
To knee his throne, and, squire-like, pension beg
To keep base life afoot. Return with her? 215
Persuade me rather to be slave and sumpter
To this detested groom. [*Pointing at Oswald.*]
Goneril: At your choice, sir.
Lear: I prithee, daughter, do not make me mad.
I will not trouble thee, my child; farewell.
We'll no more meet, no more see one another. 220
But yet thou art my flesh, my blood, my daughter;
Or rather a disease that's in my flesh,
Which I must needs call mine. Thou art a boil,
A plague sore or embossed carbuncle,
In my corrupted blood. But I'll not chide thee. 225
Let shame come when it will, I do not call it.
I do not bid the Thunder-bearer shoot,
Nor tell tales of thee to high-judging Jove.
Mend when thou canst; be better at thy leisure;
I can be patient; I can stay with Regan, 230
I and my hundred knights.
Regan: Not altogether so.
I looked not for you yet, nor am provided
For your fit welcome. Give ear, sir, to my sister;
For those that mingle reason with your passion
Must be content to think you old, and so— 235
But she knows what she does.

237 *avouch:* maintain, stand by, affirm

239 *sith that:* since; *charge and danger:* expense and risks involved in having such large numbers of unruly men about

242 *Hold amity?:* keep peace

245 *slack ye:* be neglectful of you, fall short of their duty

247 *spy:* see, perceive

248 *but:* only

249 *notice:* recognition

250 *I gave you all:* I gave you everything; *And in . . . it:* You gave up your kingdom barely in time (because you are old and senile).

251 *depositaries:* trustees. Lear thought that his rule was given in trust to his daughters, and that all the privileges of his office would remain as they had been. Goneril and Regan, of course, put no such limit on their inheritance.

252-253 *kept a reservation:* reserved the right; *to be . . . number:* to be served by my original one hundred knights

256-258 *Those wicked . . . wicked:* Some wicked persons (like Goneril) look pleasing by comparison when others (like Regan) are even more wicked; *not being . . . praise:* It is in Goneril's favour that she is not as bad as Regan.

261 *What need you:* what need have you of

262 *twice so many:* fifty (of my servants)

264-265 *O, reason not the need:* Do not examine the exact need; *Our basest . . . superfluous:* Even the poorest beggars have things that they do not actually need.

266-267 *Allow not . . . beast's:* If you allow a person no more than what is absolutely necessary, that person is no better than an animal.

268-270 *If only . . . thee warm:* If warmth alone were all you require of clothing, then your dazzling dress is obviously unnecessary, since gorgeousness is not naturally essential.

Lear: Is this well spoken?
Regan: I dare avouch it, sir. What, fifty followers?
Is it not well? What should you need of more?
Yea, or so many, sith that both charge and danger
Speak 'gainst so great a number? How in one house 240
Should many people, under two commands,
Hold amity? 'Tis hard; almost impossible.
Goneril: Why might not you, my lord, receive attendance
From those that she calls servants, or from mine?
Regan: Why not, my lord? If then they chanced to slack
ye, 245
We could control them. If you will come to me
(For now I spy a danger), I entreat you
To bring but five-and-twenty. To no more
Will I give place or notice.
Lear: I gave you all—
Regan: And in good time you gave it! 250
Lear: Made you my guardians, my depositaries;
But kept a reservation to be followed
With such a number. What, must I come to you
With five-and-twenty, Regan? Said you so?
Regan: And speak it again, my lord. No more with me. 255
Lear: Those wicked creatures yet do look well-favoured
When others are more wicked; not being the worst
Stands in some rank of praise. [*To Goneril.*] I'll go with
thee.
Thy fifty yet doth double five-and-twenty,
And thou art twice her love.
Goneril: Hear me, my lord. 260
What need you five-and-twenty, ten, or five,
To follow in a house where twice so many
Have a command to tend you?
Regan: What need one?
Lear: O, reason not the need! Our basest beggars
Are in the poorest thing superfluous. 265
Allow not nature more than nature needs,
Man's life is cheap as beast's. Thou art a lady:
If only to go warm were gorgeous,
Why, nature needs not what thou gorgeous wearest,

270-271 *But, for . . . I need:* As Lear is about to explain the difference between true need and frivolous need, he stops to pray for his own need at the moment – patience.

275-276 *fool me . . . tamely:* Do not make such a fool of me that I will take all this meekly.

277 *women's weapons, water drops:* tears

Stage direction – *Sounds of an approaching storm:* The storm and Lear's madness approach together.

289 *bestowed:* lodged, sheltered

290 *blame:* fault; *hath put himself from rest:* has caused his own frustration and downfall

291 *taste his folly:* endure the effects of his foolish actions

292 *his particular:* himself alone

297 *will I know not whither:* I do not know where he intends to go.

298 *give him way:* let him go; *leads himself:* does as he wishes, and will not be hindered

301 *Do sorely ruffle:* are very blustery

Which scarcely keeps thee warm. But, for true need— 270
You heavens, give me that patience, patience I need!
You see me here, you gods, a poor old man,
As full of grief as age; wretched in both.
If it be you that stirs these daughters' hearts
Against their father, fool me not so much 275
To bear it tamely; touch me with noble anger,
And let not women's weapons, water drops,
Stain my man's cheeks! No, you unnatural hags!
I will have such revenges on you both
That all the world shall—I will do such things— 280
What they are yet, I know not; but they shall be
The terrors of the earth! You think I'll weep.
No, I'll not weep. [*Sounds of an approaching storm.*]
I have full cause of weeping, but this heart
Shall break into a hundred thousand flaws 285
Or ere I'll weep. O fool, I shall go mad!
[*Exeunt Lear, Gloucester, Kent, and Fool.*]
Cornwall: Let us withdraw, 'twill be a storm.
Regan: This house is little; the old man and's people
Cannot be well bestowed.
Goneril: 'Tis his own blame; hath put himself from rest 290
And must needs taste his folly.
Regan: For his particular, I'll receive him gladly,
But not one follower.
Goneril: So am I purposed.
Where is my Lord of Gloucester?
Cornwall: Followed the old man forth.
[*Enter Gloucester.*] He is returned. 295
Gloucester: The King is in high rage.
Cornwall: Whither is he going?
Gloucester: He calls to horse, but will I know not whither.
Cornwall: 'Tis best to give him way, he leads himself.
Goneril: My lord, entreat him by no means to stay.
Gloucester: Alack, the night comes on, and the bleak winds 300
Do sorely ruffle. For many miles about
There's scarce a bush.
Regan: O, sir, to wilful men
The injuries that they themselves procure

304 *Must be their schoolmasters:* must teach them wisdom

305 *desperate train:* violent group of followers

306 *incense:* provoke

307 *To have his ear abused:* to be misled by evil advisers; *wisdom bids fear:* It would be wise to fear (the "desperate train").

Must be their schoolmasters. Shut up your doors.
He is attended with a desperate train, 305
And what they may incense him to, being apt
To have his ear abused, wisdom bids fear.
Cornwall: Shut up your doors, my lord; 'tis a wild night.
My Regan counsels well. Come out o' the storm.
[*Exeunt.*]

Act 2, Scene 4: Activities

1. The Fool delivers two puzzling speeches in this scene (lines 46–55 and 67–84). In groups, determine how these speeches fit into the fabric of the play. Write a new speech for the Fool that would summarize these two speeches. Insert your speech into the scene in an appropriate place, and share it with others in the class. Remember to compose your speech so that your audience will understand its context.

2. In this scene, King Lear appears bewildered by Regan's absence from her home and by Kent's imprisonment. Discuss why you think Lear cannot comprehend what is happening. If you were Kent in this scene, what might you say to Lear who seems to be more interested in his own plight than in yours? Where would you place this speech?

3. In your journal, record your responses to Lear's behaviour in this scene, remembering that he is a former king, a father, and an ordinary human being. If you had an opportunity to speak to Lear at this point, what would you say to him?

4. With your group, discuss how you feel about Regan's treatment of her father in this scene. Do you feel she is justified? Prepare an argument that Regan might use to defend her position if she were interviewed on a current affairs program on television. Conduct the interview for other groups in the class.

5. Regan implies that suffering is a good teacher (lines 302–04). With your group, discuss whether or not you agree with her. Cite as many current examples as you feel appropriate, as well as any significant examples from the play so far. If you could choose one character from the play to hear your observations, who would it be? How do you think he or she would respond?

Act 2: Consider the Whole Act

1. Imagine that Kent has been keeping a diary of the events in the kingdom since Lear's abdication. Write his diary entries for this act. Be certain to indicate his feelings about who can and cannot be trusted, since he may use these notes to provide information to Cordelia at some later date.

2. In Scene 4, when Kent asks the Fool why Lear now has so few followers, he is told that men desert leaders when they sense that fortune has turned against them. As a member of Lear's retinue, how would you respond to this criticism? Create a brief dialogue between you and another of Lear's knights in which you give your thoughts on this issue.

3. Cornwall makes a number of brief appearances in this act. With a partner or in your group, determine what you think Cornwall understands about the events that have occurred in this act. What do you think motivates him? Is he in control of events or is his wife the motivator for his actions? What is your opinion of Cornwall as a character? Do you think he is a good or bad leader? If you could speak to him, what questions might you ask him?

4. If you were given the opportunity to add one more illustration to this text that would best capture the essence of Act 2, what would you draw? Sketch or describe your illustration and compare it with those already included with the act.

5. Create a chart, listing on one side the factors and events that suggest the collapse of Lear's former kingdom and, on the other, those that suggest that total collapse may not occur. From the evidence on your chart, predict the action that could possibly transpire. You may wish to add to your chart as the play unfolds.

6. Prepare a list of five or six questions that you would like to ask one character from this act. Make sure that your questions are worded in such a way that they will get full responses. Ask a classmate to assume the character you have chosen and interview him or her, using your prepared questions. You have five minutes to conduct your interview. What other questions do you wish you had asked?

7. There are a number of repeated words and images in this act that help both to underscore key ideas and to reinforce characterization. Brainstorm with your group and make a list of these words and images. Decide whether these words and images help to identify characters as either clearly good or clearly evil. From your list, decide which words and images are better related to themes than to characters. What do you think the most important themes are?

   Keep your list current as the play progresses and decide whether or not the observations you have made are consistent throughout. Feel free to alter your point of view as you continue.

8. You have been asked to make a one-page summary of the action, the characters, and the main themes of the play so far. You will use this summary as the basis of a children's story based on *King Lear*. You must make certain that your summary is very clear, easy to follow, and easy to understand. Write your summary and share it with others in the class. How do the summaries differ? How do you account for these differences? After reading several summaries, make an entry in your journal in which you decide whether or not there is such a thing as the "right" story.

9. In your journal, write a series of questions that you would like to ask Shakespeare about his play if you could

speak to him at this point. You may wish to use some of the following starters as a guide:

- Why did you . . . ?
- Why didn't you . . . ?
- I can't figure out . . . ?
- I am really confused by . . . ?
- Why did you introduce . . . (character)?
- I really like . . .
- Why is . . . ?
- How did you stage . . . ?

For the next scene . . .

Imagine that you lived in a country that was in social and political turmoil. What circumstances would concern you?

Act 3, Scene 1

In this scene . . .

In the barren countryside, Kent meets one of Lear's gentlemen. Kent learns that Lear is wandering about in the raging storm, accompanied only by the Fool.

Kent tells the gentleman that a dispute is brewing between Albany and Cornwall and that Cordelia and France have been kept informed of the situation by their spies. The King of France is now sending troops to invade England and to rescue Lear. Kent sends the gentleman to Dover with a message for Cordelia, and gives him a ring with which he can identify himself. Kent and the gentleman separate in search of Lear.

2 *minded like . . . unquietly:* with an unquiet (uneasy) mind

4 *Contending with the fretful elements:* struggling with the weather

6 *curled waters:* waves; *main:* land

7 *things:* everything, the order of the world; specifically, Lear's misfortunes

8 *blasts:* winds; *eyeless:* unseeing, blind

9 *make nothing of:* show no respect for

10 *his little world of man:* man's microcosm, in the sense that man is himself a little world

11 *to-and-fro-conflicting:* swaying around in angry conflict

12 *cub-drawn:* hungry. Literally, with udders sucked dry by cubs; *couch:* remain in shelter

13 *belly-pinched:* gaunt and ravenous

14 *unbonneted:* hatless

15 *And bids . . . all:* and invites any destructive force to take his life. A gambler, recklessly staking everything he or she has left, might call "Take all."

16-17 *labours to . . . injuries:* works hard at joking to relieve the pain caused by Lear's heart-breaking situation

18 *upon the . . . note:* on the strength or guarantee of the fact that I know you

19 *Commend:* entrust; *a dear thing:* an important matter; *division:* discord, disunity

20-21 *(Although as . . . cunning):* although the appearance of discord is cunningly concealed

22-23 *that their . . . high?:* that fate has raised to a position of great power; *who seem no less:* who appear nothing more or less

24 *speculations:* synonym for "spies"

25 *Intelligent of our state:* giving information about our government

26 *snuffs and packings:* resentments and (consequent) plottings

27-28 *hard rein . . . King:* arbitrary and cruel way in which they have treated Lear

Act 3, Scene 1

A heath.

Storm still. Enter Kent and a Gentleman, severally.

Kent: Who's there, besides foul weather?
Gentleman: One minded like the weather, most unquietly.
Kent: I know you. Where's the King?
Gentleman: Contending with the fretful elements;
Bids the wind blow the earth into the sea, 5
Or swell the curled waters 'bove the main,
That things might change or cease; tears his white hair,
Which the impetuous blasts, with eyeless rage,
Catch in their fury and make nothing of;
Strives in his little world of man to outscorn 10
The to-and-fro-conflicting wind and rain.
This night, wherein the cub-drawn bear would couch,
The lion and the belly-pinched wolf
Keep their fur dry, unbonneted he runs,
And bids what will take all.
Kent: But who is with him? 15
Gentleman: None but the fool, who labours to outjest
His heart-struck injuries.
Kent: Sir, I do know you,
And dare upon the warrant of my note
Commend a dear thing to you. There is division
(Although as yet the face of it is covered 20
With mutual cunning) 'twixt Albany and Cornwall;
Who have (as who have not, that their great stars
Throned and set high?) servants, who seem no less,
Which are to France the spies and speculations
Intelligent of our state. What hath been seen, 25
Either in snuffs and packings of the Dukes,
Or the hard rein which both of them have borne
Against the old kind King, or something deeper,

29 *furnishings:* outward evidences, trimmings, pretexts; Kent's sentence remains unfinished.

30 *power:* army

31 *scattered:* divided

32 *Wise in our negligence:* knowing that we are ill-prepared; *have secret feet:* having obtained a secret foothold

33 *at point:* on the point of, ready to

35 *If on . . . far:* if you dare to trust me as far as

36 *make your speed:* hurry

37 *making:* for making; *just:* accurate

38 *bemadding:* maddening

39 *plain:* complain of

41 *assurance:* reliable information

42 *office:* assignment, duty

45 *my out-wall:* my outer wall, exterior, or what I appear to be; Kent is in the disguise of a servant.

52 *to effect:* in their importance

53-54 *(in which . . . this):* in which your task lies this way (as he has just been instructed by Kent), while mine lies in this direction; *lights on:* discovers

55 *Holla:* shout for, summon

Whereof, perchance, these are but furnishings—
But, true it is, from France there comes a power 30
Into this scattered kingdom, who already,
Wise in our negligence, have secret feet
In some of our best ports and are at point
To show their open banner. Now to you:
If on my credit you dare build so far 35
To make your speed to Dover, you shall find
Some that will thank you, making just report
Of how unnatural and bemadding sorrow
The King hath cause to plain.
I am a gentleman of blood and breeding, 40
And from some knowledge and assurance offer
This office to you.

Gentleman: I will talk further with you.

Kent: No, do not.
For confirmation that I am much more
Than my out-wall, open this purse and take 45
What it contains. If you shall see Cordelia
(As fear not but you shall), show her this ring,
And she will tell you who that fellow is
That yet you do not know. Fie on this storm!
I will go seek the King. 50

Gentleman: Give me your hand. Have you no more to say?

Kent: Few words, but, to effect, more than all yet:
That, when we have found the King (in which your pain
That way, I'll this), he that first lights on him
Holla the other. [*Exeunt severally.*] 55

Act 3, Scene 1: Activities

1. Kent obviously knows a great deal more about what is going on in the kingdom than he has told Lear's gentleman. Assume the two have had a fuller conversation and, with a partner, create their brief but pointed dialogue. What is Kent's role in the invasion plot? What are his plans and motives? Is he completely open and honest with Lear's gentleman? Does the gentleman trust him?

   Enact your conversation for the class.

2. In this scene, Kent reveals enough to have himself killed. Who is the man to whom he is talking? What can you tell about him and his motives? Role-play a television interview with this mystery man, the source of some important information about impending events. Find out who he is and what he is up to.

3. There appears to be no coherent sense of geography in this play. Draw a map of the action so far in terms of "who went where." Use this scene as the centre of your map and position everyone else in locations that make sense for you.

4. If this scene were accidentally left out, what gaps would its exclusion create? How would the play be altered? Discuss your ideas.

For the next scene . . .

In your journal, recount an instance in which you encountered an elderly person in a position much worse than your own. What thoughts went through your mind? What thoughts do you think were going through that person's mind? What feeling do you have about becoming elderly yourself?

Act 3, Scene 2

In this scene . . .

In another part of the heath, Lear stands raging at the storm. The Fool attempts to make him take shelter, but Lear pays no attention. When Kent finds them, he persuades Lear to seek out a hovel that is close by. Lear agrees, fearing for his sanity. Kent decides to return to Gloucester's castle to persuade Goneril and Regan that they should allow Lear to return.

1 *Blow, winds . . . blow:* Old maps were often decorated with faces drawn in the act of furiously blowing air or wind.

2 *cataracts:* the floodgates of the heavens; *hurricanoes:* waterspouts

3 *cocks:* weather-vanes on the peaks of buildings

4 *thought-executing:* killing with the speed of thought

5 *Vaunt-couriers:* forerunners (from the French "avant coureurs"); *oak-cleaving:* strong enough to split an oak

7 *Strike flat . . . world:* flatten the earth

8 *Nature's molds:* shapes into which all things are first poured in their creation; i.e., the creative force of Nature, which has cheated Lear by giving him such ungrateful daughters; *germens:* seeds; *spill:* destroy, kill

10 *court holy water:* flattering words (a proverbial phrase); flatter your daughters into giving you shelter for the night.

11-12 *ask/thy daughters' blessing:* Apologize and come to terms with your daughters.

14 *thy bellyful:* Since the storm is personified, the sense is "to your heart's content," or until you have had enough.

15 *Nor:* neither

16-18 *I tax . . . subscription:* Lear feels no bitterness at the storm, which owes him nothing. He implies that what the storm can do to him is nothing compared with what has been done to him by his daughters.

21 *servile ministers:* slave-like or cringing servants

22-23 *pernicious:* evil; *join/Your high-engendered battles:* combine your heavenly (and hence, all-powerful) battalions

25 *put's:* put his

26 *headpiece:* a pun: hat and brain. Lear should have brains enough to take shelter from the storm.

27-30 *The codpiece . . . many:* The man who satisfies his sexual drives before he has a roof over his head will end up a lice-infested beggar; *codpiece:* a cover for the male genitals, worn on the outside of tight fitting hose. Here, it symbolizes sexual lust.

Scene 2

Another part of the heath.

Storm still. Enter Lear and Fool.

Lear: Blow, winds, and crack your cheeks! rage! blow!
You cataracts and hurricanoes, spout
Till you have drenched our steeples, drowned the cocks!
You sulph'rous and thought-executing fires,
Vaunt-couriers of oak-cleaving thunderbolts, 5
Singe my white head! And thou, all-shaking thunder,
Strike flat the thick rotundity o' the world,
Crack Nature's molds, all germens spill at once,
That make ingrateful man!

Fool: O nuncle, court holy water in a dry house is better 10
than this rain water out o' door. Good nuncle, in; ask
thy daughters' blessing! Here's a night pities neither
wise men nor fools.

Lear: Rumble thy bellyful! Spit, fire! Spout, rain!
Nor rain, wind, thunder, fire are my daughters. 15
I tax not you, you elements, with unkindness.
I never gave you kingdom, called you children,
You owe me no subscription. Then let fall
Your horrible pleasure. Here I stand your slave,
A poor, infirm, weak, and despised old man. 20
But yet I call you servile ministers,
That will with two pernicious daughters join
Your high-engendered battles 'gainst a head
So old and white as this! O, ho! 'Tis foul!

Fool: He that has a house to put's head in has a good 25
headpiece.

The codpiece that will house
Before the head has any,
The head and he shall louse:
So beggars marry many. 30

31-34 *The man . . . wake:* The man who pays more attention to an unimportant part of his body (his toe) rather than to an important one (his brain) will suffer harm from the part he considered significant. The implication is that Lear has brought this trouble on himself by failing to see things in the proper order of importance.

35-36 *For there . . . glass:* A reference to vanity – possibly that of Goneril and Regan or, perhaps, a reference to their practised hypocrisy.

37 *pattern:* example

40 *grace:* the King's grace or the King himself; *codpiece:* The Fool refers to himself. He leaves Kent to decide which is the wise man and which the fool.

44 *Gallow:* terrify

48 *carry:* bear, endure

50 *pudder:* turmoil

53 *Unwhipped of:* unpunished by; *bloody:* murderous

54 *simular:* simulator, pretender

55 *incestuous:* lustful after child, sibling, or parent – a desire considered abhorrent in all societies; *Caitiff:* wretch

56 *covert:* secret; *seeming:* pretence, hypocrisy

57 *practised:* plotted against; *guilts:* crimes

58-59 *Rive your concealing continents:* Shatter the containers hiding you; *summoners:* church officers who called offenders before the church courts. Here, the summoners are the vengeances against sinful man, represented by the storm; *cry/These dreadful summoners grace:* beg for mercy from

62 *lend:* give, afford

63 *hard house:* cruel palace (of Gloucester)

65 *Which:* the owners of which

66 *to come in:* entry, welcome

67 *scanted:* missing

The man that makes his toe
What he his heart should make
Shall of corn cry woe,
And turn his sleep to wake.
For there was never yet fair woman but she made 35
mouths in a glass.
[*Enter Kent.*]
Lear: No, I will be the pattern of all patience;
I will say nothing.
Kent: Who's there?
Fool: Marry, here's grace and a codpiece; that's a wise man 40
and a fool.
Kent: Alas, sir, are you here? Things that love night
Love not such nights as these. The wrathful skies
Gallow the very wanderers of the dark
And make them keep their caves. Since I was man, 45
Such sheets of fire, such bursts of horrid thunder,
Such groans of roaring wind and rain, I never
Remember to have heard. Man's nature cannot carry
The affliction nor the fear.
Lear: Let the great gods,
That keep this dreadful pudder o'er our heads, 50
Find out their enemies now. Tremble, thou wretch,
That hast within thee undivulged crimes
Unwhipped of justice. Hide thee, thou bloody hand;
Thou perjured, and thou simular of virtue
That are incestuous. Caitiff, to pieces shake 55
That under covert and convenient seeming
Hast practised on man's life. Close pent-up guilts,
Rive your concealing continents, and cry
These dreadful summoners grace. I am a man
More sinned against than sinning.
Kent: Alack, bareheaded? 60
Gracious my lord, hard by here is a hovel;
Some friendship will it lend you 'gainst the tempest.
Repose you there, while I to this hard house
(More harder than the stones whereof 'tis raised,
Which even but now, demanding after you, 65
Denied me to come in) return, and force
Their scanted courtesy.

70 *art:* Lear refers to the art of alchemy, which contrived to turn base metals into gold. He is pointing out that necessity has a strange way of changing us.

71 *vile:* paltry (such as mere straw for bedding)

74-77 *He that . . . day:* The Fool's song is an adaptation of a song in *Twelfth Night*. The meaning is that a fool must be content with whatever fortune brings, which will be poor because he is a fool. He may be referring to himself, or to Lear, or to both.

78 *True:* Lear agrees with the Fool; *bring:* show me the way

79 *cool a courtesan:* visit a prostitute. The Fool lewdly pretends that they are entering a brothel.

81 *more in word than matter:* better in preaching than in conduct

81-94 *When priests . . . feet:* The Fool speaks of a series of prophecies that are based upon common events, and pretends that they will probably never happen. Lines 81-84 refer to the actual state of affairs; lines 85-90 refer to the ideal state of affairs.

82 *malt:* an ingredient of beer and ale

83 *their tailors' tutors:* teach their tailors how to make clothes

84 *No heretics . . . suitors:* accepted religious belief. They were frequently burned at the stake. The Fool is punning: "burned" means suffering from the pox (syphilis).

86 *squire:* boy apprenticed to a knight to learn the art of knighthood

88 *cutpurses:* thieves (who cut purse strings and make off with the purse)

89 *tell:* count

90 *bawds:* See line 79, a variant of courtesan or prostitute; *do churches build:* as a sign of repentance

91 *Albion:* Britain

92 *confusion:* ruin

93 *who:* if anyone

94 *That going . . . feet:* that feet shall be used for walking – an absurd truism

95 *Merlin:* the magician of King Arthur's Court. The general setting of *King Lear* is early England before the time of King Arthur.

Lear: My wits begin to turn.
Come on, my boy. How dost, my boy? Art cold?
I am cold myself. Where is this straw, my fellow?
The art of our necessities is strange, 70
And can make vile things precious. Come, your hovel.
Poor fool and knave, I have one part in my heart
That's sorry yet for thee.

Fool [*Sings.*]*:*
He that has and a little tiny wit,
With hey, ho, the wind and the rain, 75
Must make content with his fortunes fit,
Though the rain it raineth every day.

Lear: True, boy. Come, bring us to this hovel.
[*Exeunt Lear and Kent.*]

Fool: This is a brave night to cool a courtesan. I'll speak a prophecy ere I go: 80
When priests are more in word than matter;
When brewers mar their malt with water;
When nobles are their tailors' tutors,
No heretics burned, but wenches' suitors;
When every case in law is right; 85
No squire in debt nor no poor knight;
When slanders do not live in tongues;
Nor cutpurses come not to throngs;
When usurers tell their gold i' the field;
And bawds and whores do churches build: 90
Then shall the realm of Albion
Come to great confusion.
Then comes the time, who lives to see't,
That going shall be used with feet.
This prophecy Merlin shall make, for I live before his 95
time. [*Exit.*]

Act 3, Scene 2: Activities

1. You are a reporter who has been sent by a local television station to film Lear on the heath. Prepare a shooting script of that scene. A shooting script divides the text into audio and visual parts that support each other.

   To prepare your shooting script, divide a page in half and supply the words in the text on one side with the visual details that highlight and support the audio material on the other side. After you have edited the shooting script and have rehearsed your shoot, prepare a video to share with your classmates.

2. Many of the Fool's comments and songs contain obscene references. Why do you think the Fool might speak this way? Is he simply crude? Demented? Trying to make a point of some kind? Is Shakespeare using the Fool simply to amuse the audience?

   In groups, discuss your ideas about the Fool's role. Do you think the Fool is necessary in the play?

For the next scene . . .

In your journal, recall an incident in which you tried to help two parties resolve a problem, but became the villain in the eyes of both parties. Do you think you were used by one or the other party? How was the situation resolved?

Act 3, Scene 3

In this scene . . .

Gloucester trusts Edmund so implicitly that he reveals to him the contents of a letter that gives details of the invading army that has already landed in England. In addition, Gloucester tells Edmund that he is determined to help Lear despite Cornwall's commands against it.

Edmund decides to inform Cornwall that his father is a traitor. He believes that this information will induce Cornwall (who has confiscated Gloucester's possessions) to give them to Edmund.

1-2	*unnatural/dealing:* cruel treatment given to Lear
2	*pity:* take pity on
4	*perpetual displeasure:* permanent hostility
5	*sustain:* care for
8	*Go to:* roughly equivalent to "That's enough."
9	*worse matter:* i.e., the French invasion
10	*'tis dangerous to be spoken:* It's dangerous to divulge the contents in speaking.
11	*closet:* private room or, perhaps, cupboard
12	*home:* completely, to the utmost
13	*power:* army; *footed:* landed (from France); *incline to:* support
14	*look him:* look for him; *privily relieve:* secretly aid
15	*charity:* kind treatment
19	*toward:* imminent, about to happen
21	*courtesy:* service; *forbid:* forbidden
22	*Instantly know:* from Edmund
23	*a fair deserving:* a service that should bring me the reward I deserve; *draw me:* bring to me

Scene 3

Inside Gloucester's castle.

Enter Gloucester and Edmund.

Gloucester: Alack, alack, Edmund, I like not this unnatural dealing! When I desired their leave that I might pity him, they took from me the use of mine own house; charged me on pain of perpetual displeasure neither to speak of him, entreat for him, nor any way sustain him. 5

Edmund: Most savage and unnatural!

Gloucester: Go to; say you nothing. There is division between the Dukes, and a worse matter than that. I have received a letter this night—'tis dangerous to be spoken— 10 I have locked the letter in my closet. These injuries the King now bears will be revenged home; there is part of a power already footed; we must incline to the King. I will look him and privily relieve him. Go you and maintain talk with the Duke, that my charity 15 be not of him perceived. If he ask for me, I am ill and gone to bed. If I die for it, as no less is threatened me, the King my old master must be relieved. There are strange things toward, Edmund. Pray you be careful. [*Exit.*] 20

Edmund: This courtesy, forbid thee, shall the Duke
Instantly know, and of that letter too.
This seems a fair deserving, and must draw me
That which my father loses—no less than all.
The younger rises when the old doth fall. [*Exit.*] 25

Act 3, Scene 3: Activities

1. Many critics have argued that Shakespeare wrote some scenes simply to give actors time to prepare for the action that follows. This scene is often cited as an example of this argument. In groups, discuss whether or not you think this scene is necessary to the sense of the play. Does it present any new information? Does it add any new insights to your understanding of the play? Before making your decision, review the scene with your group. Consider the difference between the text and a performance of this scene on stage. How long might it take to present this scene?

2. Some people have said that this scene is repetitive and boring. Do you agree? Discuss your ideas. If you agree, explain what is repeated that bores you.

For the next scene . . .

In your journal, describe an example of human life in the most degraded form imaginable that you have either witnessed first-hand or encountered in the media. What, in your opinion, caused the situation? Do you believe that people in such conditions need help or that they must help themselves?

Act 3, Scene 4

In this scene . . .

Kent, Lear, and the Fool arrive outside the hovel. Despite Kent's pleas, Lear refuses to enter. Seemingly impervious to the storm, he rages at his two daughters for their treatment of him. He tells Kent that he wishes to remain outside and pray.

As the Fool goes inside, Lear addresses the "poor naked wretches" (line 28) of the world whom he feels he has neglected. Suddenly Edgar, disguised as Poor Tom, speaks from inside the hovel. Lear, now quite mad, thinks the beggar has been brought to his fate by ungrateful daughters – he feels that only daughters as cruel as his own could reduce a man to such a pitiful condition. Faced with this image of "unaccommodated man," Lear asks, "Is man no more than this?" In sympathy with the beggar, Lear tears off his own clothes.

Gloucester enters to offer Lear shelter. Lear eventually agrees to follow him but insists on taking Poor Tom along. Gloucester reveals to Kent that Goneril and Regan are seeking Lear's death.

2 *The tyranny . . . night's:* the harshness of the night in the open air

3 *nature:* human strength

4 *Wilt break my heart?:* Possibly Lear addressing his own heart or Lear thinking that if he remains in the storm he will be distracted from thinking about the ingratitude that has happened to him which would break his heart.

6 *'tis much:* that it much matters; *contentious:* contending (in the sense of contending or struggling against humans)

7 *Invades:* soaks

8-9 *But where . . . felt:* Where a greater illness is established, a lesser one is scarcely noticed.

11-12 *i' the mouth:* face to face; *When the . . . delicate:* When the mind is untroubled, the body is sensitive.

14 *Save what beats there:* except what troubles my heart – the ungratefulness of Goneril and Regan; *Filial ingratitude:* ungratefulness of children

16 *home:* to the fullest extent

21 *that way:* in thinking of those things; *shun:* avoid

25 *On things would:* on things that would

Scene 4

Before a hovel on the heath.

Storm still. Enter Lear, Kent, and Fool.

Kent: Here is the place, my lord. Good my lord, enter.
The tyranny of the open night's too rough
For nature to endure.
Lear: Let me alone.
Kent: Good my lord, enter here.
Lear: Wilt break my heart?
Kent: I had rather break mine own. Good my lord, enter. 5
Lear: Thou thinkest 'tis much that this contentious storm
Invades us to the skin. So 'tis to thee;
But where the greater malady is fixed,
The lesser is scarce felt. Thou'dst shun a bear;
But if thy flight lay toward the roaring sea, 10
Thou'dst meet the bear i' the mouth. When the mind's free,
The body's delicate. The tempest in my mind
Doth from my senses take all feeling else
Save what beats there. Filial ingratitude!
Is it not as this mouth should tear this hand 15
For lifting food to it? But I will punish home!
No, I will weep no more. In such a night
To shut me out! Pour on; I will endure.
In such a night as this! O Regan, Goneril!
Your old kind father, whose frank heart gave all! 20
O, that way madness lies; let me shun that!
No more of that.
Kent: Good my lord, enter here.
Lear: Prithee go in thyself; seek thine own ease.
This tempest will not give me leave to ponder
On things would hurt me more. But I'll go in. 25

26 *You houseless poverty:* you poor, homeless fellow. Here, the abstract is used for the concrete.

27 *pray:* Lear prays to the poor, not to the gods.

29 *bide:* endure; *pelting:* relentless pouring

31 *looped and windowed raggedness:* ragged clothing full of gaping holes.

33 *this:* this condition of the poor, to which I have been reduced; *Take physic, pomp:* Cure yourselves, you great ones. Lear then gives the remedy.

35-36 *shake the . . . just:* Cast away what you do not need (the "superflux" or superfluity) and give it to the poor, and show that there is more justice in life than we think.

37 *Fathom and half:* Edgar uses the call of the sailor sound, which is made to sound the depth of water in the hold of a sinking ship.

46 *Humh:* Edgar shivers from the cold and damp.

48 *Didst thou . . . daughters?:* Lear, in his madness, thinks that any misfortune evidently as great as Poor Tom's could only have been inflicted by daughters as ungrateful as his own.

50-61 *Who gives . . . there:* Edgar is begging for charity, but he is not entirely coherent. We must remember that he is playing a part.

53 *laid knives under his pillow:* for killing himself; *halters in his pew:* ropes with which to hang himself from a porch

54 *ratsbane:* rat poison; *porridge:* broth, soup

55 *bay:* brown; *trotting horse:* horse trained to move gently; *four-inched:* very narrow

56-57 *course:* chase; *for:* as; *Bless/thy five wits:* May God bless your faculties. The five wits were imagination, common wit, estimation, fantasy, memory. These are not to be confused with the five senses.

57 *O, do . . . de:* Edgar shudders from the cold.

58 *Bless thee:* May God protect you; *star-blasting:* being struck by a wandering star; *taking:* being struck by disease, infection

60-61 *There could . . . there:* Edgar pretends to clutch at a spirit or devil that haunts him and torments his body.

[*To the Fool.*] In, boy; go first.—You houseless poverty—
Nay, get thee in. I'll pray, and then I'll sleep.
[*The Fool enters the hovel.*]
Poor naked wretches, wheresoe'er you are,
That bide the pelting of this pitiless storm,
How shall your houseless heads and unfed sides, 30
Your looped and windowed raggedness, defend you
From seasons such as these? O, I have ta'en
Too little care of this! Take physic, pomp;
Expose thyself to feel what wretches feel,
That thou may'st shake the superflux to them 35
And show the heavens more just.

Edgar: [*Within.*] Fathom and half, fathom and half! Poor Tom!

[*Re-enter Fool.*]

Fool: Come not in here, nuncle, here's a spirit. Help me, help me! 40

Kent: Give me thy hand. Who's there?

Fool: A spirit, a spirit! He says his name's poor Tom.

Kent: What art thou that dost grumble there i' the straw? Come forth.

[*Enter Edgar.*]

Edgar: Away! the foul fiend follows me! Through the sharp 45 hawthorn blow the winds. Humh! Go to thy bed, and warm thee.

Lear: Didst thou give all to thy two daughters? And art thou come to this?

Edgar: Who gives anything to poor Tom? Whom the foul 50 fiend hath led through fire and through flame, through ford and whirlpool, o'er bog and quagmire; that hath laid knives under his pillow and halters in his pew, set ratsbane by his porridge, made him proud of heart, to ride on a bay trotting horse over four-inched 55 bridges, to course his own shadow for a traitor. Bless thy five wits! Tom's acold. O, do de, do de, do de. Bless thee from whirlwinds, star-blasting, and taking! Do poor Tom some charity, whom the foul fiend vexes. There could I have him now, and there, and 60 there again, and there! [*Storm still.*]

69 *Death, traitor:* Lear would condemn Kent to death for daring to suggest that anything but filial ingratitude could have caused Poor Tom's plight; *subdued nature:* reduced his powers

72 *little mercy on their flesh?:* a reference either to Edgar's horrid state or to his own flesh, in which he has stuck pins and thorns

73 *Judicious:* fitting, appropriate, suitable; *this flesh:* Lear himself; *begot:* fathered

74 *pelican:* thought to feed its young with its own blood

75-76 *Pillicock Hill:* The word "pillicock" is suggested to Edgar by the word "pelican." "Pillicock" was a term of endearment meaning, roughly, "darling"; *Alow, alow,/loo, loo:* a cry used to call a hawk.

78-80 *keep/thy word's justice:* literally, be as just in deeds as you are in words. Here the sense is, keep the word; *commit not:* do not commit adultery; *man's/sworn spouse:* another man's wife

78-81 *Take heed . . . acold:* Edgar is apparently reciting a catechism.

83 *A servingman:* either a lover or a servant who uses his good looks to advantage

89-90 *out-paramoured/the Turk:* had more mistresses than the Sultan of Turkey

90-91 *light of ear:* ready to listen to any malicious talk; *hog in sloth:* as lazy as a pig. Sloth was one of the Seven Deadly Sins.

92-94 *Let not . . . woman:* Do not fall in love with a woman as soon as you hear her shoes creak or her skirts rustle.

95 *plackets:* an opening, in the side-seam of a woman's dress or skirt, that made it easier to put the garment on. A placket was also used as a synonym for a loose woman; *lender's books:* a money-lender's record book

96-98 *Still through . . . wind:* Edgar's words are probably the refrain of a song or a poem; *suum, mun, hey, no, nonny:* possibly the sound of the wind; *Dolphin my boy, my boy:* Dolphin was a common name for a horse; *sessa:* a term used with horses, like "giddy-up."

99 *answer:* bear the brunt of

100 *extremity:* severity

Lear: Have his daughters brought him to this pass?
Couldst thou save nothing? Wouldst thou give 'em all?
Fool: Nay, he reserved a blanket, else we had been all
shamed. 65
Lear: Now all the plagues that in the pendulous air
Hang fated o'er men's faults light on thy daughters!
Kent: He hath no daughters, sir.
Lear: Death, traitor! Nothing could have subdued nature
To such a lowness but his unkind daughters. 70
Is it the fashion that discarded fathers
Should have thus little mercy on their flesh?
Judicious punishment! 'Twas this flesh begot
Those pelican daughters.
Edgar: Pillicock sat on Pillicock Hill. Alow, alow, 75
loo, loo!
Fool: This cold night will turn us all to fools and madmen.
Edgar: Take heed o' the foul fiend; obey thy parents; keep
thy word's justice; swear not; commit not with man's
sworn spouse; set not thy sweet heart on proud array. 80
Tom's acold.
Lear: What hast thou been?
Edgar: A servingman, proud in heart and mind; that curled
my hair, wore gloves in my cap; served the lust of my
mistress' heart and did the act of darkness with her; 85
swore as many oaths as I spake words, and broke
them in the sweet face of heaven; one that slept in the
contriving of lust, and waked to do it. Wine loved I
deeply, dice dearly; and in woman out-paramoured
the Turk. False of heart, light of ear, bloody of hand; 90
hog in sloth, fox in stealth, wolf in greediness, dog in
madness, lion in prey. Let not the creaking of shoes
nor the rustling of silks betray thy poor heart to
woman. Keep thy foot out of brothels, thy hand out
of plackets, thy pen from lender's books, and defy the 95
foul fiend. Still through the hawthorn blows the cold
wind; says suum, mun, hey, no, nonny. Dolphin my
boy, my boy, sessa! Let him trot by. [*Storm still.*]
Lear: Thou wert better in thy grave than to answer with
thy uncovered body this extremity of the skies. Is man 100

103-104 *cat:* the civet-cat, whose glands function like those of the skunk and provide the base for the best perfume; *on's:* of us; *sophis-/ ticated:* made artificial, wearing clothes that are not a part of themselves. Lear comments on the contrast between Edgar, who has taken nothing from the animals for himself and Lear, Kent, and the Fool, who are all fully clothed.

104 *unaccommodated:* unsheltered, unprotected

105 *forked:* two-legged

106 *lendings:* borrowed articles (his clothing)

Stage direction – *Tearing his garments:* Lear tears at his clothing, trying to remove it, to be "natural."

107 *naughty:* awful

108-110 *Now a . . . cold:* Just as a flame in a barren field will not cause a widespread fire, so the lust in a wicked old man's heart will not give energy, warmth or potency to his body.

110 *a walking fire:* Gloucester, carrying his torch

111-113 *Flibbertigibbet:* an Elizabethan devil; *curfew:* 9 p.m.; *first cock:* midnight; *the web and the/pin:* eye cataract

114 *white:* unripened

115-119 *Swithold footed . . . thee:* St. Withold travelled around the world three times, met the demon Nightmare and her nine children, ordered her to dismount from the spirits she was riding, to promise never to trouble anyone again.

125 *todpole:* tadpole; *wall-newt:* wall lizard; *water:* water newt

127 *sallets:* salads; *old rat and the ditch-dog:* dead rat and dog carcass found in a ditch

128 *green mantle:* greenish scum; *standing:* stagnant

129 *tithing:* parish or district. A district contained ten families. Elizabethan law required that vagrants be publicly whipped and sent off to another district; *stock-punished:* put into the stocks

130 *three suits:* the allowance of a servant

134 *my follower:* my attending fiend or familiar; *Smulkin:* name of another Elizabethan devil

137 *Modo . . . Mahu:* powerful Elizabethan devils

no more than this? Consider him well. Thou owest
the worm no silk, the beast no hide, the sheep no wool,
the cat no perfume. Ha! Here's three on's are sophis-
ticated! Thou art the thing itself; unaccommodated man
is no more but such a poor, bare, forked animal as 105
thou art. Off, off, you lendings! Come, unbutton here.
[*Tearing his garments.*]

Fool: Prithee, nuncle, be contented! 'Tis a naughty night
to swim in. Now a little fire in a wild field were like an
old lecher's heart—a small spark, all the rest on's
body cold. Look, here comes a walking fire. 110

[*Enter Gloucester with a torch.*]

Edgar: This is the foul Flibbertigibbet. He begins at curfew,
and walks till the first cock. He gives the web and the
pin, squints the eye, and makes the harelip; mildews
the white wheat, and hurts the poor creature of earth.
Swithold footed thrice the 'old; 115
He met the nightmare, and her nine fold;
Bid her alight
And her troth plight,
And aroint thee, witch, aroint thee!

Kent: How fares your Grace? 120

Lear: What's he?

Kent: Who's there? What is't you seek?

Gloucester: What are you there? Your names?

Edgar: Poor Tom, that eats the swimming frog, the toad,
the todpole, the wall-newt and the water; that in the 125
fury of his heart, when the foul fiend rages, eats cow-
dung for sallets, swallows the old rat and the ditch-dog,
drinks the green mantle of the standing pool; who is
whipped from tithing to tithing, and stock-punished and
imprisoned; who hath had three suits to his back, six 130
shirts to his body, horse to ride, and weapon to wear;
But mice and rats, and such small deer,
Have been Tom's food for seven long year.
Beware my follower. Peace, Smulkin! Peace, thou fiend!

Gloucester: What, hath your Grace no better company? 135

Edgar: The prince of darkness is a gentleman!
Modo he's called, and Mahu.

138 *Our flesh and blood:* our children – Edgar, Goneril and Regan. Gloucester links all of these people together because he considers them to be villains; *is grown:* has become

139 *gets:* begets, is father to

141 *suffer:* permit, allow

147 *philosopher:* scientist. In Elizabethan English, "philosophy" meant science or the accumulation of knowledge.

148 *What is . . . thunder?:* a scientific question, frequently discussed before the facts were known.

150 *learned Theban:* learned Greek, a scholar

151 *study?:* particular field of study or research

152 *prevent:* avoid, keep ahead of

154 *Importune:* beg, implore. Pronounced with the stress on "por."

160 *outlawed from my blood:* outcast from my family

164 *cry you mercy, sir:* I beg your pardon. (Lear did not hear Gloucester.)

170 *soothe him:* Let him have his way.

Gloucester: Our flesh and blood, my lord, is grown so vile,
That it doth hate what gets it.
Edgar: Poor Tom's acold. 140
Gloucester: Go in with me. My duty cannot suffer
T' obey in all your daughters' hard commands.
Though their injunction be to bar my doors
And let this tyrannous night take hold upon you,
Yet have I ventured to come seek you out 145
And bring you where both fire and food is ready.
Lear: First let me talk with this philosopher.
What is the cause of thunder?
Kent: Good my lord, take his offer; go into the house.
Lear: I'll talk a word with this same learned Theban. 150
What is your study?
Edgar: How to prevent the fiend and to kill vermin.
Lear: Let me ask you one word in private.
Kent: Importune him once more to go, my lord.
His wits begin to unsettle.
Gloucester: Canst thou blame him? 155
[*Storm still.*]
His daughters seek his death. Ah, that good Kent!
He said it would be thus—poor banished man!
Thou sayest the King grows mad: I'll tell thee, friend,
I am almost mad myself. I had a son,
Now outlawed from my blood. He sought my life 160
But lately, very late. I loved him, friend—
No father his son dearer. True to tell thee,
The grief hath crazed my wits. What a night's this!
I do beseech your Grace—
Lear: O, cry you mercy, sir.
Noble philosopher, your company. 165
Edgar: Tom's acold.
Gloucester: In, fellow, there, into the hovel; keep thee warm.
Lear: Come, let's in all.
Kent: This way, my lord.
Lear: With him!
I will keep still with my philosopher.
Kent: Good my lord, soothe him; let him take the
fellow. 170

171 *Take him you on:* You take Poor Tom to the hovel, and I'll go along with the King.

173 *Athenian:* philosopher, thinker

175 *Child:* a candidate for knighthood; *Rowland:* nephew of Charlemagne and the chief knight of his time, according to legends; *Child Rowland . . . came:* probably a line from a lost ballad

176 *word:* motto; *still:* ever, always

177-178 *Fie, foh . . . man:* a couplet from "Jack the Giant Killer," which is madly unsuitable for a chivalrous knight to use as a motto for his coat of arms.

Gloucester: Take him you on.
Kent: Sirrah, come on; go along with us.
Lear: Come, good Athenian.
Gloucester: No words, no words! hush.
Edgar: Child Rowland to the dark tower came; 175
His word was still
Fie, foh, and fum!
I smell the blood of a British man.
[*Exeunt.*]

Act 3, Scene 4: Activities

1. Choose one of the following:

   a) Create a crossword puzzle using only words that appear in the glossary in this scene. Keep your puzzle simple – twenty words at most, and exchange it with another group. Follow standard crossword-puzzle format to avoid confusion.

   b) Extract Edgar's speeches and paraphrase them. Make special note of the key ideas and visual images they contain. Create a shortened, updated version of these speeches and present them as a monologue to the class. Make sure that, while your speech may sound like nonsense, it communicates meaning to an astute listener.

2. Prepare a two-minute dramatization of one important part of this scene. You might choose to use a reader's theatre presentation in which you read the text, using facial expressions and gestures to give meaning and feeling to the words you read.

   Make sure you communicate essentials of the plot, conflict, and theme in your presentation. Perform your reading with a partner or with a group.

3. Select a modern piece of music, or portions of one, that you think best captures the mood of this scene. Tape the music and play it for your group or the whole class. Be sure to identify the portion of the scene you are illustrating. Discuss the effectiveness of each choice.

4. Write a detailed description or draw a picture of how you think Edgar as a Bedlam beggar appears in this scene.

5. As a director for this scene, decide how you might present this scene to create dramatic effect on your audience.

Make diagrams to show where you would place characters in relation to each other. Decide what effects you want to create and how you would do this. Share your ideas with your classmates.

6. King Lear undergoes a profound change in this scene. Assume you are a reporter who has interviewed Kent about events on the heath. Write an article for your newspaper, outlining what you have learned. How will you portray Lear? What term or terms will you use to describe the change in him? What will your headline be? To what audience will you appeal? What will you suggest might happen to Lear from this point on?

7. Write a poem or piece of prose that captures the mood, the weather, and the action in this scene. Share your selection with a partner. Select the words and phrases that most effectively convey the atmosphere and movement of the scene.

8. As King Lear, write a monologue in which you recall what has happened to you, examine the causes of your present plight, and outline your future actions and their projected outcomes.

For the next scene . . .

Why do you think loyalty is so important to people and betrayal is so upsetting?

Act 3, Scene 5

In this scene . . .

In this brief scene, we learn that Edmund continues to be successful. He has informed Cornwall that his father plans to support France. As a reward for this information, he has been granted the earldom of Gloucester. Cornwall commands Edmund to find his father so that punishment can be administered. Edmund hopes he will find Gloucester helping Lear, which will cast even greater suspicion on Edmund's father.

1 *I will have my revenge:* Edmund has told Cornwall that Gloucester intends to help Lear and to support the invading French army.

2 *censured:* judged; *nature:* human nature, the natural bond between father and son

3 *loyalty:* to Cornwall, rather than his father; *fears me:* makes me worry

6 *provoking merit:* something deserved that motivates action; *reprovable badness:* wickedness deserving punishment. Cornwall claims that it was not only the evil in Edgar that made his plot against his father. Gloucester's evil was also to blame although Edgar's wickedness was a motivating factor.

8-9 *repent/to be just:* remorse for doing the right thing; *approves:* proves

10 *an intelligent party:* a well-informed person, spy; *to the advantages of:* on behalf of

11 *were not:* did not exist; *or not I:* or that I were not

16 *True or false:* The letter itself is evidence enough; the exact facts do not matter.

18 *apprehension:* arrest

19 *comforting:* aiding

20 *stuff:* reinforce, strengthen; *his suspicion:* the suspicion that already rests on Gloucester

Scene 5

Inside Gloucester's castle.

Enter Cornwall and Edmund.

Cornwall: I will have my revenge ere I depart his house.
Edmund: How, my lord, I may be censured, that nature thus gives way to loyalty, something fears me to think of.
Cornwall: I now perceive it was not altogether your brother's evil disposition made him seek his death; but a provoking merit, set a-work by a reprovable badness in himself. 5
Edmund: How malicious is my fortune that I must repent to be just! This is the letter he spoke of, which approves him an intelligent party to the advantages of France. O heavens! That this treason were not, or not I the detector! 10
Cornwall: Go with me to the Duchess.
Edmund: If the matter of this paper be certain, you have mighty business in hand. 15
Cornwall: True or false, it hath made thee Earl of Gloucester. Seek out where thy father is, that he may be ready for our apprehension.
Edmund: [*Aside.*] If I find him comforting the King, it will stuff his suspicion more fully. [*Aloud.*] I will persevere in my course of loyalty, though the conflict be sore between that and my blood. 20
Cornwall: I will lay trust upon thee, and thou shalt find a dearer father in my love. [*Exeunt.*]

Act 3, Scene 5: Activities

1. Imagine that you knew nothing whatsoever about events in King Lear's England and you happened to overhear this exchange between Cornwall and Edmund. What would you assume was going on? As a loyal subject of the king, what would you do? Who would you tell about what you overheard? Record your responses in your journal.

2. As Cornwall, write a diary entry explaining why you trust Edmund implicitly.

3. You have discovered a lost soliloquy given by Edmund at the end of this scene. In the soliloquy, Edmund reveals that he has no intentions of being satisfied with the title of Earl of Gloucester. Write the soliloquy, revealing what other schemes you have devised and how you (as Edmund) will attempt to accomplish them.

For the next scene . . .

How would you define justice? Does justice mean bringing to trial all people who have committed wrongs so that the court may identify their crimes and make them repent? Is justice a form of revenge? Do you think our justice system saves wrongdoers by reprimanding them for the sins they have committed? How do you think a judge's definition of justice might be similar to or different from your own?

Act 3, Scene 6

In this scene . . .

Lear is taking shelter in the outbuilding or farmhouse provided by Gloucester. Overcome with a desire for revenge, he insists that his daughters be tried for their sins against him. He convenes a court with Edgar, Kent, and the Fool as judges and proceeds to try two stools which he sees as his daughters. Throughout the trial, Edgar sings irrelevant songs and the Fool clowns through the part he is given to play. Finally, Edgar is so overwhelmed by pity that he cannot continue.

Kent persuades the old king to lie down and rest, but as Lear is settling down, Gloucester brings the news that there is a plot against Lear's life. He tells Kent to take Lear to Dover where friends will assist him. Kent and the Fool carry Lear away. Left alone, Edgar comments on the extent of Lear's suffering and hopes the king will escape.

After this point in the play, the Fool is not seen again.

6 *Frateretto:* another devil's name; *Nero:* Nero was condemned to playing the fiddle in hell; Edgar may be confusing Nero with Trajan, who was doomed to fish for frogs in hell.

7 *innocent:* fool

10 *yeoman:* a freeholder: that is, one who owned his own land but was lower in status than a gentleman

12-14 *No, he's . . . him:* This statement has been explained as a reference by Shakespeare to his own efforts to acquire a coat of arms for his father. To Edgar, the words would convey only nonsense. Lear understands them in the light of his own experience.

15 *To have a thousand;* Lear exaggerates the number of his offspring in the vehemence of his desire to torture them; *spits:* iron rods, used to pierce meat in order to turn it over a fire and roast it

16 *hizzing:* hissing (from the heat)

19 *horse's health:* likely the seller's account of the health of the horse

20 *arraign:* bring to trial; *them:* his daughters; *straight:* immediately. Lear is now intent on bringing his daughters to trial instead of to torture, as he first decided. He is at the height of his madness here.

21 *justicer:* judge

22-23 *sapient:* wise; *she-/foxes:* symbols of cunning deception and ingratitude

24 *he:* a fiend; or Lear

25 *eyes;* watchers, spectators; *madam?:* Edgar pretends to address Goneril and Regan, turning to the two stools that Lear thinks are his daughters.

26 *Come o'er . . . me:* Edgar sings the first line of an old song in which the singer calls upon his love to come closer to him across a brook ("bourn").

Scene 6

An outbuilding near Gloucester's castle.

Enter Gloucester and Kent.

Gloucester: Here is better than the open air; take it thankfully. I will piece out the comfort with what addition I can. I will not be long from you.

Kent: All the power of his wits have given way to his impatience. The gods reward your kindness! 5

[*Exit Gloucester.*]

[*Enter Lear, Edgar, and Fool.*]

Edgar: Frateretto calls me, and tells me Nero is an angler in the lake of darkness. Pray, innocent, and beware the foul fiend.

Fool: Prithee, nuncle, tell me whether a madman be a gentleman or a yeoman. 10

Lear: A king, a king!

Fool: No, he's a yeoman that has a gentleman to his son; for he's a mad yeoman that sees his son a gentleman before him.

Lear: To have a thousand with red burning spits 15
Come hizzing in upon 'em—

Edgar: The foul fiend bites my back.

Fool: He's mad that trusts in the tameness of a wolf, a horse's health, a boy's love, or a whore's oath.

Lear: It shall be done; I will arraign them straight. 20
[*To Edgar.*] Come, sit thou here, most learned justicer.
[*To the Fool.*] Thou, sapient sir, sit here. Now, you she-foxes!

Edgar: Look, where he stands and glares! Wantest thou eyes at trial, madam? 25

Come o'er the bourn, Bessy, to me.

27-29 *Her boat . . . thee:* The Fool completes the song, modifying the lines, perhaps to imply that the case of Goneril and Regan is not a sound one.

31 *nightingale:* Edgar believes that the Fool's voice is that of a fiend disguised as a nightingale; *Hoppedance:* another Elizabethan devil; *in Tom's belly:* a reference to a rumbling caused by hunger

32 *white herring:* unsmoked or fresh herring; *Croak not:* another reference to his rumbling stomach

34 *How do you:* How do you feel?; *amazed:* dumbfounded, stunned

36 *evidence:* witnesses to testify against Goneril and Regan – an abstract term used for the concrete

38 *yokefellow of equity:* partner in law

39 *Bench:* take your place on the bench; *o' the commission:* of those commissioned as justices or law officers

42-45 *Sleepest or . . . harm:* the words of an old song; *And for one blast:* and if you take time to play just one tune (on the shepherd's pipe); *minikin:* little, dainty

46 *Purr:* Edgar pretends to see a fiend in the form of a cat.

47 *Arraign:* try

48 *kicked:* an action conceived in Lear's tortured imagination

52 *Cry you mercy:* I beg your pardon; *joint-stool:* a low stool of three or four legs that were carefully fitted into the seat. The whole phrase is an apology for not noticing someone, equivalent to "I didn't know you were there."

53 *another:* Regan; *warped:* twisted by evil thoughts

54 *store:* substance; *on;* of; *Stop her there:* Lear imagines Regan is escaping from the court.

55 *Corruption in the place:* There is evil in this court (because Regan is being allowed to escape).

58 *Sir:* He addresses Lear.

61 *counterfeiting:* pretending

62-63 *The little . . . me:* Lear imagines that even his own pets have turned against him.

Fool: Her boat hath a leak,
And she must not speak
Why she dares not come over to thee.
Edgar: The foul fiend haunts poor Tom in the voice of a 30
nightingale. Hoppedance cries in Tom's belly for two
white herring. Croak not, black angel; I have no food
for thee.
Kent: How do you, sir? Stand you not so amazed.
Will you lie down and rest upon the cushions? 35
Lear: I'll see their trial first. Bring in their evidence.
[*To Edgar.*] Thou, robed man of justice, take thy place.
[*To the Fool.*] And thou, his yokefellow of equity,
Bench by his side. [*To Kent.*] You are o' the commission,
Sit you too. 40
Edgar: Let us deal justly.
Sleepest or wakest thou, jolly shepherd?
Thy sheep be in the corn;
And for one blast of thy minikin mouth
Thy sheep shall take no harm. 45
Purr! the cat is grey.
Lear: Arraign her first. 'Tis Goneril. I here take my oath
before this honourable assembly, she kicked the poor
King her father.
Fool: Come hither, mistress. Is your name Goneril? 50
Lear: She cannot deny it.
Fool: Cry you mercy, I took you for a joint-stool.
Lear: And here's another, whose warped looks
proclaim
What store her heart is made on. Stop her there!
Arms, arms! Sword! Fire! Corruption in the place! 55
False justicer, why hast thou let her scape?
Edgar: Bless thy five wits!
Kent: O pity! Sir, where is the patience now
That you so oft have boasted to retain?
Edgar: [*Aside.*] My tears begin to take his part so much 60
They mar my counterfeiting.
Lear: The little dogs and all,
Tray, Blanch, and Sweetheart, see, they bark at me.
Edgar: Tom will throw his head at them. Avaunt, you curs!

74 *thy horn is dry:* An animal horn was apparently used by Bedlam beggars for drinking.

75 *anatomize:* dissect; *breeds:* is growing

77 *entertain:* engage

78 *hundred:* his former group of knights

79 *Persian:* Persian clothing was a symbol of gorgeous attire. Lear turns Edgar's rags into rich garments.

82 *curtains:* There are none, of course, and no cushions – only straw.

83 *So, so:* words spoken as he settles down, as his delirium subsides; *supper i' the morning:* Lear remembers that he has had no meal.

84 *And I'll . . . noon:* The Fool, jokingly, takes Lear at his word and decides that, if breakfast is at supper time, bedtime must surely be noon.

89 *litter:* a type of stretcher. Some litters had a tent-like covering that would shelter the person being carried.

90 *drive:* The litter was probably designed to be suspended between two horses, in tandem, one at each end of the litter. Gloucester is also urging great haste.

94 *Stand in assured loss:* are certain to be lost; *Take up:* Lift up the litter.

96 *Oppressed nature sleeps:* Lear overwhelmed by a deep hurt, has fallen into a deep sleep.

97 *balmed:* comforted, helped to cure, healed

98 *convenience:* circumstances, the present situation

99 *Stand in hard cure:* will be difficult to cure

Be thy mouth or black or white, 65
Tooth that poisons if it bite;
Mastiff, greyhound, mongrel grim,
Hound or spaniel, brach or lym,
Bobtail tyke or trundle-tail—
Tom will make him weep and wail; 70
For, with throwing thus my head,
Dogs leap the hatch, and all are fled.

Do de, de, de. Sessa! Come, march to wakes and fairs and market towns. Poor Tom, thy horn is dry.

Lear: Then let them anatomize Regan. See what breeds about 75 her heart. Is there any cause in nature that makes these hard hearts? [*To Edgar.*] You, sir, I entertain for one of my hundred; only I do not like the fashion of your garments. You'll say they are Persian; but let them be changed. 80

Kent: Now, good my lord, lie here and rest awhile.

Lear: Make no noise, make no noise; draw the curtains.
So, so. We'll go to supper i' the morning.

Fool: And I'll go to bed at noon.

[*Enter Gloucester.*]

Gloucester: Come hither, friend. Where is the King my master? 85

Kent: Here, sir; but trouble him not; his wits are gone.

Gloucester: Good friend, I prithee take him in thy arms.
I have o'erheard a plot of death upon him.
There is a litter ready; lay him in it
And drive toward Dover, friend, where thou shalt meet 90
Both welcome and protection. Take up thy master.
If thou shouldst dally half an hour, his life,
With thine, and all that offer to defend him,
Stand in assured loss. Take up, take up!
And follow me, that will to some provision 95
Give thee quick conduct.

Kent: Oppressed nature sleeps.
This rest might yet have balmed thy broken sinews
Which, if convenience will not allow,
Stand in hard cure. [*To the Fool.*] Come, help to bear thy master.
Thou must not stay behind.

101 *our betters:* those like Lear; *our woes:* the same sort of ills that we ordinary people must endure

102 *We scarcely . . . foes:* We scarcely think our misfortunes are serious.

103 *Who alone . . . mind:* "Alone" and "most" are the words to be emphasized. The one who suffers alone suffers most deeply.

104 *free:* carefree; *happy shows:* all appearances of happiness

105 *sufferance:* misery; *o'erskip:* avoid

106 *mates:* companions, company; *bearing fellowship:* when the endurance of misfortune is made bearable by companionship

107 *portable:* bearable, endurable

108 *When that . . . bow:* when what afflicts me also afflicts the King

109 *He childed as I fathered:* He had children as cruel as the father I had (and our sorrows are therefore the same).

110-111 *Mark the high noises:* Pay attention to the disagreements among those who are powerful in the country; *thyself bewray/ . . . thee:* reveal yourself when false opinion that deforms you is reversed by your own proof that restores (reconciles) you to your true character.

113 *What will . . . King:* Whatever else may occur tonight, may the King escape safely!

114 *Lurk:* hide

Gloucester: Come, come, away! 100
[*Exeunt all but Edgar.*]

Edgar: When we our betters see bearing our woes,
We scarcely think our miseries our foes.
Who alone suffers suffers most i' the mind,
Leaving free things and happy shows behind;
But then the mind much sufferance doth o'erskip 105
When grief hath mates, and bearing fellowship.
How light and portable my pain seems now,
When that which makes me bend makes the King bow,
He childed as I fathered! Tom, away!
Mark the high noises, and thyself bewray 110
When false opinion, whose wrong thoughts defile thee,
In thy just proof repeals and reconciles thee.
What will hap more tonight, safe scape the King!
Lurk, lurk. [*Exit.*]

Act 3, Scene 6: Activities

1. The Fool makes his last appearance in this scene. In your journal, explain why, in your opinion, he disappears. What happens to him? Do you think there may be a piece missing from the play? If you were the Fool and had one last speech, what would you say? To whom would you address it? Write your speech and present it to your group for their reaction.

2. a) To many directors, Edgar, in what is to be his final speech (lines 101–114), seems very artificial and stilted. The lines have contrived rhymes that many feel are not Shakespearean at all. What is your response to this criticism? Does the speech add to what the audience already knows? Explain.

   b) If you were Shakespeare, how would you answer the questions in part a?

3. You are Kent and have decided to help Lear at any cost. Record in your diary why you are so ineffectual.

4. Review the scene to observe what speeches characters make when they are *not* talking to each other. What speeches do they make when they *are* talking to each other? What (if any) pattern do you note? Discuss your ideas.

   If you were presenting this scene to any audience, what (if any) changes would you make? Why?

For the next scene . . .

Recall the most horrible scene you have ever encountered, either in real life or in the media. What made this scene horrible for you? How do you define "horror"?

In your opinion, is there any purpose in displaying horrifying scenes for people to watch? What do you think is the effect of these scenes on the people who watch them?

Act 3, Scene 7

In this scene . . .

Cornwall gives Goneril and Edmund instructions to inform the Duke of Albany of the arrival of the French army. Oswald enters to tell Cornwall that Lear and his party, advised by Gloucester, have escaped to Dover.

After Goneril and Edmund leave, Gloucester is arrested and brought before Cornwall. When Gloucester admits to having warned Lear, Cornwall gouges out one of his eyes. One of Cornwall's own servants protests this cruelty and fatally wounds Cornwall in the fight that ensues. Regan stabs the servant and then gouges out Gloucester's other eye. Gloucester asks for Edmund and is told that he is Gloucester's betrayer. Thus, at the moment of his blinding, Gloucester sees his sons in their true roles and prays for forgiveness.

Gloucester is thrown outside his castle gates and told to "smell his way to Dover." One of Cornwall's servants chooses to follow Gloucester and to have Poor Tom lead him to safety.

7 *sister:* sister-in-law

9-11 *Advise the . . . preparation:* Tell Albany, to whose palace you are going, to make the swiftest possible preparation for war; *festinate:* urgent; *preparation:* for war; *We are . . . like:* We will do the same.

11 *intelligent:* giving information

14 *hence:* from here

16 *Hot questrists:* eager, anxious searchers

17 *lord's:* Gloucester's.

22 *Pinion:* tie his arms; *thief:* The word had a stronger sense than it has now.

Scene 7

Inside Gloucester's castle.

Enter Cornwall, Regan, Goneril, Edmund the Bastard, and Servants.

Cornwall: [*To Goneril.*] Post speedily to my lord your husband, show him this letter. The army of France is landed.—Seek out the traitor Gloucester.
[*Exeunt some of the Servants.*]

Regan: Hang him instantly.

Goneril: Pluck out his eyes. 5

Cornwall: Leave him to my displeasure. Edmund, keep you our sister company. The revenges we are bound to take upon your traitorous father are not fit for your beholding. Advise the Duke where you are going, to a most festinate preparation. We are bound to the 10 like. Our posts shall be swift and intelligent betwixt us. Farewell, dear sister; farewell, my Lord of Gloucester.
[*Enter Oswald the Steward.*]
How now? Where's the King?

Oswald: My Lord of Gloucester hath conveyed him hence.
Some five or six and thirty of his knights, 15
Hot questrists after him, met him at gate;
Who, with some other of the lord's dependants,
Are gone with him toward Dover, where they boast
To have well-armed friends.

Cornwall: Get horses for your mistress.

Goneril: Farewell, sweet lord, and sister. 20

Cornwall: Edmund, farewell.
[*Exeunt Goneril, Edmund, and Oswald.*]
Go seek the traitor Gloucester,
Pinion him like a thief, bring him before us.
[*Exeunt other Servants.*]

23-25 *Though well . . . justice:* although we may not truly pass judgement on him without some form of trial; *our power/ . . . wrath:* My power as Duke will enable me to satisfy the anger I feel towards him.

26 *blame:* criticize

28 *corky:* stiff, dry, withered (by age)

30 *foul play:* injustice

31 *Hard:* tightly

32 *none:* no traitor

34 *ignobly done:* dishonourable, mean

36 *white:* Goneril looks at the hairs of Gloucester's beard and observes, mockingly, that they are white and symbolic of purity; *Naughty:* wicked, evil

37 *ravish:* pluck, tear

38 *quicken:* come alive; *host:* Gloucester protests against the dishonouring of the age-old rule that courtesy between host and guest is inviolable.

39 *hospitable favours:* my face, which has an expression of hospitality on it

40 *ruffle:* do violence to

41 *late:* lately, recently

42 *simple-answered:* straightforward

43 *confederacy:* unauthorized alliance or agreement, conspiracy

44 *footed:* landed

47 *guessingly set down:* written down without firm knowledge

48 *of a neutral heart:* taking neither side

49 *Cunning:* Now he is using cunning; *And false:* and he is false as well

52 *charged at peril:* ordered on pain of death

Though well we may not pass upon his life
Without the form of justice, yet our power
Shall do a court'sy to our wrath, which men 25
May blame, but not control.
[*Enter Gloucester, brought in by two or three.*]
Who's there? The traitor?

Regan: Ingrateful fox! 'Tis he.

Cornwall: Bind fast his corky arms.

Gloucester: What mean your Graces? Good my friends, consider
You are my guests. Do me no foul play, friends. 30

Cornwall: Bind him, I say. [*Servants bind him.*]

Regan: Hard, hard. O filthy traitor!

Gloucester: Unmerciful lady as you are, I am none.

Cornwall: To this chair bind him. Villain, thou shalt find—
[*Regan pulls his beard.*]

Gloucester: By the kind gods, 'tis most ignobly done
To pluck me by the beard. 35

Regan: So white, and such a traitor!

Gloucester: Naughty lady,
These hairs which thou dost ravish from my chin
Will quicken, and accuse thee. I am your host.
With robber's hands my hospitable favours
You should not ruffle thus. What will you do? 40

Cornwall: Come, sir, what letters had you late from France?

Regan: Be simple-answered, for we know the truth.

Cornwall: And what confederacy have you with the traitors
Late footed in the kingdom?

Regan: To whose hands you have sent the lunatic King? 45
Speak.

Gloucester: I have a letter guessingly set down,
Which came from one that's of a neutral heart,
And not from one opposed.

Cornwall: Cunning.

Regan: And false.

Cornwall: Where hast thou sent the King? 50

Gloucester: To Dover.

Regan: Wherefore to Dover? Wast thou not charged at peril—

54-55 *I am . . . course:* I am like a bear chained to a post and must endure as best I can – a reference to bear-baiting, in which bears were attacked by dogs.

59 *anointed:* blessed with holy oil at his coronation (Therefore, to attack the King is sacrilege); *rash:* slash, as with a tusk, like a boar

61-62 *hell-black night:* night as black as hell itself; *would have . . . fires:* would have risen in one great wave and extinguished the fire of the stars.

63 *holp the heavens rain:* helped the heavens to rain (with his tears)

64 *If:* even if; *dern:* dreadful

65 *turn the key:* open the door (and let them in)

66 *All cruels else subscribe:* Disregard all other cruelties, i.e., other than inflicted upon Lear, since all are less diabolical.

67 *winged vengeance:* the vengeance of the gods, vengeance like a bird of prey

72 *One side will mock another:* An eye remaining would make the eyeless socket look worse; *The other too:* Gouge out the other eye as well.

76 *How now:* What do you think you are doing?

78 *shake it on this quarrel:* insult you to provoke an immediate quarrel over this cause – Gloucester's treatment

79 *villain:* used here in the double sense of scoundrel and serf

80 *Nay, then:* a denial that he is a serf; *come on:* an invitation to fight; *take the chance of anger:* take the risk of fighting when angry (and therefore, rash)

81 *peasant:* Regan interprets Cornwall's punning use of "villain."

Stage direction – *takes a . . . behind:* stabs him in the back.

83 *mischief:* injury

84 *Lest:* in case that; *vile jelly:* Gloucester's remaining eye

85 *lustre:* brightness of the living eye

Cornwall: Wherefore to Dover? Let him answer that.
Gloucester: I am tied to the stake, and I must stand the
    course. 55
Regan: Wherefore to Dover?
Gloucester: Because I would not see thy cruel nails
  Pluck out his poor old eyes; nor thy fierce sister
  In his anointed flesh rash boarish fangs.
  The sea, with such a storm as his bare head 60
  In hell-black night endured, would have buoyed up
  And quenched the stelled fires.
  Yet, poor old heart, he holp the heavens to rain.
  If wolves had at thy gate howled that dern time,
  Thou shouldst have said, "Good porter, turn the key." 65
  All cruels else subscribe: but I shall see
  The winged vengeance overtake such children.
Cornwall: See it shalt thou never. Fellows, hold the chair.
  Upon these eyes of thine I'll set my foot.
Gloucester: He that will think to live till he be old, 70
  Give me some help!—O cruel! O you gods!
[*Gloucester's eye is put out.*]
Regan: One side will mock another. The other too!
Cornwall: If you see vengeance—
First Servant: Hold your hand, my lord!
  I have served you ever since I was a child,
  But better service have I never done you 75
  Than now to bid you hold.
Regan: How now, you dog?
First Servant: If you did wear a beard upon your chin,
  I'd shake it on this quarrel.
Regan: What do you mean?
Cornwall: My villain! [*They draw and fight.*]
First Servant: Nay, then, come on, and take the chance of
    anger. 80
Regan: Give me thy sword. A peasant stand up thus?
[*She takes a sword and runs at him behind.*]
First Servant: O, I am slain! My lord, you have one eye
    left
  To see some mischief on him. O! [*He dies.*]
Cornwall: Lest it see more, prevent it. Out, vile jelly!
  Where is thy lustre now? 85

87 *enkindle:* summon up; *sparks of nature:* feelings of filial affection

88 *quit:* repay, requite, avenge; *Out:* an interjection, expressing hatred; abbreviated from "Out upon you!"

90-91 "That" and "who" have the same antecedent: "he" (line 87); *overture:* disclosure, revelation

92 *abused:* wronged

93 *that:* Edgar's wrong; *prosper him:* May he (Edgar) prosper.

95 *How look you?:* How are you feeling?

97 *slave:* the servant who attempted to defend Gloucester

98 *apace:* quickly, freely

99 *Untimely:* at the wrong time in my life; *hurt:* wound

101-103 *If she . . . monsters:* If she lives to a ripe age and dies a normal death, then all women will become wicked (since they will not have to fear punishment for their crimes).

104 *bedlam:* Edgar, evidently known to the servant

105-106 *His roguish . . . anything:* Since the bedlam beggar is mad, he will not be called to account and can, therefore, safely lead Gloucester.

Gloucester: All dark and comfortless! Where's my son
Edmund?
Edmund, enkindle all the sparks of nature
To quit this horrid act.
Regan: Out, treacherous villain!
Thou callest on him that hates thee. It was he
That made the overture of thy treasons to us, 90
Who is too good to pity thee.
Gloucester: O my follies! Then Edgar was abused.
Kind gods, forgive me that, and prosper him!
Regan: Go thrust him out at gates, and let him smell
His way to Dover. [*Exit a Servant with Gloucester.*]
How is't, my lord? How look you? 95
Cornwall: I have received a hurt. Follow me, lady.
Turn out that eyeless villain. Throw this slave
Upon the dunghill. Regan, I bleed apace.
Untimely comes this hurt. Give me your arm.
[*Exit Cornwall, led by Regan.*]
Second Servant: I'll never care what wickedness I do, 100
If this man come to good.
Third Servant: If she live long,
And in the end meet the old course of death,
Women will all turn monsters.
Second Servant: Let's follow the old Earl, and get the bedlam
To lead him where he would. His roguish madness 105
Allows itself to anything.
Third Servant: Go thou. I'll fetch some flax and whites of
eggs
apply to his bleeding face. Now heaven help him!
[*Exeunt.*]

Act 3, Scene 7: Activities

1. Discuss with your group how you would stage the blinding of Gloucester. Would you make the act of blinding graphic or would you rely on the imagination of the audience to create their own images of horror? In your decision, consider the purpose of the scene in general rather than focusing on the act of blinding itself.

2. Whenever characters in this play ask for divine assistance, they meet either with indifference or with outright hostility.

   In Act 3, Scene 6, Kent thanks Gloucester for his kindness to Lear by saying, "The gods reward your kindness" (line 5). In this scene Gloucester is brutally maimed. In your journal, consider whether or not the gods play any role in this play. You may wish to share some of your ideas with others in a group.

3. Unlike many of the scenes in this play, this one is packed with action. How might you stage the killing of the servant that occurs in this scene to make it fit smoothly into the flow of the action? Could the killing, rather than the blinding of Gloucester be the focus of the scene? If the killing was omitted, would the play suffer at all? Discuss your ideas.

4. Irony is a figure of speech in which the literal meaning of an expression is the opposite of that intended, particularly when the expression understates the effect intended. One example of irony occurs in line 30. Select as many other examples as you can from this scene and, in a group discussion, determine what effect they have on the scene. Do you believe that the irony is always deliberate on the part of the speaker? What effect would the removal of all the irony have on the scene?

Act 3: Consider the Whole Act

1. There are obvious parallels between what happens to Lear and what happens to Gloucester. Divide a page in half; on one side, list what happens to Lear in this act and, on the other, what happens to Gloucester. With your group, discuss what you think is the purpose of this parallelism. Do you think it is a deliberate dramatic device or just an accident of the plot?

2. You are Kent. Before Cordelia left the kingdom, she asked you to keep her informed about her father and events in the kingdom. Write a report to her telling of the significant events that have occurred in this act.

3. Imagine that you are the Fool. You are very concerned about your master, King Lear. Unknown to anyone you have been keeping a record of what has been happening to him. Write the journal that you have kept for this act.

4. If one of the characters from this act could speak to you, what comment might he or she make about the events that have occurred? What might the person have done differently (if anything)? In your journal, script the conversation you and the character might have based on what has happened in this act.

5. There is an expression, "Children and fools tell the truth." From your observation of the characters in this act, who would you say are "children" and who would you say are "fools"? Share your observations with others in the class. Write an editorial explaining your interpretation of the expression for publication in a magazine.

6. You are Edmund. Considering that illegitimate children have no social standing whatsoever, what alternatives do you have in terms of your future? In a television interview, explain what you have done and the reasons for your actions. Your object is to elicit sympathy both from your interviewer and your audience.

7. There are numerous ways in which Shakespeare develops characters in this scene. Create a chart with three headings: "Physical Appearance," "Actions," and "Personality Traits." Fill in the chart for each character. Share your discoveries with a partner and add any details that you have missed. Write a character sketch of the figure you find to be the most complete.

For the next scene . . .

In your opinion, is it possible for a seemingly insensitive person to change? Have you ever known someone who did just that? If so, what do you think prompted the person to change? Write your ideas in a journal entry.

Act 4, Scene 1

In this scene . . .

Edgar believes his fortunes have reached their lowest possible ebb and that anything that happens from this point on is bound to be a change for the better. No sooner does he express this belief than his blind father appears, led by another old man.

Gloucester tells the old man to leave, saying in despair that, since he had nowhere to go, he has no need of direction. His one wish is to meet his son Edgar again. Edgar realizes that, in fact, he has not yet seen the worst.

Meeting Poor Tom, Gloucester asks the old man to bring the beggar some clothes, and asks Poor Tom to lead him to Dover. He is planning to end his misery by jumping off one of the cliffs there. Edgar, still in disguise, consents to guide him.

1-2 *thus:* as a bedlam beggar; *known to be:* aware of being; *contemned:* despised; *Than still contemned and flattered:* than to live unaware that one is despised in the midst of flattery

2-5 *To be . . . best:* When one's fortunes are at the very worst, there is only hope for the better; thus, the creature whose fortune is at the lowest ebb has everything to hope for and nothing to fear.

6 *The worst returns to laughter:* The worst circumstances can only change to those inspiring laughter.

7 *unsubstantial:* having little substance, not being able to sustain human life

8 *wretch:* Edgar himself

9 *Owes nothing to:* has nothing to fear from

10-12 *poorly led?:* led by a poor old man or led like a poor man (beggar); *World, world . . . age:* O, world, if the strange changes in our fortunes did not make us hate you, we should not surrender to old age and to the consequent approach of death.

14 *fourscore:* eighty

19-21 *I stumbled . . . commodites:* When I was in full possession of my faculties, I was careless (stumbled). Very often, we observe that our own faculties (means) make us feel overconfident (secure us), and our very weaknesses (defects) prove to be beneficial in causing us to take notice of our circumstances.

22 *The food . . . wrath:* the object or victim of your deceived father's anger

23-24 *Might I . . . again:* If only I might live to touch you, I'd feel as if my sight were restored.

24 *How now?:* What's that?

Act 4, Scene 1

The heath.

Enter Edgar.

Edgar: Yet better thus, and known to be contemned,
Than still contemned and flattered. To be worst,
The lowest and most dejected thing of fortune,
Stands still in esperance, lives not in fear.
The lamentable change is from the best; 5
The worst returns to laughter. Welcome then,
Thou unsubstantial air that I embrace!
The wretch that thou hast blown unto the worst
Owes nothing to thy blasts.
[*Enter Gloucester, led by an Old Man.*]
But who comes here?
My father, poorly led? World, world, O world! 10
But that thy strange mutations make us hate thee,
Life would not yield to age.

Old Man: O my good lord,
I have been your tenant, and your father's tenant,
These fourscore years.

Gloucester: Away, get thee away! Good friend, be gone. 15
Thy comforts can do me no good at all;
Thee they may hurt.

Old Man: You cannot see your way.

Gloucester: I have no way, and therefore want no eyes;
I stumbled when I saw. Full oft 'tis seen
Our means secure us, and our mere defects 20
Prove our commodities. O dear son Edgar,
The food of thy abused father's wrath;
Might I but live to see thee in my touch,
I'd say I had eyes again!

Old Man: How now? Who's there?

26 *I am . . . was:* Edgar sees his father's pitiful condition and realizes that circumstances are worse than ever.

27-28 *The worst . . . worst:* The worst has not befallen us as long as we can assure ourselves that it is the worst. Thus, we are not without hope.

31 *He has some reason:* he seems to have some intelligence

33 *a worm:* a thing of no consequence

34 *Came then . . . mind:* either because he saw something of Edgar beneath his disguise or because he thought that Edgar must have become a homeless wanderer.

35 *scarce:* scarcely; *friends:* friendly

36 *wanton:* carelessly playful

37 *How should this be?:* "Why should this be the case?", "How did he come to forigve me?", or "How did he lose his eyes?"

38-39 *Bad is . . . others:* It is bad business (trade) that I must disguise myself as a Bedlamite, making myself and others angry, when my father is in such sorrow.

43 *I' the way:* on the path or track; *ancient love:* love dating from earlier days

44 *covering:* clothing

45 *entreat:* humbly request

46 *'Tis the . . . blind:* It is the curse of our time that the leaders of the country are mad and that the people whom they lead are blind.

47 *thy pleasure:* what you please

48 *Above the rest:* above all

49 *'parel:* apparel, clothing

50 *Come on't what will:* no matter what happens to me

52 *daub it:* pretend. The metaphor is taken from the skill of plastering.

Edgar: [*Aside.*] O gods! Who is't can say, "I am at the worst"? 25
I am worse than e'er I was.
Old Man: 'Tis poor mad Tom.
Edgar: [*Aside.*] And worse I may be yet. The worst is not
So long as we can say, "This is the worst."
Old Man: Fellow, where goest?
Gloucester: Is it a beggarman?
Old Man: Madman and beggar too. 30
Gloucester: He has some reason, else he could not beg.
I' the last night's storm I such a fellow saw,
Which made me think a man a worm. My son
Came then into my mind, and yet my mind
Was then scarce friends with him. I have heard more since. 35
As flies to wanton boys are we to the gods.
They kill us for their sport.
Edgar: [*Aside.*] How should this be?
Bad is the trade that must play fool to sorrow,
Angering itself and others.—Bless thee, master!
Gloucester: Is that the naked fellow?
Old Man: Ay, my lord. 40
Gloucester: Get thee away. If for my sake
Thou wilt o'ertake us hence a mile or twain
I' the way toward Dover, do it for ancient love;
And bring some covering for this naked soul,
Which I'll entreat to lead me.
Old Man: Alack, sir, he is mad! 45
Gloucester: 'Tis the time's plague when madmen lead the blind.
Do as I bid thee, or rather do thy pleasure.
Above the rest, be gone.
Old Man: I'll bring him the best 'parel that I have,
Come on't what will. [*Exit.*] 50
Gloucester: Sirrah, naked fellow—
Edgar: Poor Tom's acold. [*Aside.*] I cannot daub it further.
Gloucester: Come hither, fellow.
Edgar: [*Aside.*] And yet I must.—Bless thy sweet eyes, they bleed. 55

58 *horseway:* a path used by horseback riders

61 *Obidicut:* another Elizabethan devil

63-64 *mopping and/mowing:* grimacing and making faces

64 *possesses:* possesses the souls of

65 *heavens' plagues:* afflictions, misfortunes of the gods

67-68 *humbled to all strokes:* reduced to the lowest kind of misery; *That I . . . still:* The fact that I am wretched makes you appear happier than I. May the gods continue to inflict this kind of punishment – to make my suffering the common experience of the powerful whenever they abuse their power.

69-72 *Let the . . . excess:* Let the pampered man who treats the commands of the gods as if these commands were his slaves, and who will not see the truth because he is insensitive, feel your power quickly. If this were done, the man with excessive wealth would be willing to distribute it more justly.

75 *bending:* overhanging

76 *fearfully:* in such a manner as to inspire terror; *the confirmed deep:* the channel; the Strait of Dover

78-79 *And I'll . . . me:* and I will reward you (lessen your misery) by giving you something of value that I have on my person

Gloucester: Knowest thou the way to Dover?
Edgar: Both stile and gate, horseway and footpath. Poor
Tom hath been scared out of his good wits. Bless thee,
good man's son, from the foul fiend! Five fiends have 60
been in poor Tom at once: of lust, as Obidicut; Hob-
bididence, prince of dumbness; Mahu, of stealing;
Modo, of murder; Flibbertigibbet, of mopping and
mowing, who since possesses chambermaids and waiting
women. So, bless thee, master! 65
Gloucester: Here, take this purse, thou whom the heavens'
plagues
Have humbled to all strokes. That I am wretched
Makes thee the happier. Heavens, deal so still!
Let the superfluous and lust-dieted man,
That slaves your ordinance, that will not see 70
Because he does not feel, feel your power quickly;
So distribution should undo excess,
And each man have enough. Dost thou know Dover?
Edgar: Ay, master.
Gloucester: There is a cliff, whose high and bending head 75
Looks fearfully in the confirmed deep.
Bring me but to the very brim of it,
And I'll repair the misery thou dost bear
With something rich about me. From that place
I shall no leading need.
Edgar: Give me thy arm. 80
Poor Tom shall lead thee. [*Exeunt.*]

Act 4, Scene 1: Activities

1. As Edgar imagine that you are being interviewed by a television host about your behaviour and attitudes in this scene. You are asked the following questions:
   - Since your father was blind when you met him, why did you continue to remain disguised?
   - Since you already heard him express a desire to see you again, why didn't you tell him who you were?

   With a partner, role-play this interview for others in the class.

2. You have been asked to make a presentation to a group on the topic of "divine justice." Brainstorm with a group to gather ideas on your topic, based on the events of the play so far and this scene in particular. Prepare your presentation and deliver it to another group making your argument as concise, yet thorough, as you can.

   Based on what you have discovered, what do you think Shakespeare might have thought about "divine justice"? If you could ask him three questions on this topic, what would they be?

3. One of the issues raised towards the end of the scene is the unfair distribution of wealth. With your group, consider what is said about affluent people in this scene. Do you agree or disagree with Gloucester's opinion? Write a short article for a business magazine in which you use the play as the basis for your economic ideas. Share your article with classmates for their responses.

4. Gloucester's solution to his problem is to commit suicide by jumping off a cliff. In groups, discuss what you think of this as a solution. How might a modern psychiatrist respond to Gloucester's planned action?

   As a psychiatrist, what would you say to Gloucester at this point? Record your thoughts in your journal.

For the next scene . . .

What does physical courage mean to you? What does moral courage mean? Can a person who is considered to be passive show physical and/or moral courage? Discuss your ideas with classmates.

Act 4, Scene 2

In this scene . . .

Edmund and Goneril meet outside the Duke of Albany's palace. Oswald brings news that the Duke's behaviour has changed greatly, and that the Duke has reacted oddly to the news of Gloucester's supposed treason. Goneril interprets the change in his behaviour as cowardice in the face of the French invasion. She sends Edmund back to Cornwall to warn him to speed his efforts to prepare his army. Before Edmund leaves, she declares her love for him and hints that she will be calling on Edmund to murder Albany.

Albany enters and confronts Goneril, condemning her for her cruelty to Lear. As they argue, a messenger delivers the news of Gloucester's blinding and Cornwall's death. Albany is horrified, particularly when he learns of Edmund's part in the torture of his own father. Goneril, on the other hand, is excited by the news of Cornwall's death. She thinks that she and Edmund will now be able to seize Regan's part of the kingdom. However, she is also troubled by the thought that Regan may steal Edmund from her, now that Cornwall is dead.

1 *Welcome:* i.e., to my palace; *our mild husband:* Goneril reveals to Edmund her true feeling towards her husband.

2 *your master?:* Albany

3 *so changed:* The ruthlessness of Goneril and Regan have appalled Albany, but he seems incapable of positive action.

7 *loyal service:* denouncing his father to Cornwall; *son:* Edmund

8 *sot:* blockhead, fool

9 *I had . . . out:* I had seen good as evil, and evil as good.

10-11 *What most . . . offensive:* Oswald asserts that it is Albany, not himself, who has reversed good and evil.

11 *Then shall . . . further:* You will not accompany me at this point.

12 *cowish terror:* cowardly fear

13 *undertake:* transform conviction into action; *feel:* notice or appear to notice; He will ignore wrongs that demand some responsible action from him.

14-15 *Our wishes . . . effects:* The desire we have for each other may possibly be fulfilled.

17-18 *I must . . . hands:* I must take my husband's sword and present him with a distaff (a staff used for spinning and associated, therefore, with women); *This trusty servant:* Oswald

19 *pass between us:* be our intermediary or go-between; *like:* likely

20 *(If you . . . behalf):* if you have the initiative to advance yourself (Goneril implies that Edmund should kill Albany.)

Stage direction – *favour:* trinket (recognizing Edmund as her lover)

22 *Decline your head:* Bend your head (to be kissed or to put a chain around his neck).

23 *Would stretch . . . air:* would raise your spirits to the skies. Goneril changes from the formal "your" to the intimate "thy" and "thee."

24 *Conceive:* understand (what I am suggesting about our future – without Albany)

Scene 2

Outside the Duke of Albany's palace.

Enter Goneril and Edmund the Bastard.

Goneril: Welcome, my lord. I marvel our mild husband
Not met us on the way.
[*Enter Oswald the Steward.*]
Now where's your master?
Oswald: Madam, within, but never man so changed.
I told him of the army that was landed:
He smiled at it. I told him you were coming: 5
His answer was, "The worse." Of Gloucester's treachery
And of the loyal service of his son
When I informed him, then he called me sot
And told me I had turned the wrong side out.
What most he should dislike seems pleasant to him; 10
What like, offensive.
Goneril: [*To Edmund.*] Then shall you go no further.
It is the cowish terror of his spirit,
That dares not undertake. He'll not feel wrongs
Which tie him to an answer. Our wishes on the way
May prove effects. Back, Edmund, to my brother. 15
Hasten his musters and conduct his powers.
I must change arms at home and give the distaff
Into my husband's hands. This trusty servant
Shall pass between us. Ere long you are like to hear
(If you dare venture in your own behalf) 20
A mistress's command. Wear this; [*Gives a favour.*]
Spare speech;
Decline your head: this kiss, if it durst speak,
Would stretch thy spirits up into the air.
Conceive, and fare thee well.

28 *My foot usurps my body:* My husband enjoys my body (but Edmund possesses my heart).

29 *I have . . . whistle:* This line is evidently based on an old proverb: It is a poor dog that is not worth the whistling.

31 *I fear your disposition:* I am appalled at your character.

32 *nature:* character; *contemns:* despises; *it:* its; *origin:* source, i.e., Lear (whom Albany admires)

33 *Cannot be . . . itself:* cannot be kept within set limits

34 *sliver and disbranch:* be cut off

35-36 *material sap:* essential nourishment – in this case, the characteristics Goneril should have received from Lear; *perforce:* of necessity, necessarily; *must wither/ . . . use:* must be as a dead branch, fit only for burning (or for death)

37 *text:* Goneril means: A sermon from you is not worth hearing, since the text is foolish.

39 *savour:* relish, have a liking for

42 *Whose reverence . . . lick:* who would be (affectionately) licked even by a bear that is being tugged along via a head harness

43 *madded:* driven mad

44 *brother:* brother-in-law (Cornwall)

45 *him:* Lear

46 *If that:* if; *visible spirits:* avenging spirits in visible form.

47 *offences:* offenders

49-50 *Humanity must . . . deep:* People will devour one another, like the creatures of the ocean; *Milk-livered:* cowardly

51 *a cheek for blows:* See Matthew 5:39; *a head for wrongs:* a head that would endure injustices against it

52-53 *Who hast . . . suffering:* who has no insight to tell you what should be accepted honourably and what should not.

54-55 *Fools do . . . mischief:* Only fools pity the villains who are punished before they have committed evil acts; *Where's thy drum?:* i.e., your war drum

Edmund: Yours in the ranks of death! [*Exit.*]
Goneril: My most dear
Gloucester! 25
O, the difference of man and man!
To thee a woman's services are due;
My foot usurps my body.
Oswald: Madam, here comes my lord.
[*Exit.*]

[*Enter Albany.*]
Goneril: I have been worth the whistle.
Albany: O Goneril,
You are not worth the dust which the rude wind 30
Blows in your face! I fear your disposition.
That nature which contemns it origin
Cannot be bordered certain in itself.
She that herself will sliver and disbranch
From her material sap, perforce must wither 35
And come to deadly use.
Goneril: No more! The text is foolish.
Albany: Wisdom and goodness to the vile seem vile;
Filths savour but themselves. What have you done?
Tigers, not daughters, what have you performed? 40
A father, and a gracious aged man,
Whose reverence even the head-lugged bear would lick,
Most barbarous, most degenerate, have you madded.
Could my good brother suffer you to do it?
A man, a prince, by him so benefited! 45
If that the heavens do not their visible spirits
Send quickly down to tame these vile offences,
It will come,
Humanity must perforce prey on itself,
Like monsters of the deep.
Goneril: Milk-livered man! 50
That bearest a cheek for blows, a head for wrongs;
Who hast not in thy brows an eye discerning
Thine honour from thy suffering; that not knowest
Fools do those villains pity who are punished
Ere they have done their mischief. Where's thy drum? 55
France spreads his banners in our noiseless land,
With plumed helm thy state begins to threat,

58 *a moral fool:* a fool who moralizes when action is necessary

59 *See thyself:* See yourself as others see you.

60-61 *Proper deformity . . . woman:* Physical or moral deformity, expected in a fiend, looks much more horrid in woman, where it is not expected.

62 *changed:* transformed; *self-covered:* with your real self covered with a woman's body

63 *Bemonster:* Do not change your appearance into that of a fiend; *Were't my fitness:* if it were proper to me

64 *blood:* impulses

66 *Howe'er:* in whatever ways

68 *Marry:* By the Virgin Mary; *your manhood – mew:* Confine (or coop up) your feeble manhood until it is strong enough for a man's work. Alternatively, Goneril may be making a scornful sound, imitating a cat's cry, in an expression of contempt.

73 *bred:* reared, brought up; *thrilled with remorse:* moved or excited by compassion

74 *Opposed against:* tried to prevent; *bending:* turning, directing

76 *amongst them felled him dead:* Among the lot of them, they killed him.

77 *harmful stroke:* fatal wound

78 *plucked him after:* drew him along to death after the murdered servant

79 *justicers:* judges, dispenses of justice, gods; *neither crimes:* crimes on earth, crimes committed here and now

84-86 *But being . . . life:* But since Regan is now a widow, and my lover Edmund is with her, my dreams of a life with Edmund may be shattered, and escape from my hated life with Albany may be impossible.

87 *tart:* sour, unpleasant

88 *son:* Edmund

Whiles thou, a moral fool, sittest still, and cries
"Alack, why does he so?"
Albany: See thyself, devil!
Proper deformity shows not in the fiend 60
So horrid as in woman.
Goneril: O vain fool!
Albany: Thou changed and self-covered thing, for shame!
Bemonster not thy feature! Were't my fitness
To let these hands obey my blood,
They are apt enough to dislocate and tear 65
Thy flesh and bones. Howe'er thou art a fiend,
A woman's shape doth shield thee.
Goneril: Marry, your manhood—mew!
[*Enter a Gentleman.*]
Albany: What news?
Gentleman: O, my good lord, the Duke of Cornwall's dead, 70
Slain by his servant, going to put out
The other eye of Gloucester.
Albany: Gloucester's eyes?
Gentleman: A servant that he bred, thrilled with remorse,
Opposed against the act, bending his sword
To his great master; who, there at enraged, 75
Flew on him, and amongst them felled him dead;
But not without that harmful stroke which since
Hath plucked him after.
Albany: This shows you are above,
You justicers, that these our nether crimes
So speedily can venge! But O poor Gloucester! 80
Lost he his other eye?
Gentleman: Both, both, my lord.
This letter, madam, craves a speedy answer.
'Tis from your sister.
Goneril: [*Aside.*] One way I like this well;
But being widow, and my Gloucester with her,
May all the building in my fancy pluck 85
Upon my hateful life. Another way
The news is not so tart.—I'll read, and answer. [*Exit.*]
Albany: Where was his son when they did take his eyes?
Gentleman: Come with my lady hither.
Albany: He is not here.

90 *back:* on his way back

93-94 *And quit . . . course:* and left deliberately so that those dealing with Gloucester might have a freer hand in punishment

Gentleman: No, my good lord; I met him back again. 90
Albany: Knows he the wickedness?
Gentleman: Ay, my good lord: 'twas he informed against
him,
And quit the house on purpose, that their punishment
Might have the freer course.
Albany: Gloucester, I live
To thank thee for the love thou show'dst the King, 95
And to revenge thine eyes. Come hither, friend.
Tell me what more thou knowest. [*Exeunt.*]

Act 4, Scene 2: Activities

1. As Albany, write a diary entry explaining why it took you so long to understand what was happening both in your own life and in the kingdom in general. How do you respond to the accusations of cowardice levelled at you? What were your motivations for marrying Goneril? What did you really think of Cornwall? Are you motivated by a desire for revenge? Explain.

2. Goneril and Edmund believe that human beings design their own fates. Albany believes the opposite. Do you agree with Goneril and Edmund or with Albany? Using the three characters and their situations to illustrate your point of view, share your response with others. You might create a short tale with a moral (a fable) or create a comic strip to illustrate your philosophy.

3. The medieval convention of courtly love – the chivalric relationship between a knight and a lady – followed a strict etiquette. Goneril and Edmund use the language of courtly love with each other in this scene. Do you think they really behave this way?

   Write a short scene suitable for a daytime soap opera in which you show the two of them together in an intimate conversation.

For the next scene . . .

If you were in an army at war, how would you feel about having a woman lead you into battle?

Act 4, Scene 3

In this scene . . .

Kent arrives at the French camp near Dover only to discover that the King has been recalled to France to deal with an emergency. The army has been left in control of the Marshal of France under the guidance of Cordelia, who remains in England.

Kent learns that Cordelia is distressed over the plight of her father and, reveals that, although Lear knows she is in Dover, he refuses to see her out of guilt for the wrongs he has done her.

As the scene closes, Kent is told that the combined forces of Albany and Cornwall are approaching.

4 *imports:* portends (indicates beforehand, as an omen does), signifies

7 *general?:* as general, in charge of the army

9 *pierce:* impel; move

12 *trilled:* trickled

13 *delicate:* lovely

13-15 *It seemed . . . her:* It appeared that she was in control of her feelings ("passion") which seemed to be trying to control her.

16-17 *Patience and . . . goodliest:* Her self-control struggled with her sorrow as to which would give her the most appropriate (or beautiful) expression.

19 *A better way:* i.e., of expressing the ideas; *smilets:* little smiles

21 *guests:* tears (visiting her eyes)

22 *As pearls from diamonds dropped:* a courtly and therefore exaggerated compliment from the messenger, who compares her tears to pearls and her eyes to diamonds

23-24 *Sorrow would . . . it:* Sorrow would be a prized jewel if it was as becoming to others (made them as attractive).

24 *Made she no verbal question?:* Did she say nothing apart from what you gathered from her tears?

25 *Faith:* in faith (a mild oath); *heaved:* spoke with difficulty

Scene 3

The French camp near Dover.

Enter Kent and a Gentleman.

Kent: Why the King of France is so suddenly gone back; know you no reason?

Gentleman: Something he left imperfect in the state, which since his coming forth is thought of, which imports to the kingdom so much fear and danger that his personal return was most required and necessary. 5

Kent: Who hath he left behind him general?

Gentleman: The Marshal of France, Monsieur La Far.

Kent: Did your letters pierce the Queen to any demonstration of grief? 10

Gentleman: Ay, sir. She took them, read them in my presence,
And now and then an ample tear trilled down
Her delicate cheek. It seemed she was a queen
Over her passion, who, most rebel-like,
Sought to be king o'er her.

Kent: O, then it moved her? 15

Gentleman: Not to a rage. Patience and sorrow strove
Who should express her goodliest. You have seen
Sunshine and rain at once: her smiles and tears
Were like. A better way: those happy smilets
That played on her ripe lip seemed not to know 20
What guests were in her eyes, which parted thence
As pearls from diamonds dropped. In brief,
Sorrow would be a rarity most beloved,
If all could so become it.

Kent: Made she no verbal question?

Gentleman: Faith, once or twice she heaved the name of father 25
Pantingly forth, as if it pressed her heart;
Cried, "Sisters, sisters! Shame of ladies! Sisters!

29	*Let pity not be believed:* Let it not be believed that pity can exist in a world that sees such deeds, and let it not be believed for the sake of human pity.
29-31	*There she . . . moistened:* The general sense is that Cordelia's emotion was calmed by a great outburst of tears, but probably also that the outbursts of tears punctuated her exclamations.
31-32	*Then away . . . alone:* Then she simply gave way to her feelings of grief.
32-33	*It is . . . conditions:* The stars themselves control our characters.
34-35	*Else one . . . issues:* Otherwise, the same husband and wife could not produce children so utterly unalike.
39	*in his better tune:* when he is comparatively rational
41	*yield to see:* submit to seeing
42	*sovereign:* overwhelming; *elbows:* jogs his elbow, reminds him of what he did to Cordelia
43	*stripped her from his benediction:* cut her off from his blessings
44	*foreign casualties:* hazards encountered in foreign countries
45	*dog-hearted:* cruel, fierce, pitiless
48	*powers:* armies
49	*afoot:* on the march
51	*Some dear cause:* an important matter
52	*Will in . . . awhile:* will occupy my time and conceal my true identity
53	*aright:* in my true character
54	*Lending me this acquaintance:* for having been acquainted with me

Kent! Father! Sisters! What, i' the storm? I' the night?
Let pity not be believed!" There she shook
The holy water from her heavenly eyes, 30
And clamour moistened. Then away she started
To deal with grief alone.

Kent: It is the stars,
The stars above us, govern our conditions;
Else one self mate and make could not beget
Such different issues. You spoke not with her since? 35

Gentleman: No.

Kent: Was this before the King returned?

Gentleman: No, since.

Kent: Well, sir, the poor distressed Lear's i' the town;
Who sometime, in his better tune, remembers
What we are come about, and by no means 40
Will yield to see his daughter.

Gentleman: Why, good sir?

Kent: A sovereign shame so elbows him; his own unkindness,
That stripped her from his benediction, turned her
To foreign casualties, gave her dear rights
To his dog-hearted daughters—these things sting 45
His mind so venomously that burning shame
Detains him from Cordelia.

Gentleman: Alack, poor gentleman!

Kent: Of Albany's and Cornwall's powers you heard not?

Gentleman: 'Tis so; they are afoot.

Kent: Well, sir, I'll bring you to our master Lear 50
And leave you to attend him. Some dear cause
Will in concealment wrap me up awhile.
When I am known aright, you shall not grieve
Lending me this acquaintance. I pray you go
Along with me. [*Exeunt.*] 55

Act 4, Scene 3: Activities

1. This scene is frequently omitted from productions of *King Lear*. With your group, prepare an argument as to whether you, as directors, would cut the scene or leave it in the play. Present your argument to classmates.

2. As the person in charge of the French troops, what qualities do you think Cordelia might have that are not revealed to us? In your group, reread the descriptions of Cordelia in this scene.

   a) Create a written portrait of her from your observations.

   b) Using your written description, make a sketch of Cordelia that could be used as an illustration for this scene.

3. You are the King of France. Before you return to your country, you leave Cordelia a letter explaining how you feel about your leaving, the situation in which you are leaving her, and your feelings toward her. Write that letter in your journal.

   In a brief statement, describe the relationship between Cordelia and her husband. Share your statement with others in the class.

For the next scene . . .

In your journal, describe a friend, relative, or neighbour who is considered to be an epitome of patience, compassion, and goodness. You may wish to share your portrait with others.

Act 4, Scene 4

In this scene . . .

Cordelia sends her soldiers to search for her father, who is wandering aimlessly in the countryside, dressed in garlands of weeds and wild flowers. A doctor comforts her with the reassurance that Lear can be cured with rest and relaxation. Cordelia is concerned, however, that he will die before she can find and help him.

A messenger enters to warn of the approach of the British forces. Cordelia is prepared to meet this army, but makes it clear that her French forces are entering into this war only to aid her father, not to gain political control.

3 *rank:* luxuriant; *fumiter:* fumitory, a plant with bitter leaves. Its juice was used to help in cases of hypochondria and jaundice; *furrow-weeds:* Weeds that spring up in the furrows of plowed land.

4 *hardocks:* white burdocks; *hemlock:* swamp hemlock, a deadly poisonous weed used as a narcotic; *nettles:* weeds with fine stinging needles

5 *Darnel:* hurtful weed

5-6 *idle weeds . . . corn:* worthless rather than sustaining as is corn which provides us with food

6 *century:* force of one hundred soldiers

8-9 *What can . . . sense?:* What power has man's accumulated knowledge in restoring his impaired faculties?

10 *helps:* cures; *outward:* material; *worth:* possessions

11 *means:* a way

13 *That to provoke:* to cause that (sleep)

14 *simples operative:* effective medicinal plants (called simples, because they were not compounds)

15 *eye of anguish:* eye of one suffering from deep sorrow; *secrets:* remedies, once regarded as the special secrets of the physician

16 *All you . . . earth:* a more impressive way of referring to the secrets; *virtues:* here, medicinal plants

17 *Spring:* grow; *aidant and remediate:* as aids and remedies

19 *rage:* insane frenzy

20 *wants:* lacks; *the means:* here, the reason, the rationality; *lead:* guide, control

21 *hitherward:* this way, in this direction

22-23 *Our preparation . . . them:* Our troops are ready to meet them.

23-24 *O dear . . . about:* Likely a reference to *Luke* 2:49: "I must go about my father's business."

Scene 4

Same.

Enter, with Drum and Colours,
Cordelia, Doctor, and Soldiers.

Cordelia: Alack, 'tis he! Why, he was met even now
As mad as the vexed sea, singing aloud,
Crowned with rank fumiter and furrow-weeds,
With hardocks, hemlock, nettles, cuckoo-flowers,
Darnel, and all the idle weeds that grow 5
In our sustaining corn. A century send forth.
Search every acre in the high-grown field
And bring him to our eye. [*Exit an Officer.*] What can
man's wisdom
In the restoring his bereaved sense?
He that helps him take all my outward worth. 10
Doctor: There is means, madam.
Our foster nurse of nature is repose,
The which he lacks. That to provoke in him
Are many simples operative, whose power
Will close the eye of anguish.
Cordelia: All blest secrets, 15
All you unpublished virtues of the earth,
Spring with my tears! be aidant and remediate
In the good man's distress! Seek, seek for him!
Lest his ungoverned rage dissolve the life
That wants the means to lead it.
[*Enter Messenger.*]
Messenger: News, madam. 20
The British powers are marching hitherward.
Cordelia: 'Tis known before. Our preparation stands
In expectation of them. O dear father,
It is thy business that I go about.

25-26 *Therefore great . . . pitied:* For that reason, the King of France has taken pity on my mourning and my importunate (urging) tears.

27 *blown:* mighty

Therefore great France 25
My mourning and importuned tears hath pitied.
No blown ambition doth our arms incite,
But love, dear love, and our aged father's right.
Soon may I hear and see him! [*Exeunt.*]

Act 4, Scene 4: Activities

1. In this scene we learn that Lear is wearing weeds and wild flowers. Some of these are fumiter, hardocks, nettles, and darnell. Find out what these look like, what they smell like, and if they have special properties, such as a medical cure. Decide why Lear is dressed in such a manner. Who dressed him? What is he thinking about?

2. Cordelia and a doctor discuss possible cures for Lear. Research with your group what sorts of cures were used for madness in Elizabethan times and prescribe a cure of your own.

3. As Cordelia, you are concerned that you will be accused of using the rescue of Lear as an excuse for taking over Britain. Prepare a written defence that Cordelia could present to a court of law, if necessary.

For the next scene . . .

What experience have you had with sibling rivalry? Describe one in your journal. Is competition more keen between siblings than it is between unrelated people? If so, what might be the reason for this?

Act 4, Scene 5

In this scene . . .

Regan is hoping to read the letter that Goneril has sent with Oswald to Edmund. She is clearly looking for evidence that Goneril and Edmund are having an affair. Regan tells Oswald that she and Edmund are lovers and, because she is already a widow, Edmund is more likely to marry her than Goneril.

Goneril also tells Oswald that Edmund, meanwhile, has gone to find and kill his father. Gloucester, now a potential object of pity, might turn public opinion against the lovers and endanger their common cause. Oswald, who has previously shunned violence, now eagerly agrees to join the hunt for Gloucester, on Regan's instructions.

1 *brother's:* brother-in-law's, i.e., Albany's

2 *ado:* fuss; said sarcastically. Oswald is really Goneril's servant and has little to do with Albany.

3 *Your sister . . . soldier:* because of Albany's reluctance to take arms against Lear. "Soldier" is pronounced as three syllables.

6 *What might . . . him?:* The topic of the letter was obviously discussed before the beginning of the scene. Regan probably suspects that the letter is a love letter.

8 *serious matter:* important business. This is information that Oswald must have given to Regan previously.

9 *ignorance:* foolishness, lack of judgement

12 *In pity of his misery:* the comment is intentional irony; *dispatch:* take

13 *nighted:* darkened, because of his blindness; *descry:* discover

18 *charged my duty:* gave me strict instructions

20 *Transport her purposes:* carry her instructions; *Belike:* probably

21 *Some things . . . what:* Regan conveys her suspicion that Goneril and Edmund are lovers; *I'll love thee much:* I'll reward you generously.

22 *Madam, I had rather:* Oswald refuses to give up the letter.

25 *eliads:* loving looks

26 *her bosom:* in her confidence

Scene 5

Inside Gloucester's castle.

Enter Regan and Oswald the Steward.

Regan: But are my brother's powers set forth?
Oswald: Ay, madam.
Regan: Himself in person there?
Oswald: Madam, with much ado:
Your sister is the better soldier.
Regan: Lord Edmund spake not with your lord at home?
Oswald: No, madam. 5
Regan: What might import my sister's letter to him?
Oswald: I know not, lady.
Regan: Faith, he is posted hence on serious matter.
It was great ignorance, Gloucester's eyes being out,
To let him live. Where he arrives he moves 10
All hearts against us. Edmund, I think, is gone,
In pity of his misery, to dispatch
His nighted life; moreover, to descry
The strength o' the enemy.
Oswald: I must needs after him, madam, with my letter. 15
Regan: Our troops set forth tomorrow. Stay with us.
The ways are dangerous.
Oswald: I may not, madam.
My lady charged my duty in this business.
Regan: Why should she write to Edmund? Might not you
Transport her purposes by word? Belike, 20
Some things—I know not what—I'll love thee much—
Let me unseal the letter.
Oswald: Madam, I had rather—
Regan: I know your lady does not love her husband;
I am sure of that; and at her late being here
She gave strange eliads and most speaking looks 25
To noble Edmund. I know you are of her bosom.

29 *take this note:* take note of this (not a reference to her letter)

30 *talked:* talked about marriage, or, have come to an understanding

31 *convenient;* fitting

32 *You may gather more:* You may assume more (that we are already lovers).

33 *this:* a love-token or trinket, like that Goneril gave Edmund

34 *thus much:* what I have already told you

35 *call her wisdom to her:* have the good sense to accept the situation

38 *Preferment:* promotion

Oswald: I, madam?
Regan: I speak in understanding. Y'are! I know't.
Therefore I do advise you take this note.
My lord is dead; Edmund and I have talked, 30
And more convenient is he for my hand
Than for your lady's. You may gather more.
If you do find him, pray you give him this;
And when your mistress hears thus much from you,
I pray desire her call her wisdom to her. 35
So fare you well.
If you do chance to hear of that blind traitor,
Preferment falls on him that cuts him off.
Oswald: Would I could meet him, madam! I should show
What party I do follow.
Regan: Fare thee well. [*Exeunt.*] 40

Act 4, Scene 5: Activities

1. This scene shows the development of what we commonly call a "love triangle." In groups, determine how the triangle came about, what events you can assume have taken place, and who you think is to blame.

   Such triangles are common in television shows and in movies. How do they usually turn out, from your observations? How do you think this one will turn out?

2. Suddenly, it has become important to kill Gloucester. You are a reporter preparing for a six o'clock newscast. How will you handle the Gloucester story? Will you be sympathetic to Gloucester's plight or openly hostile towards him? Make a video of your broadcast to share with the class. Remember that you are broadcasting to a country that is essentially leaderless.

3. If you were preparing a two-minute television report of the action at this point, how would you present the background war scenes? Describe the camera shots and write the documentary dialogue that you would use to tie Scenes 3, 4, and 5 together. What kind of mood are you trying to convey to your viewing audience?

For the next scene . . .

In your journal, recall an incident in your life that made you feel there was no justice in the world. How did you respond? Have your views on the world's justice changed as a result of your experience? Comment.

Act 4, Scene 6

In this scene . . .

Edgar has led Gloucester to some fields near Dover. He tells his father that they have climbed to the top of a cliff. Believing this to be true, Gloucester thanks Edgar, gives him a purse containing a jewel, and dismisses him. Then Gloucester jumps off what he believes to be the cliff. Although he does not fall far, he faints, overwhelmed by his action. When he revives, he is greeted by Edgar pretending to be a peasant who has seen Gloucester fall. Edgar convinces Gloucester that his survival is a miracle, a sign from the gods that they want him to live. As a result, Gloucester determines that he must endure his suffering until the gods decide that he should die.

Lear now enters, wearing garlands of wild flowers. He raves about the hypocrisy of human beings and decides, in garbled speech, that all of humanity is guilty of sin and that suffering is the lot for all of us. When one of Cordelia's gentlemen attempts to take him in charge, Lear flees.

Oswald appears, delighted to have found Gloucester. Before he can murder the blind man, however, he is attacked by Edgar and killed in the course of their duel. Before he dies, Oswald asks Edgar to take a letter he is carrying to Edmund. Edgar reads the letter in which Goneril confirms her plot with Edmund to murder Albany. Edgar vows to inform Albany and then leads Gloucester away to a friend who will take care of him.

2 *labour:* i.e., at going uphill

3 *Methinks:* it seems to me; *the ground is even:* The ground is indeed even. Edgar has only pretended to lead his blind father to where the cliff is "Horrible steep"; *Horrible:* terrifyingly

4 *Hark:* listen

5-6 *Why, then . . . anguish:* Then your other sense must be dulled by pain caused by the loss of your eyes.

7-8 *Methinks thy . . . didst:* Edgar uses several different accents during his period of disguise (see Act 4, Scene 1, lines 52-55). Apparently, he has dropped part of his assumed character.

10 *Methinks y'are better spoken:* You speak with a better accent (than you did before).

13 *choughs:* jackdaws, birds that were common on the cliffs (pronounced "chuffs")

14 *gross:* large

15 *sampire:* sampire or *herbe de Saint Pierre*, a plant used with vinegar to produce a meat relish and gathered from the cliff face at Dover by men suspended on a rope from the top of the cliff; hence, Edgar's comment "Dreadful trade!"

18 *bark:* ship

19 *Diminished to her cock:* reduced in size (by the distance) to seem no bigger then her cockboat, the small boat used by the crew to reach shore from the ship; *her cock, a buoy:* the tiny cockboat is similarly reduced in size to that of a buoy

20 *surge:* surf, breaking waves

21 *unnumbered:* numberless; *idle:* moved by a continuous agitation for no purpose; *pebble:* pebbles

23-24 *the deficient . . . headlong:* And my sight failing me, I fall headlong down the cliff.

Scene 6

Open country near Dover.

Enter Gloucester, and Edgar, clothed as a countryman.

Gloucester: When shall I come to the top of that same hill?
Edgar: You do climb up it now. Look how we labour.
Gloucester: Methinks the ground is even.
Edgar: Horrible steep.
Hark, do you hear the sea?
Gloucester: No, truly.
Edgar: Why, then, your other senses grow imperfect 5
By your eyes' anguish.
Gloucester: So may it be indeed.
Methinks thy voice is altered, and thou speakest
In better phrase and matter than thou didst.
Edgar: Y'are much deceived. In nothing am I changed
But in my garments.
Gloucester: Methinks y'are better spoken. 10
Edgar: Come on, sir; here's the place. Stand still. How fearful
And dizzy 'tis to cast one's eyes so low!
The crows and choughs that wing the midway air
Show scarce so gross as beetles. Halfway down
Hangs one that gathers sampire—dreadful trade! 15
Methinks he seems no bigger than his head.
The fishermen that walk upon the beach
Appear like mice; and yond tall anchoring bark,
Diminished to her cock; her cock, a buoy
Almost too small for sight. The murmuring surge 20
That on the unnumbered idle pebble chafes
Cannot be heard so high. I'll look no more,
Lest my brain turn, and the deficient sight
Topple down headlong.

27 *leap upright:* He is so close to the cliff that if he jumped straight up in the air, he still could fall over the edge.

29 *Fairies:* possibly a reference to a superstition that hidden treasure is guarded by fairies

33-34 *Why I . . . it:* The reason that I humour my father's despair is to cure it – a necessary explanation for the audience, who would otherwise be puzzled by Edgar's behaviour.

38 *To quarrel with:* rebel against; *opposeless:* not to be opposed, not to be resisted, irresistible

39 *My snuff . . . nature:* the darkened and hated remainder of my life

42-44 *how conceit . . . theft:* how imagination may be robbing life's treasury of all its strength when life itself surrenders or consents (yields) to the theft. Edgar is fearful that, even though his father has not jumped off the cliff, simply imagining the fall may be enough of a shock to kill him.

45 *had:* would have

46 *Ho you . . . Speak:* Edgar tries to rouse Gloucester, who has fallen down on the ground from a slight height.

47 *pass:* die

49 *Hadst thou:* if you had; *aught:* anything; *gossamer:* thread of a spider's web

50 *precipating:* falling

51 *Thou'dst:* you would have; *shivered:* shattered

52 *Hast heavy substance:* are of normal weight, subject to gravity

53 *Ten masts at each:* ten masts of a tall ship, one on top of the other

54 *fell:* fallen

57 *bourn:* boundary of the sea (the cliffs at Dover are composed of chalk)

Gloucester: Set me where you stand.
Edgar: Give me your hand; you are now within a foot 25
Of the extreme verge; for all beneath the moon
Would I not leap upright.
Gloucester: Let go my hand.
Here, friend, 's another purse; in it a jewel
Well worth a poor man's taking. Fairies and gods
Prosper it with thee! Go thou further off; 30
Bid me farewell, and let me hear thee going.
Edgar: Now fare ye well, good sir.
Gloucester: With all my heart.
Edgar: [*Aside.*] Why I do trifle thus with this despair
Is done to cure it.
Gloucester: O you mighty gods! [*He kneels.*]
This world I do renounce, and, in your sights, 35
Shake patiently my great affliction off.
If I could bear it longer and not fall
To quarrel with your great opposeless wills,
My snuff and loathed part of nature should
Burn itself out. If Edgar live, O, bless him! 40
Now, fellow, fare thee well.
[*He falls forward and faints.*]
Edgar: Gone, sir, farewell.—
And yet I know not how conceit may rob
The treasury of life when life itself
Yields to the theft. Had he been where he thought,
By this had thought been past.—Alive or dead? 45
Ho you, sir! Friend! Hear you, sir? Speak!—
Thus might he pass indeed. Yet he revives.
What are you, sir?
Gloucester: Away, and let me die.
Edgar: Hadst thou been aught but gossamer, feathers, air,
So many fathom down precipitating, 50
Thou'dst shivered like an egg; but thou dost breathe;
Hast heavy substance; bleedest not; speakest; art sound.
Ten masts at each make not the altitude
Which thou hast perpendicularly fell.
Thy life's a miracle. Speak yet again. 55
Gloucester: But have I fallen, or no?
Edgar: From the dread summit of this chalky bourn.

58 *a-height:* on high, to the height above; *shrill-gorged:* shrill-throated, shrill-voiced

61-64 *Is wretchedness . . . death?:* Am I, in my misfortune, to be deprived of the benefit of death? *'Twas yet . . . will:* After all, it was some comfort to know that in my unhappiness I could cheat the tyrant's (Cornwall's) tyranny and foil his aims by suicide.

65 *Up – so:* Edgar is straining to get Gloucester to his feet again; *Feel you:* either "Can you use?" or "Have you any feeling in?"

66 *above all strangeness:* the strangest thing I have ever seen

67-68 *Upon the . . . you:?* Edgar pretends to be a new rescuer. He is no longer the Bedlam beggar who led Gloucester to the cliff.

69-72 *As I . . . fiend:* Edgar further confuses Gloucester by convincing him that a fiend, not Poor Tom, led him to the cliff, and that the gods pitied him and saved him.

71 *whelked:* twisted; *enridged:* furrowed

73-74 *Think that . . . thee:* Believe that the most glorious gods, who make themselves honoured by performing miracles impossible to men, have saved you (from the fiend).

77 *die:* disappear. Gloucester determines to bear his suffering until affliction itself recognizes he has been hurt enough and dies.

79 *"The fiend, the fiend":* Edgar's words during his pretended madness

80 *free:* i.e., free from despair

81-82 *The safer . . . thus:* The sane judgement of a man would not permit him to dress in this fashion. Edgar implies that the man he sees must be mad because of his strange dress.

83 *touch:* charge, arrest; *coining:* making counterfeit money. The king in early days coined all the legal money of the realm.

86 *Nature's above . . . respect:* A born (or natural) king is superior to one dependent upon legal supports.

Look up a-height. The shrill-gorged lark so far
Cannot be seen or heard. Do but look up.
Gloucester: Alack, I have no eyes! 60
Is wretchedness deprived that benefit
To end itself by death? 'Twas yet some comfort
When misery could beguile the tyrant's rage
And frustrate his proud will.
Edgar: Give me your arm.
Up—so. How is't? Feel you your legs? You stand. 65
Gloucester: Too well, too well.
Edgar: This is above all strangeness.
Upon the crown o' the cliff what thing was that
Which parted from you?
Gloucester: A poor unfortunate beggar.
Edgar: As I stood here below, methought his eyes
Where two full moons; he had a thousand noses, 70
Horns whelked and waved like the enridged sea:
It was some fiend; therefore, thou happy father,
Think that the clearest gods, who make them honours
Of men's impossibilities, have preserved thee.
Gloucester: I do remember now. Henceforth I'll bear 75
Affliction till it do cry out itself,
"Enough, enough," and die. That thing you speak of,
I took it for a man. Often 'twould say,
"The fiend, the fiend"—he led me to that place.
Edgar: Bear free and patient thoughts.
[*Enter Lear, mad, garlanded with wild flowers.*]
But who comes here? 80
The safer sense will ne'er accommodate
His master thus.
Lear: No, they cannot touch me for coining;
I am the King himself.
Edgar: O thou side-piercing sight! 85
Lear: Nature's above art in that respect. There's your press money. That fellow handles his bow like a crowkeeper. Draw me a clothier's yard. Look, look, a mouse! Peace, peace; this piece of toasted cheese will do it. There's my gauntlet; I'll prove it on a giant. Bring up the 90 brown bills. O, well flown, bird! I' the clout, i' the clout! Hewgh! Give the word.

93 *Sweet marjoram:* wild flower; also a remedy for mental illness

96-98 *Ha! Goneril with a white beard?:* Lear mistakes Gloucester for Goneril; *They flattered . . . there:* They flattered me by telling me I had white hair and was therefore wise, although I proved myself foolish.

103-105 *men:* women; *ague:* fever

106 *trick:* individual peculiarity or intonation

109 *cause?:* charge or offence

111 *Die for adultery?:* Adultery was not a capital offence in Elizabethan England nor in the imagined time of the play.

112 *gilded:* deceptively and superficially beautiful

113 *lecher:* copulate

117 *To it:* Go to it; *luxury:* lust

119 *forks:* legs; *presages snow:* promises chastity, seems to be frigidly chaste.

120 *minces virtue:* coyly affects the timidity of virtue

121 *To hear of pleasure's name:* even to hear the word "pleasure"

122 *fitchew:* polecat (weasel) – prostitute

123 *riotous:* unrestrained

124 *Centaurs:* legendary creatures half-horse and half-human

126-127 *But to . . . fiend's:* Down to the waist, they belong to the gods; below the waist, to the devil.

Edgar: Sweet marjoram.
Lear: Pass.
Gloucester: I know that voice. 95
Lear: Ha! Goneril with a white beard? They flattered me like a dog, and told me I had white hairs in my beard ere the black ones were there. To say "ay" and "no" to everything that I said! "Ay" and "no" too was no good divinity. When the rain came to wet me once, 100 and the wind to make me chatter; when the thunder would not peace at my bidding; there I found 'em, there I smelt 'em out. Go to, they are not men o' their words! They told me I was everything. 'Tis a lie—I am not ague-proof. 105
Gloucester: The trick of that voice I do well remember.
Is't not the King?
Lear: Ay, every inch a king!
When I do stare, see how the subject quakes.
I pardon that man's life. What was thy cause?
Adultery? 110
Thou shalt not die. Die for adultery? No.
The wren goes to it, and the small gilded fly
Does lecher in my sight.
Let copulation thrive; for Gloucester's bastard son
Was kinder to his father than my daughters 115
Got 'tween the lawful sheets.
To it, luxury, pell-mell! For I lack soldiers.
Behold yond simpering dame,
Whose face between her forks presages snow,
That minces virtue, and does shake the head 120
To hear of pleasure's name.
The fitchew nor the soiled horse goes to it
With a more riotous appetite.
Down from the waist they are Centaurs,
Though women all above. 125
But to the girdle do the gods inherit,
Beneath is all the fiend's.
There's hell, there's darkness, there is the sulphurous pit; burning, scalding, stench, consumption. Fie, fie, fie! Pah, pah! Give me an ounce of civet; good apothecary, 130 sweeten my imagination. There's money for thee.

133 *mortality:* death or existence (or the bitter experience of life)

134-135 *O ruined . . . naught:* What a masterpiece of nature (Lear) is ruined! In such a way will the universe eventually be worn down to nothing.

137 *blind Cupid:* the god of love, whose images was used commonly in Shakespeare's day on signs for brothels.

138 *mark:* observe; *penning:* handwriting

140 *I would . . . report:* I would not believe this if it had been reported to me; *is:* is so

143 *case of eyes?:* eye socket

144 *are you there with me?:* Are you like me in that respect?

145-146 *in a heavy/case:* in a serious condition; *light:* empty

148 *feelingly:* by touch, by pain

151 *justice:* judge; *rails upon:* scolds, lectures; *simple:* ordinary

152 *handy-dandy:* a children's game in which one child hides a prize in one of his or her closed hands and another guesses which hand holds the prize

153-158 *Thou hast . . . office:* Lear says that anyone in power is obeyed regardless of his character.

156 *creature:* beggar

159 *beadle:* parish constable; *hold thy bloody hand:* Restrain yourself from giving out punishment.

162 *cozener:* cheat

164 *Robes and . . . all:* fine dress of those in office hides all evil

164-166 *Plate sin . . . it:* Dress a sinner in expensive clothing and he will be untouched by the law; dress him in rags and the law fails him.

167 *None does . . . 'em:* No person shall be considered guilty. I will authorize all to act as they wish.

169 *glass eyes:* glasses – an anachronism

170 *scurvy politician:* vile trickster

Gloucester: O, let me kiss that hand!
Lear: Let me wipe it first; it smells of mortality.
Gloucester: O ruined piece of nature! This great world
Shall so wear out to naught. Dost thou know me? 135
Lear: I remember thine eyes well enough. Dost thou squint
at me? No, do thy worst, blind Cupid! I'll not love.
Read thou this challenge; mark but the penning of it.
Gloucester: Were all thy letters suns, I could not see.
Edgar: [*Aside.*] I would not take this from report. It is, 140
And my heart breaks at it.
Lear: Read.
Gloucester: What, with the case of eyes?
Lear: O, ho, are you there with me? No eyes in your head,
nor no money in your purse? Your eyes are in a heavy 145
case, your purse in a light. Yet you see how this
world goes.
Gloucester: I see it feelingly.
Lear: What, art mad? A man may see how this world goes
with no eyes. Look with thine ears. See how yond 150
justice rails upon yond simple thief. Hark in thine
ear. Change places and, handy-dandy, which is the
justice, which is the thief? Thou hast seen a farmer's
dog bark at a beggar?
Gloucester: Ay, sir. 155
Lear: And the creature run from the cur? There thou mightst
behold the great image of authority: a dog's obeyed
in office.
Thou rascal beadle, hold thy bloody hand!
Why dost thou lash that whore? Strip thine own back. 160
Thou hotly lusts to use her in that kind
For which thou whippest her. The usurer hangs the
cozener.
Through tattered clothes small vices do appear;
Robes and furred gowns hide all. Plate sin with gold,
And the strong lance of justice hurtless breaks; 165
Arm it in rags, a pygmy's straw does pierce it.
None does offend, none, I say, none; I'll able 'em:
Take that of me, my friend, who have the power
To seal th' accuser's lips. Get thee glass eyes
And, like a scurvy politician, seem 170

172	*So:* said as his boots come off – an expression of relief. Lear thinks that he has just completed a journey or tour of inspection.
173	*matter and impertinency:* sense and incoherence
175-176	*If thou . . . Gloucester:* Lear's mind clears for a moment, and he recognizes his old supporter.
177	*We came crying hither:* We come into the world crying.
179	*mark:* Listen carefully.
182	*this great stage:* this great world; *This' a good block:* This is a stylish hat.
183	*a delicate stratagem:* a very difficult plan
184	*felt:* material of specially matted fur from which hats are made, and a fanciful means by which a whole troop of horses could be made to move quietly; *put't in proof:* put in to the test
185	*stolen upon:* with a troop of felt-shod horses; *sons-in-law:* Albany and Cornwall
186	*kill, kill . . . kill:* a cry used by soldiers, meaning "No mercy."
189	*What, a prisoner?:* Lear feels he has been taken prisoner.
190	*The natural fool of fortune:* a plaything of fortune
192	*cut:* wounded
193	*seconds?:* supporters
194	*Why, this . . . salt:* This would make any man weep.
195-196	*To use . . . dust:* to weep more copiously; *bravely:* in fine dress
197	*smug:* trim, neat
198	*masters:* gentlemen
200	*Then there's life in't:* Then there's still hope; *an:* if
201	*Sa, sa, sa, sa:* a hunting cry to urge on the hounds
204	*general:* universal
205	*twain:* a pair
206	*speed you:* God bless you; *What's your will?:* What do you wish?

To see the things thou dost not. Now, now, now, now!
Pull off my boots. Harder, harder! So.
Edgar: O, matter and impertinency mixed!
Reason in madness!
Lear: If thou wilt weep my fortunes, take my eyes. 175
I know thee well enough; thy name is Gloucester.
Thou must be patient. We came crying hither;
Thou knowest, the first time that we smell the air
We wawl and cry. I will preach to thee: mark.
Gloucester: Alack, alack the day! 180
Lear: When we are born, we cry that we are come
To this great stage of fools. This' a good block.
It were a delicate stratagem to shoe
A troop of horse with felt. I'll put't in proof,
And when I have stolen upon these sons-in-law, 185
Then kill, kill, kill, kill, kill, kill!
[*Enter a Gentleman with Attendants.*]
Gentleman: O, here he is! Lay hand upon him.—Sir,
Your most dear daughter—
Lear: No rescue? What, a prisoner? I am even
The natural fool of fortune. Use me well; 190
You shall have ransom. Let me have surgeons;
I am cut to the brains.
Gentleman: You shall have anything.
Lear: No seconds? All myself?
Why, this would make a man a man of salt,
To use his eyes for garden waterpots, 195
Ay, and laying autumn's dust. I will die bravely,
Like a smug bridegroom. What! I will be jovial.
Come, come, I am king; masters, know you that?
Gentleman: You are a royal one, and we obey you.
Lear: Then there's life in't. Come, an you get it, you shall 200
get it by running. Sa, sa, sa, sa!
[*Exit running followed by Attendants.*]
Gentleman: A sight most pitiful in the meanest wretch,
Past speaking of in a king! Thou hast one daughter
Who redeems nature from the general curse
Which twain have brought her to. 205
Edgar: Hail, gentle sir.
Gentleman: Sir, speed you. What's your will?

207 *toward?:* about to take place, in preparation

208 *Most sure and vulgar:* most certain, and a matter of common knowledge

209 *Which can distinguish sound:* who can hear at all

211-212 *and on speedy foot:* moving swiftly; *The main . . . thought:* The main body of troops is expected to be in view within the hour.

213-214 *Though that . . . on:* Though Cordelia is here for a special reason (to seek her father), her troops have moved ahead.

215 *take my breath from me:* choose when to make me die

216 *worser spirit:* the evil side of my nature

217 *father:* This word would not reveal Edgar's identity to Gloucester, since it was used as a term of respect by younger to older men.

219 *made tame:* resigned

220-221 *Who, by . . . pity:* who, through the instruction provided by heart-felt sorrow, am easily moved to pity. More simply, Edgar says: Since I have experienced deep sorrow, I can readily feel pity for others.

222 *biding:* shelter, lodging

223 *bounty and the benison:* reward and the blessing

224 *To boot, and boot:* in the highest degree; *A proclaimed prize:* a criminal with a reward on his head; *Most happy:* This is a happy opportunity for me!

225 *framed:* created

227 *thyself remember:* Pray for your sins; *the sword is out:* Oswald draws his sword as he speaks.

228 *friendly:* because it offers the death Gloucester wants

230 *published:* proclaimed

231-232 *Lest that . . . thee:* lest his ill-luck become yours

233 *Chill:* I'll. Edgar adopts conventional stage rustic dialect, much like that of rural Somerset; *zir:* sir; *'casion:* occasion, reason

Edgar: Do you hear aught, sir, of a battle toward?
Gentleman: Most sure and vulgar. Every one hears that
Which can distinguish sound.
Edgar: But, by your favour,
How near's the other army? 210
Gentleman: Near and on speedy foot. The main descry
Stands on the hourly thought.
Edgar: I thank you, sir. That's
all.
Gentleman: Though that the Queen on special cause is here,
Her army is moved on.
Edgar: I thank you, sir.
[*Exit Gentleman.*]
Gloucester: You ever-gentle gods, take my breath from me; 215
Let not my worser spirit tempt me again
To die before you please!
Edgar: Well pray you, father.
Gloucester: Now, good sir, what are you?
Edgar: A most poor man, made tame to fortune's blows,
Who, by the art of known and feeling sorrows, 220
Am pregnant to good pity. Give me your hand;
I'll lead you to some biding.
Gloucester: Hearty thanks.
The bounty and the benison of heaven
To boot, and boot!
[*Enter Oswald the Steward.*]
Oswald: A proclaimed prize! Most happy!
That eyeless head of thine was first framed flesh 225
To raise my fortunes. Thou old unhappy traitor,
Briefly thyself remember: the sword is out
That must destroy thee.
Gloucester: Now let thy friendly hand
Put strength enough to't. [*Edgar interposes.*]
Oswald: Wherefore, bold peasant,
Darest thou support a published traitor? Hence! 230
Lest that th' infection of his fortune take
Like hold on thee. Let go his arm.
Edgar: Chill not let go, zir, without vurther 'casion.
Oswald: Let go, slave, or thou diest!

235 *go your gait:* Go your way; *volk:* folk, people

235-236 *An chud . . . vortnight:* If I could have been frightened out of my life by bold words, I should have been dead a couple of weeks ago. (Edgar accuses Oswald of mere braggery, not real courage.)

238-240 *Keep out . . . you:* Stand back, I warn you, or I shall try to find out whether your head or my club (ballow) is the harder. I'll be plain with you.

241 *dunghill:* born on a dunghill; low-born

242-243 *Chill pick . . . foins:* I'll knock your teeth out, sir. Come at me. I don't care about your sword thrusts (foins).

244 *Villain:* serf (in contrast to Edgar's use of "villain," line 249)

248 *Upon the English party:* on the side of the English

249 *serviceable villain:* evil fellow ready to be used

250 *duteous:* obedient

254 *May be my friends:* may be able to help me

255 *deathsman:* executioner

256 *Leave:* by your leave; *wax:* with which the letter was sealed; *manners, blame us not:* the ordinary respect with which we view the letters of others should not count here.

257-258 *To know . . . lawful:* To know what our enemies are thinking, we would tear their hearts from their bodies; to rip open their letters is more justifiable.

259 *reciprocal vows:* See Act 4, Scene 2, lines 21-24.

260-261 *to cut him off:* to murder Albany; *If your will want/not:* if you are not lacking in desire

261 *time and place;* i.e., for his murder

266 *would:* would like to: *servant:* lover

267 *O indistinguished . . . will:* O, the limitless scope of a woman's lust.

269 *sands:* Gloucester believes they are on the beach; perhaps Edgar is speaking for his father's benefit.

270 *rake up:* cover up, bury; *post unsanctified:* unholy messenger

Edgar: Good gentleman, go your gait, and let poor volk pass. An chud ha' bin zwagger'd out of my life, 'twould not ha' bin zo long as 'tis by a vortnight. Nay, come not near the old man. Keep out, che vor' ye, or Ise try whither your costard or my ballow be the harder. Chill be plain with you. 235–240

Oswald: Out, dunghill!

Edgar: Chill pick your teeth, zir. Come! No matter vor your foins. [*They fight and Oswald falls.*]

Oswald: Slave, thou hast slain me. Villain, take my purse.
If ever thou wilt thrive, bury my body, 245
And give the letters which thou find'st about me
To Edmund Earl of Gloucester. Seek him out
Upon the English party. O, untimely death! Death!
[*He dies.*]

Edgar: I know thee well. A serviceable villain,
As duteous to the vices of thy mistress 250
As badness would desire.

Gloucester: What, is he dead?

Edgar: Sit you down, father; rest you.
Let's see these pockets; the letters that he speaks of
May be my friends. He's dead; I am only sorry
He had no other deathsman. Let us see. 255
Leave, gentle wax; and manners, blame us not:
To know our enemies' minds, we rip their hearts;
Their papers is more lawful. [*Reads the letter.*]
"Let our reciprocal vows be remembered. You have many opportunities to cut him off. If your will want not, time and place will be fruitfully offered. There is nothing done if he return the conqueror. Then am I the prisoner, and his bed my jail; from the loathed warmth whereof deliver me, and supply the place for your labour. 260–265
Your (wife, so I would say) affectionate servant,"
GONERIL.
O indistinguished space of woman's will!
A plot upon her virtuous husband's life,
And the exchange my brother! Here in the sands
Thee I'll rake up, the post unsanctified 270

271 *murderous lechers:* lustful and murderous persons (Goneril and Edmund); *in the mature time:* when the proper moment arrives

272-273 *ungracious paper:* evil letter; *strike the . . . Duke:* show to the Duke of Albany, whose death is plotted

275 *vile sense:* vile, because his senses make him fully aware of his losses and sorrows but do not give him the relief of insanity

276 *ingenious:* conscious

277 *distract:* mad

278-280 *So should . . . themselves:* If I were mad (like Lear), my thoughts and griefs would be separated, and my sorrows would be lost amid mad illusions (wrong imaginations).

282 *bestow you with:* leave you in the care of; *friend:* How Edgar managed to get in touch with a friend is anybody's guess.

Of murderous lechers; and in the mature time
With this ungracious paper strike the sight
Of the death-practised Duke. From him 'tis well
That of thy death and business I can tell.

Gloucester: The King is mad. How stiff is my vile sense, 275
That I stand up, and have ingenious feeling
Of my huge sorrows! Better I were distract.
So should my thoughts be severed from my griefs,
And woes by wrong imaginations lose
The knowledge of themselves. [*A drum afar off.*]

Edgar: Give me your hand. 280
Far off methinks I hear the beaten drum.
Come, father, I'll bestow you with a friend. [*Exeunt.*]

Act 4, Scene 6: Activities

1. The segment of this scene in which Gloucester tries to jump off the cliff has often been criticized as being so contrived to be unbelievable. In groups, decide how you might stage this segment so that it can be believed by an audience. Assume that you have nothing to work with but a bare stage. Present your ideas to classmates.

   If you were to film the segment for a movie, how realistic would you make Gloucester's fall? Why?

2. A symbol is usually defined as something that stands for or represents something else. A friend of yours has just seen a production of *King Lear* for the first time and has no prior knowledge of the play. Your friend senses there is something symbolic in the suicide sequence in this scene. How do you explain it to him or her? Share your understanding with others.

3. Many people regard the coming together of Lear and Gloucester in this scene as representational, standing for many things other than two old men meeting by chance. Discuss with classmates what their meeting may represent in light of your understanding of the play to this point.

4. Lear's speeches in this scene appear initially to make no sense at all. Upon careful examination, however, it becomes clear that there are threads tying them together. In groups, sort out what Lear is recalling. What do his recollections reveal about him that we did not know previously? How do you think an audience seeing the play for the first time would respond to these speeches? How much sense do you think they would make of them?

   In modern fiction, the technique Shakespeare uses in Lear's speeches is referred to as "stream of consciousness" – a narrative in which a character recounts different experiences, responses, and ideas in a continuous flow. Assume that Gloucester, on hearing Lear's voice, also goes mad. Write a speech for him employing the stream-of-consciousness technique, drawing on events from Gloucester's past.

5. Some productions of *King Lear* use this scene to emphasize the idea that the world is essentially evil and that all good is eventually crushed out of it. In your group, discuss to what extent you believe this to be the theme of this scene.

6. In this scene, Lear continues to rail bitterly against women. What kind of woman do you think his wife might have been? Do you think she may have been partly responsible for the way Lear's daughters turned out? Write the dialogue that could result from a conversation you have with Lear's wife in which you ask her what it was like to have been married to Lear. Be sure to include questions on the way each of them treated their children.

7. After Oswald is killed, his diary is discovered. In it, he reveals why he acted in the way he did. Write an excerpt from this diary that you might give to someone developing a character profile on Oswald.

8. You are preparing a short film documentary on the life of Oswald. What would you include in it? Prepare the narrative you would use to create the impression you want. Is Oswald a sympathetic and misled character? Is he a dupe? Or is he primarily evil?

For the next scene . . .

What do you know about parent-child bonding? Describe an experience you had in which you became aware of a special bond that was developing between a parent and child.

Act 4, Scene 7

In this scene . . .

In the French camp, Cordelia thanks Kent for his loyalty to her father. She invites him to remove his disguise but he tells her that he still requires it. We learn that Cordelia has finally rescued her father and that he has been attended to by a doctor.

After he has been sleeping for some time, Lear is awakened and brought to Cordelia. She asks him for his blessing and, now that his mind is calmed, Lear begs her forgiveness. As they leave together, we hear that the enemy is approaching and that a bloody battle is about to ensue.

The scene closes with news of Cornwall's death and of Edgar's leading his troops. Kent observes that the outcome of this battle will determine whether or not he has reached his objectives.

3 *measure:* attempt

4 *To be acknowledged:* to be recognized (for one's work)

5 *All my . . . truth:* Everything I have reported (about Lear) conforms to the simple truth.

6 *Nor more nor clipped:* no more, no less; *so:* as I say; *suited:* dressed

7 *weeds:* clothes; *memories:* reminders; *worser:* worst

8 *I prithee:* I beg you.

9 *Yet to . . . intent:* If I am to reveal myself now, I shall not be able to carry out my intentions.

10 *boon:* request

11 *meet:* suitable

15 *breach in his abused nature:* damage in his disturbed mind

16-17 *Th' untuned . . . father:* Tune the untuned and discordant senses of this father who has been made mad (also made into a child) by the savagery of his children. The image is based upon the tuning of a stringed musical instrument.

18 *That we may:* may we

19 *Be governed by:* act according to

20 *I' the sway of:* according to

Scene 7

A tent in the French camp.
Enter Cordelia, Kent, Doctor,
and Gentleman.

Cordelia: O thou good Kent, how shall I live and work
To match thy goodness? My life will be too short
And every measure fail me.
Kent: To be acknowledged, madam, is o'erpaid.
All my reports go with the modest truth; 5
Nor more nor clipped, but so.
Cordelia: Be better suited:
These weeds are memories of those worser hours:
I prithee put them off.
Kent: Pardon, dear madam.
Yet to be known shortens my made intent.
My boon I make it that you know me not 10
Till time and I think meet.
Cordelia: Then be it so, my good lord. [*To the Doctor.*] How
does the King?
Doctor: Madam, sleeps still.
Cordelia: O you kind gods,
Cure this great breach in his abused nature! 15
Th' untuned and jarring senses, O, wind up
Of this child-changed father!
Doctor: So please your Majesty
That we may wake the King? He hath slept long.
Cordelia: Be governed by your knowledge, and proceed
I' the sway of your own will. Is he arrayed? 20
[*Enter Lear in a chair carried by Servants.*]
Gentleman: Ay, madam. In the heaviness of sleep.
We put fresh garments on him.

23 *Be by:* Be nearby, remain close at hand.

24 *I doubt . . . temperance:* I have no doubt that his sanity will have returned; I am certain he will be calm.

26-27 *restoration hang/ . . . lips:* May my kiss serve as medicine to restore you to your former state.

29 *in thy reverence:* to you, to whom all showed reverence

30 *Had you not been:* even if you had not been; *these white flakes:* these strands of white hair

31 *Had challenged:* would have called for; *of:* from

33 *dread-bolted:* with its dreadful thunderbolts

35 *perdu:* lost one

36 *this thin helm?:* this head, with scanty hair

38 *fain:* glad

39 *To hovel thee:* to take shelter; *rogues:* vagabonds, tramps

40 *short and musty:* broken and damp

41 *at once:* at a single moment

42 *concluded all:* come to an end

43 *fittest:* most fitting, most suitable, best

47 *that:* so that

50 *far wide:* far wide of the mark, far away from sanity

51 *scarce:* scarcely

53 *mightily abused:* greatly deceived, greatly deluded

54 *thus:* in my present state

Doctor: Be by, good madam, when we do awake him.
I doubt not of his temperance.
Cordelia: Very well. [*Music.*]
Doctor: Please you draw near. Louder the music there! 25
Cordelia: O my dear father, restoration hang
Thy medicine on my lips, and let this kiss
Repair those violent harms that my two sisters
Have in thy reverence made!
Kent: Kind and dear princess!
Cordelia: Had you not been their father, these white flakes 30
Had challenged pity of them. Was this a face
To be opposed against the warring winds?
To stand against the deep dread-bolted thunder?
In the most terrible and nimble stroke
Of quick, cross lightning? to watch—poor perdu!— 35
With this thin helm? Mine enemy's dog,
Though he had bit me, should have stood that night
Against my fire; and wast thou fain, poor father,
To hovel thee with swine and rogues forlorn,
In short and musty straw? Alack, alack! 40
'Tis wonder that thy life and wits at once
Had not concluded all.—He wakes; speak to him.
Doctor: Madam, do you; 'tis fittest.
Cordelia: How does my royal lord? How fares your Majesty?
Lear: You do me wrong to take me out o' the grave. 45
Thou art a soul in bliss; but I am bound
Upon a wheel of fire, that mine own tears
Do scald like molten lead.
Cordelia: Sir, do you know me?
Lear: You are a spirit, I know. Where did you die?
Cordelia: Still, still, far wide! 50
Doctor: He's scarce awake. Let him alone awhile.
Lear: Where have I been? Where am I? Fair daylight?
I am mightily abused. I should e'en die with pity,
To see another thus. I know not what to say.
I will not swear these are my hands. Let's see: 55
I feel this pin prick. Would I were assured
Of my condition!
Cordelia: O, look upon me, sir,

58 *benediction:* blessing

60 *fond:* senile

61 *Fourscore:* eighty years

65 *mainly:* entirely

66 *skill:* sense

77 *abuse:* deceive

78 *rage:* frenzy, madness

79-80 *and yet . . . lost:* and yet it is dangerous to make him try to fill in the gap in the time that he does not recollect

81 *Desire him:* ask him

82 *Till further settling:* till his mind settles still further

84 *bear with:* be sympathetic towards, be understanding towards

85 *Holds it true:* Is it confirmed as truth?

88 *conductor:* leader

And hold your hands in benediction o'er me.
No, sir, you must not kneel.

Lear: Pray, do not mock me.
I am a very foolish fond old man, 60
Fourscore and upward, not an hour more nor less;
And, to deal plainly,
I fear I am not in my perfect mind.
Methinks I should know you, and know this man;
Yet I am doubtful; for I am mainly ignorant 65
What place this is; and all the skill I have
Remembers not these garments; nor I know not
Where I did lodge last night. Do not laugh at me;
For (as I am a man) I think this lady
To be my child Cordelia.

Cordelia: And so I am, I am. 70

Lear: Be your tears wet? Yes, faith. I pray weep not.
If you have poison for me, I will drink it.
I know you do not love me, for your sisters
Have, as I do remember, done me wrong:
You have some cause, they have not.

Cordelia: No cause, no cause. 75

Lear: Am I in France?

Kent: In your own kingdom, sir.

Lear: Do not abuse me.

Doctor: Be comforted, good madam. The great rage
You see is killed in him; and yet it is danger
To make him even o'er the time he has lost. 80
Desire him to go in. Trouble him no more
Till further settling.

Cordelia: Will't please your Highness walk?

Lear: You must bear with me.
Pray you now, forget and forgive. I am old and foolish.
[*Exeunt Lear, Cordelia, Doctor, and Attendants.*]

Gentleman: Holds it true, sir, that the Duke of Cornwall was so slain? 85

Kent: Most certain, sir.

Gentleman: Who is conductor of his people?

Kent: As 'tis said, the bastard son of Gloucester.

92 *changeable:* unreliable

93 *powers:* military forces; *apace:* speedily

94 *The arbitrement . . . bloody:* The deciding encounter, or battle, is likely to be a bloody one.

96 *My point and period:* the end of my life ("point" and "period" are synonyms); *wrought:* worked out

97 *Or . . . or:* either . . . or

Gentleman: They say Edgar, his banished son, is with the Earl of Kent in Germany. 90

Kent: Report is changeable. 'Tis time to look about; the powers of the kingdom approach apace.

Gentleman: The arbitrement is like to be bloody.
Fare you well, sir. [*Exit.*] 95

Kent: My point and period will be throughly wrought.
Or well or ill, as this day's battle's fought. [*Exit.*]

Act 4, Scene 7: Activities

1. a) Children sometimes suffer greatly at the hands of their parents, as Cordelia has done. Some people find that the reconciliation between Lear and Cordelia is unrealistic because no child so wronged could be so all-forgiving. Decide what you might say to Cordelia if you had a chance to talk to her at this moment. How do you think she would respond to you?

   In your journal, record what advice you might give to parents and children who have differences.

   b) What might Shakespeare argue in defense of his characterization of Cordelia? Consider exchanges that Lear and Cordelia had previously. Is there any similarity between the exchange in this scene and previous ones? Explain your response.

2. Some directors feel that this scene is too long and slows down the action of the play. As a director, how might you shorten it and still retain its essence? Present your shortened version to classmates.

3. Some directors claim that this scene serves no dramatic purpose and is simply intended to play on the emotions of the audience. How would you respond to this criticism? Write an article for a theatre review magazine in which you argue your case.

4. As Cordelia, you know that your father is dying. You have decided to prepare his obituary. When a person of high importance dies, the obituary usually appears on the front page of the newspaper. Keep this convention in mind, and make certain that you include all the positive contributions Lear has made during his lifetime without exaggerating the truth.

5. Some readers and audiences believe that part of the blame for what happens in the play belongs to Cordelia. She knew what her father was like and should never have confronted him as she did in Act 1. These people may think that, in this scene, she is simply attempting to ease her own guilty conscience. How would you respond to this observation? Present your view in a debate. Prepare your argument and defend your position against others in the class who hold opposing points of view.

Act 4: Consider the Whole Act

1. As Lear's lawyer before he divided his kingdom, how would you have worded the contract between Lear and his daughters? In Lear's defence, and considering what has happened, whom would you sue and on what grounds?

2. As a strategic consultant accompanying the French army, you have observed Lear's actions in this scene and have decided that he is just play-acting in order to get attention and sympathy. Write the report that you would send to Cordelia, justifying your theory.

3. As a doctor, reflect on Lear's actions in this scene. Decide what his actions suggest about his state of mind. How would you classify what is wrong with him? Write a report on his condition in which you label the disease and make recommendations for treatment.

4. You are Edgar's friend. Write a diary entry describing what you have been doing to help him since he was forced to leave home. What did you do for Gloucester when Edgar took him to you? What are your observations about what has been going on in the country?

5. Frequently, our perceptions trick us into believing illusions. As Gloucester, recount what is going through your mind as you prepare to jump off the cliffs at Dover.

In your own opinion, can the mind create its own reality? How does your opinion affect your response to events in this act?

6. You are a resident of Lear's kingdom and have observed that the weather has been terrible for some time. You know that the king has abdicated. What connections do you make between the weather and political events? Create a conversation in which you communicate your beliefs to someone you know well. What do you tell him or her? What is this person's reaction?

7. We have all met someone whom we believe is just too good to be true. As a television journalist, you have interviewed Cordelia in this act and have decided that she is not all she appears to be. On your program, called "Expose," reveal what you have discovered.

8. *King Lear* is an exceptionally long play and, as a member of the audience, you have endured two or more hours of it to this point. You have been both "lulled" and "jolted." What in this act lulled you and what jolted you? As a director, would you choose to emphasize or play down the lulls and jolts? In your director's log, outline how you would treat several examples of each. Be sure to explain what effect you would hope to have on the audience.

9. You are an Elizabethan and have just seen the first performance of this play. You are particularly puzzled by some of the things that have gone on in this act. In talking to a prospective theatre-goer, you mention these things. What things do you tell him or her?

For the next scene . . .

Describe a time when you created an elaborate plan to advance yourself at the expense of someone else, only to have the plan backfire. What actually happened? How did you feel when you were finally exposed? Would you ever do something similar again?

Act 5, Scene 1

In this scene . . .

Edmund and Regan are in command of an army to repel the French invading force. They are joined by Albany and Goneril leading their own army. Albany states that his main intention is to drive the French out of Britain, rather than to assist Lear. In the meantime, Regan is preoccupied with trying to keep Goneril and Edmund apart, while Goneril is so jealous of her sister that she would rather lose the battle than give Edmund up to Regan.

Edgar, now disguised in the uniform of a knight, draws Albany aside briefly and gives him the letter he took from Oswald. Edgar offers to prove the truth of the letter in personal combat: he is proposing to challenge Edmund to a duel to the death, according to the rules of proper knightly combat.

When Edmund is left alone on stage, he reveals that, no matter which sister he marries, his aim is to destroy Albany, Lear, and Cordelia leaving himself the undisputed ruler.

1 *Know of:* ask; *purpose:* plan or decision; *hold:* remains the same

2 *aught:* any chance, anything

5 *miscarried:* came to grief

6 *doubted:* feared

7 *intend upon:* intend to grant

9 *honoured:* honourable

10 *brother's:* brother-in-law

11 *forfended place?:* forbidden place. Regan asks if Edmund has committed adultery with Goneril; *abuses:* both deceives and is unworthy of

12-13 *doubtful:* fearful; *conjunct/And bosomed:* joined in the most intimate way; *as far . . . hers:* in the fullest possible way

16 *Fear:* distrust

19 *loosen:* separate

20 *well bemet:* a greeting. We are fortunate in meeting you.

22 *rigour of our state:* oppression of our rule

23 *cry out:* protest; *honest:* honourable

Act 5, Scene 1

The British camp near Dover.

Enter, with Drum and Colours, Edmund, Regan, Gentlemen, and Soldiers.

Edmund: Know of the Duke if his last purpose hold,
Or whether since he is advised by aught
To change the course. He's full of alteration
And self-reproving. Bring his constant pleasure.
[*Exit an Officer.*]
Regan: Our sister's man is certainly miscarried. 5
Edmund: 'Tis to be doubted, madam.
Regan: Now, sweet lord,
You know the goodness I intend upon you.
Tell me, but truly, but then speak the truth,
Do you not love my sister?
Edmund: In honoured love.
Regan: But have you never found my brother's way 10
To the forfended place?
Edmund: That thought abuses you.
Regan: I am doubtful that you have been conjunct
And bosomed with her, as far as we call hers.
Edmund: No, by mine honour, madam.
Regan: I never shall endure her. Dear my lord, 15
Be not familiar with her.
Edmund: Fear me not.
She and the Duke her husband!
[*Enter, with Drum and Colours, Albany, Goneril, Soldiers.*]
Goneril: [*Aside.*] I had rather lose the battle than that sister
Should loosen him and me.
Albany: Our very loving sister, well bemet. 20
Sir, this I hear: the King is come to his daughter,
With others whom the rigour of our state
Forced to cry out. Where I could not be honest,

24-27 *For this . . . oppose:* This business (of Cordelia's returning to her father) concerns us, not because it assists Lear and some others who oppose us, but because the King of France is invading our territory.

28 *Why is this reasoned?:* How do you arrive at that conclusion?

30 *these domestic and particular broils:* these family and personal quarrels

32 *ancient:* those with experience

33 *presently:* immediately

36 *convenient:* fitting

37 *riddle:* hidden reason

39 *overtake you:* catch up to you (spoken to Goneril, Regan, and Edmund)

41 *ope:* open

44 *champion:* a knight who is willing to undergo trial of combat with another knight, in place of a pitched battle between two armies; *prove:* by the trial of single combat

45 *avouched:* claimed, asserted, maintained; *If you miscarry:* if you should have an accident (i.e., are defeated and killed)

47 *machination:* plotting to take your life; *Fortune love you:* Good luck!

49 *When time shall serve:* when it is the right time; *herald:* official appointed to announce and organize knightly challenges and the order of combat

51 *o'erlook:* look over

52 *draw up your powers:* Deploy your forces.

53 *Here:* Edmund holds up a paper; *guess:* estimate

54 *By diligent discovery:* by careful observation

I never yet was valiant. For this business,
It touches us as France invades our land, 25
Not bolds the King, with others, whom, I fear,
Most just and heavy causes make oppose.
Edmund: Sir, you speak nobly.
Regan: Why is this reasoned?
Goneril: Combine together 'gainst the enemy;
For these domestic and particular broils 30
Are not the question here.
Albany: Let's then determine
With th' ancient of war on our proceeding.
Edmund: I shall attend you presently at your tent.
Regan: Sister, you'll go with us?
Goneril: No. 35
Regan: 'Tis most convenient; pray go with us.
Goneril: [*Aside.*] O, ho, I know the riddle.—I will go.
[*As they are going out, enter Edgar disguised.*]
Edgar: If e'er your Grace had speech with man so poor,
Hear me one word.
Albany: I'll overtake you.
[*Exeunt all but Albany and Edgar.*]
Speak. 40
Edgar: Before you fight the battle, ope this letter.
If you have victory, let the trumpet sound
For him that brought it. Wretched though I seem,
I can produce a champion that will prove
What is avouched there. If you miscarry, 45
Your business of the world hath so an end,
And machination ceases. Fortune love you!
Albany: Stay till I have read the letter.
Edgar: I was forbid it.
When time shall serve, let but the herald cry,
And I'll appear again. 50
Albany: Why, fare thee well. I will o'erlook thy paper.
[*Exit Edgar.*]
[*Enter Edmund.*]
Edmund: The enemy's in view; draw up your powers.
Here is the guess of their true strength and forces
By diligent discovery; but your haste
Is now urged on you.

55 *We will greet the time:* We will face the crisis promptly.

57-58 *jealous:* suspicious; *as the . . . adder:* just as those who are bitten by a snake are suspicious of it; i.e., both know only too well what has happened to them

62 *carry out my side:* successfully complete my plans

64 *countenance:* authority

69-70 *my state/ . . . debate:* My future demands that I act rather than think about these issues, weighing their pros and cons.

Albany: We will greet the time. [*Exit.*] 55
Edmund: To both these sisters have I sworn my love;
Each jealous of the other, as the stung
Are of the adder. Which of them shall I take?
Both? One? Or neither? Neither can be enjoyed
If both remain alive. To take the widow 60
Exasperates, makes mad her sister Goneril;
And hardly shall I carry out my side,
Her husband being alive. Now then, we'll use
His countenance for the battle, which being done,
Let her who would be rid of him devise 65
His speedy taking off. As for the mercy
Which he intends to Lear and to Cordelia,
The battle done, and they within our power,
Shall never see his pardon; for my state
Stands on me to defend, not to debate. [*Exit.*] 70

Act 5, Scene 1: Activities

1. Edmund could easily be a character in a modern television soap opera with his essential traits of greed, desire for power, and driving sexuality. Goneril likewise, as a seductress with nothing but adultery and property on her mind, could fit into a soap opera cast of characters. As one of the writers for the soap opera starring Edmund and Goneril, create an outline of a soap story for the two characters.

   Share your ideas in a group. Each group might present its story idea to a panel of judges.

   Develop and present the winning story entry to an audience.

2. As Albany, explain why you do not immediately read the letter Edgar has given you. How do you respond to the contents of the letter once you do read it? Write a short explanation of your behaviour and responses. Share your ideas with classmates.

3. Paraphrase Edmund's speech in lines 56–70. What are your feelings towards him when you read this soliloquy? Do you identify with any of the sentiments? Write a response to him and share it with others.

4. Write five questions you would like to ask one of Albany, Edmund, or Regan. Have one member of your group ask the questions and another, in the role of the character you are questioning, respond. Decide what additional information you have learned about the chosen character as a result of being able to interview him or her. Remember, the information must fit logically into the framework of the play and be consistent with the character.

For the next scene . . .

Imagine you were about to go into a risk-taking situation, such as driving in a bad snowstorm, writing an important exam, or fighting in physical warfare. What might you think about just before you entered the situation?

Act 5, Scene 2

In this scene . . .

Cordelia's army is on its way to confront the English forces. Edgar leaves Gloucester out of harm's way, but returns to report that the French have been defeated and both Lear and Cordelia have been captured. Gloucester must run for his life.

Stage direction – *Alarum:* alarm, a call on trumpets accompanied by drums, signifying that troops must press forward to the attack

2 *host:* shelter

5 *Away:* Leave this place.

6 *ta'en:* taken prisoner, captured

8 *rot:* die

9 *in ill thoughts:* in a despairing mood

11 *Ripeness:* readiness (for death)

Scene 2

A field between the two camps.

Alarum within. Enter, with Drum and Colours, Lear, Cordelia, and the Powers of France over the stage, and exeunt.
Enter Edgar and Gloucester.

Edgar: Here, father, take the shadow of this tree
For your good host. Pray that the right may thrive.
If ever I return to you again,
I'll bring you comfort.
Gloucester: Grace go with you, sir!
[*Exit Edgar.*]
[*Alarum and retreat within. Enter Edgar.*]
Edgar: Away, old man! Give me thy hand! Away! 5
King Lear hath lost, he and his daughter ta'en.
Give me thy hand! Come on!
Gloucester: No further, sir. A man may rot even here.
Edgar: What, in ill thoughts again? Men must endure
Their going hence, even as their coming hither; 10
Ripeness is all. Come on.
Gloucester: And that's true too. [*Exeunt.*]

Act 5, Scene 2: Activities

This is the shortest scene in the play. As a director, decide if you are justified in combining this scene with Act 5, Scene 1 or Act 5, Scene 3. Discuss your decision with a partner. What would you lose or gain by taking the course of action you have decided?

For the next scene . . .

Stories don't always end in the way we want; however, if you could end this story the way you wanted, how would you end it?

Act 5, Scene 3

In this scene . . .

Lear and Cordelia have been captured. They are brought before Edmund who sends them to prison under the charge of a captain with secret instructions to kill them both. Lear and Cordelia are reconciled. Lear is completely happy in the reunion and seems oblivious to everything else.

Albany appears with Goneril and Regan. He takes command, declaring Edmund a traitor. Regan claims power for Edmund, asserting that he is Cornwall's successor; Goneril, too, defends Edmund but argues that he has no need of Regan's protection. It becomes clear that Regan is, in fact, in no position to protect Edmund since she has been poisoned by Goneril. Albany challenges Edmund to defend his name in a duel, either against Albany himself or against any other knight who chooses to come forward.

In response to a herald's call for challengers, Edgar enters. Because he is wearing full armour, his identity is hidden. Edmund agrees to fight his unknown challenger and is mortally wounded. As Edmund lies dying, Albany confronts Goneril with her letter to her lover. Horrified by the turn of events, she rushes away.

Edgar reveals his identity and tells the court of Gloucester's death and Kent's loyalty to Lear. On the point of death, Edmund shows signs of remorse. A gentleman enters, bringing the news that Regan has died from her sister's poison and Goneril has stabbed herself.

As the bodies of the sisters are brought in, Kent arrives and reminds Albany of the prisoners, Lear and Cordelia. Edmund confesses the plot against them, but his confession comes too late. Lear arrives with Cordelia's body in his arms. Broken-hearted, Lear then dies.

The action draws to a close as Albany invites Edgar and Kent to rule the kingdom. Kent indicates that he also is dying and will not live to rule. Edgar ends the play with his contemplation that those who have lived longest have endured the most and that his generation "shall never see so much, nor live so long."

1-3 *Good guard . . . them:* Guard them strictly until the desires of those in command, who will pass judgement upon them, are known.

4 *meaning:* intention; *incurred:* suffered; *worst:* worst outcome

6 *else outfrown false fortune's frown:* otherwise overlook misfortune; i.e., fortune cannot cast me down

13 *gilded butterflies:* perhaps a reference to courtiers; *rogues:* vagabonds (the opposite of courtiers)

16-17 *And take . . . spies:* and pretend that we can solve all the mysteries of nature as if God had given us special powers of observation; *wear out:* outlast

18 *pacts and sects:* in groups and parties; i.e., parties at court

19 *That ebb . . . moon:* that change monthly

20 *sacrifices:* renunciation of the world; also the sacrifice Cordelia has made

22 *brand:* flame

23 *fire us hence like foxes:* part us as hunters part (or drive) foxes from their burrows with fire

24 *goodyears:* a strange word that has inspired much speculation. Lear means that some misfortune – probably disease or pestilence – will overtake those who try to hurt him and Cordelia again; *fell:* skin

Scene 3

The British camp, near Dover.

Enter, in conquest, with Drum and Colours, Edmund; Lear and Cordelia as prisoners; Soldiers, Captain.

Edmund: Some officers take them away. Good guard
Until their greater pleasures first be known
That are to censure them.
Cordelia: We are not the first
Who with best meaning have incurred the worst.
For thee, oppressed king, I am cast down; 5
Myself could else outfrown false Fortune's frown.
Shall we not see these daughters and these sisters?
Lear: No, no, no, no! Come, let's away to prison.
We two alone will sing like birds i' the cage.
When thou dost ask me blessing, I'll kneel down 10
And ask of thee forgiveness. So we'll live,
And pray, and sing, and tell old tales, and laugh
At gilded butterflies, and hear poor rogues
Talk of court news; and we'll talk with them too,
Who loses and who wins; who's in, who's out; 15
And take upon's the mystery of things,
As if we were God's spies; and we'll wear out,
In a walled prison, packs and sects of great ones
That ebb and flow by the moon.
Edmund: Take them away.
Lear: Upon such sacrifices, my Cordelia, 20
The gods themselves throw incense. Have I caught thee?
He that parts us shall bring a brand from heaven
And fire us hence like foxes. Wipe thine eyes.
The goodyears shall devour 'em, flesh and fell,

27 *hark:* Listen, pay attention

28 *note:* death warrant

31-32 *that men/ . . . is:* that men must act as the circumstances dictate; i.e., that they must act cruelly in time of war

33 *sword:* soldier active in war; *employment:* assignment

34 *bear question:* permit discussion

36 *About it:* Go to it, then! *write happy:* regard yourself as happy; i.e., consider yourself fortunate because I shall reward you; *th':* thou

37 *Mark:* note, observe

38 *set it down:* planned it (in the warrant he has given)

39 *I cannot . . . oats:* I'm not a horse – a beast of burden – but a man.

41 *valiant strain:* courageous lineage or descent

43 *opposites:* opponents, enemies

44 *I do . . . you:* I ask you to turn them over to me

45 *merits:* what they deserve

48 *retention:* detention, imprisonment; *guard:* where he can be kept and properly guarded

49-52 *Whose age . . . them:* whose age and whose royal rank attract the sympathy of the people and turn the conscripted forces, which we command, against us.

53 *My reason all the same:* for the same reason

54 *at further space:* at a later time

55-56 *session:* trial; *At this . . . bleed:* in this battle barely over, we are in no condition to judge this matter calmly

57-58 *And the . . . sharpness:* The best causes may be poorly judged by those who have been poorly affected by them, and whose emotions have not yet cooled

59-60 *The question . . . place:* Lear and Cordelia would not get a fair trial under the circumstances. Edmund is speaking hypocritically; *fitter:* more suitable

Ere they shall make us weep! We'll see 'em starved first. 25
Come. [*Exeunt Lear and Cordelia, guarded.*]

Edmund: Come hither, Captain; hark.
Take thou this note. [*Gives a paper.*] Go follow them to prison.
One step I have advanced thee; if thou dost
As this instructs thee, thou dost make thy way 30
To noble fortunes. Know thou this, that men
Are as the time is; to be tender-minded
Does not become a sword. Thy great employment
Will not bear question; either say thou'lt do't,
Or thrive by other means.

Captain: I'll do't, my lord. 35

Edmund: About it! And write happy when th' hast done.
Mark—I say, instantly; and carry it so
As I have set it down.

Captain: I cannot draw a cart, nor eat dried oats;
If it be man's work, I'll do't. [*Exit.*] 40

[*Flourish. Enter Albany, Goneril, Regan, Soldiers.*]

Albany: Sir, you have showed today your valiant strain,
And fortune led you well. You have the captives
Who were the opposites of this day's strife;
I do require them of you, so to use them
As we shall find their merits and our safety 45
May equally determine.

Edmund: Sir, I thought it fit
To send the old and miserable King
To some retention and appointed guard;
Whose age had charms in it, whose title more,
To pluck the common bosom on his side 50
And turn our impressed lances in our eyes
Which do command them. With him I sent the Queen,
My reason all the same; and they are ready
Tomorrow, or at further space, t' appear
Where you shall hold your session. At this time 55
We sweat and bleed: the friend hath lost his friend,
And the best quarrels, in the heat, are cursed
By those that feel their sharpness.
The question of Cordelia and her father
Requires a fitter place.

61 *subject:* subordinate

62 *brother:* equal; *That's as . . . him:* That is the manner in which we wish to regard him (i.e., as an equal).

65-67 *Bore the . . . brother:* acted as my deputy, and his present rank of general justifies his being considered your equal

67 *hot:* fast

68 *grace:* merit; *exalt himself:* become more powerful

69 *in your addition:* the titles and offices you have given him

70 *invested:* granted; *compeers:* equals

71 *were:* would be; *the most:* fully accomplished; *husband:* marry

72 *Jesters do oft prove prophets:* Many a true word is spoken in jest; *Holla, holla:* Hello, hello!

73 *asquint:* cross-eyed

75 *From a full-flowing stomach:* with a flood of anger

76 *patrimony:* inheritance from my father

77 *the walls are thine:* You have gained victory by overcoming the outer defences.

80 *The let-alone . . . will:* The prevention is not within your power.

81 *Half-blooded fellow:* bastard

82 *prove:* by trial of combat

84 *On capital treason:* on the charge of high treason; *attaint:* infection

85 *This gilded serpent:* Goneril beautiful, but venemous; *sister:* sister-in-law, i.e., Regan

87 *sub-contracted:* already betrothed, bound by a contract

88 *contradict your banes:* protest against the announcement of your marriage to him; *banes:* banns, the proclamations made in church to announce a forthcoming marriage. The announcements are made to provide an opportunity for anyone to give valid reasons against performing the marriage within the church.

90 *bespoke:* promised, engaged; *interlude:* little play, comedy

Albany: Sir, by your patience, 60
I hold you but a subject of this war,
Not as a brother.
Regan: That's as we list to grace him.
Methinks our pleasure might have been demanded
Ere you had spoke so far. He led our powers,
Bore the commission of my place and person, 65
The which immediacy may well stand up
And call itself your brother.
Goneril: Not so hot!
In his own grace he doth exalt himself
More than in your addition.
Regan: In my rights
By me invested, he compeers the best. 70
Goneril: That were the most if he should husband you.
Regan: Jesters do oft prove prophets.
Goneril: Holla, holla!
That eye that told you so looked but asquint.
Regan: Lady, I am not well; else I should answer
From a full-flowing stomach. General, 75
Take thou my soldiers, prisoners, patrimony;
Dispose of them, of me; the walls are thine.
Witness the world that I create thee here
My lord and master.
Goneril: Mean you to enjoy him?
Albany: The let-alone lies not in your good will. 80
Edmund: Nor in thine, lord.
Albany: Half-blooded fellow, yes.
Regan: [*To Edmund.*] Let the drum strike, and prove my title thine.
Albany: Stay yet; hear reason. Edmund, I arrest thee
On capital treason; and, in thine attaint,
This gilded serpent. [*Points to Goneril.*] For your claim, fair sister, 85
I bar it in the interest of my wife.
'Tis she is sub-contracted to this lord,
And I, her husband, contradict your banes.
If you will marry, make your loves to me;
My lady is bespoke.
Goneril: An interlude! 90

91 *armed:* in full armour. Edmund has just come from battle; *Let the trumpet sound:* See Act 5, Scene 1, line 42.

92 *prove:* See line 82.

93 *heinous:* villainous, monstrous

94 *pledge:* to do battle; *make it on thy heart:* I'll prove the truth of my allegation by trying to take your life.

95 *Ere I taste bread:* before I eat again; *thou art:* that you are

96 *Sick, O, sick:* I am very sick.

97 *medicine:* poison. Goneril has poisoned her sister.

98 *exchange:* signifying that Edmund has accepted the challenge

99 *he lies:* This was by convention a direct challenge to mortal combat. It was called the "lie direct."

101 *On him . . . not:* on anybody at all

103 *A herald . . . herald:* They call for an official to organize their duel and make the necessary announcements.

104 *thy single virtue:* your unaided courage

105 *levied:* recruited

106 *Took:* taken

111 *of quality or degree:* of rank and social standing

112 *lists:* list of names, catalogue of soldiers

113-114 *manifold/traitor:* a traitor without equal, has all the attributes of a traitor

Stage direction – *Enter Edgar, armed:* Edgar wears full armour. His face is concealed by a closed helmet; *a Trumpet before him:* a trumpeter ahead of him. Trumpets were part of the formal procedure of duels among knights.

118 *purposes:* intentions

120 *quality?:* rank

Albany: Thou art armed, Gloucester. Let the trumpet sound.
If none appear to prove upon thy person
Thy heinous, manifest, and many treasons,
There is my pledge! [*Throws down a glove.*] I'll make it on thy heart,
Ere I taste bread, thou art in nothing less 95
Than I have here proclaimed thee.
Regan: Sick, O, sick!
Goneril: [*Aside.*] If not, I'll ne'er trust medicine.
Edmund: There's my exchange. [*Throws down a glove.*] What in the world he is
That names me traitor, villain-like he lies.
Call by thy trumpet. He that dares approach, 100
On him, on you, who not? I will maintain
My truth and honour firmly.
Albany: A herald, ho!
Edmund: A herald, ho, a herald!
Albany: Trust to thy single virtue; for thy soldiers,
All levied in my name, have in my name 105
Took their discharge.
Regan: My sickness grows upon me.
Albany: She is not well. Convey her to my tent.
[*Exit Regan, led.*]
[*Enter a Herald.*]
Come hither, herald. Let the trumpet sound,
And read out this.
Captain: Sound, trumpet! [*A trumpet sounds.*] 110
Herald: [*Reads.*] "If any man of quality or degree within the lists of the army will maintain upon Edmund, supposed Earl of Gloucester, that he is a manifold traitor, let him appear by the third sound of the trumpet. He is bold in his defense." [*First trumpet.*] 115
Herald: Again! [*Second trumpet.*]
Herald: Again! [*Third trumpet.*]
[*Trumpet answers within.*]
[*Enter Edgar, armed, a Trumpet before him.*]
Albany: Ask him his purposes, why he appears
Upon this call o' the trumpet.
Herald: What are you?
Your name, your quality? And why you answer 120

122 *By treason's . . . canker-bit:* by the caterpillar, treason

124 *cope:* meet, encounter

127 *That:* so that

128 *arm:* weapon and insignia embossed on a knight's shield; *mine:* Edgar stretches out his right hand, having drawn his sword.

129-130 *Behold, it . . . profession:* It is the privilege of my knighthood to draw my sword. I do this to challenge a traitor and it is my privilege as a knight to have my challenge answered.

131 *Maugre:* in spite of; *place:* high command; *eminence:* status

132 *victor sword:* victory in the recent battle; *fire-new fortune;* completely new (recently forged) wealthy and power

136 *extremest upward:* topmost part

137 *descent:* lowest part of the body

138 *toad-spotted:* covered with the poisonous marks of treason as a toad is covered with warts; *Say:* if you say

139 *spirits:* courage; *bent:* directed

141 *liest:* See line 99; *name:* Edmund would not be obliged under the rules of combat to accept the challenge of one who was not a gentleman.

143 *say:* indication, proof

144 *safe and nicely:* cautiously, with precise, legal justification; *delay:* postpone

145 *spurn:* cast aside, ignore

147 *the hell-hated lie:* the lie (of high treason), hated even in hell, or hated as hell is hated

148 *Which:* the treason; *for they . . . bruise:* since as yet they do not harm you (since the accusations which I give back to you merely bounce off you)

149-150 *This sword . . . ever:* This sword of mine will return (them) with more force upon your head, where they will remain forever.

151 *Save:* spare his life, do not kill him; *practice:* trickery

This present summons?
Edgar: Know my name is lost;
By treason's tooth bare-gnawn and canker-bit.
Yet am I noble as the adversary
I come to cope.
Albany: Which is that adversary?
Edgar: What's he that speaks for Edmund Earl of
Gloucester? 125
Edmund: Himself. What sayest thou to him?
Edgar: Draw thy
sword,
That, if my speech offend a noble heart,
Thy arm may do thee justice. Here is mine.
Behold, it is the privilege of mine honours,
My oath, and my profession. I protest, 130
Maugre thy strength, place, youth, and eminence,
Despite thy victor sword and fire-new fortune,
Thy valour and thy heart, thou art a traitor,
False to thy gods, thy brother, and thy father;
Conspirant 'gainst this high illustrious prince; 135
And from th' extremest upward of thy head
To the descent and dust beneath thy foot,
A most toad-spotted traitor. Say thou "no,"
This sword, this arm, and my best spirits are bent
To prove upon thy heart, whereto I speak, 140
Thou liest.
Edmund: In wisdom I should ask thy name;
But since thy outside looks so fair and warlike,
And that thy tongue some say of breeding breathes,
What safe and nicely I might well delay
By rule of knighthood, I disdain and spurn; 145
Back do I toss those treasons to thy head,
With the hell-hated lie o'erwhelm thy heart,
Which, for they yet glance by and scarcely bruise,
This sword of mine shall give them instant way
Where they shall rest for ever. Trumpets, speak! 150
[*Alarums. Fight. Edmund falls.*]
Albany: Save him, save him!
Goneril: This is mere practice,
Gloucester.

152-153 *By the . . . opposite:* See line 141; *opposite:* opponent

154 *cozened and beguiled:* deceived and fooled

155 *Hold, sir:* Just a moment; wait a minute

158-159 *Say if I do:* You say, if you like, whether I know the letter or not; *the laws . . . for't?:* The laws are mine to make, not yours (since I am the ruling sovereign). Who can bring me to trial? As sovereign, I am above the law.

160 *this paper?:* the letter

161 *desperate:* distraught, not in her right mind; *govern:* control, restrain

164-165 *But what . . . me?:* But who are you that has won this victory over me?

166 *charity:* forgiveness

167 *blood:* lineage, nobility

168 *more:* more noble in blood since Edmund, being illegitimate, is only half-noble

170 *The gods are just:* because they hate sin and wickedness; *pleasant:* pleasure-giving

172-173 *The dark . . . eyes:* the secret and sinful place where Edmund was conceived. Edgar suggests that the dark sin of adultery has earned Gloucester darkness (blindness). In other words, one is suitably punished for one's sins.

174 *The wheel . . . circle:* The Wheel of Fortune has made a complete revolution. Edmund began at the bottom, rose to the top, and now finds himself at the bottom again, as the goddess Fortune sat by and turned the wheel to which all mortals were said to cling. See Act 2, Scene 2, line 169.

175 *gait:* manner of walking, movement, posture; *prophesy:* suggest

178 *thee:* Edgar

181 *By nursing them:* by caring for them; *List:* listen to

By the law of arms thou wast not bound to answer
An unknown opposite. Thou art not vanquished,
But cozened and beguiled.
Albany: Shut your mouth, dame,
Or with this paper shall I stop it. [*Shows her her letter to Edmund.*]—[*To Edmund.*] Hold, sir. 155
[*To Goneril.*] Thou worse than any name, read thine own evil.
No tearing, lady! I perceive you know it.
Goneril: Say if I do—the laws are mine, not thine.
Who can arraign me for't?
Albany: Most monstrous! O!
Knowest thou this paper?
Goneril: Ask me not what I know. 160
[*Exit.*]
Albany: Go after her. She's desperate; govern her.
[*Exit an Officer.*]
Edmund: What you have charged me with, that have I done,
And more, much more. The time will bring it out.
'Tis past, and so am I. But what art thou
That hast this fortune on me? If thou'rt noble, 165
I do forgive thee.
Edgar: Let's exchange charity.
I am no less in blood than thou art, Edmund;
If more, the more th' hast wronged me.
My name is Edgar and thy father's son.
The gods are just, and of our pleasant vices 170
Make instruments to plague us.
The dark and vicious place where thee he got
Cost him his eyes.
Edmund: Th' hast spoken right; 'tis true.
The wheel is come full circle; I am here.
Albany: Methought thy very gait did prophesy 175
A royal nobleness. I must embrace thee.
Let sorrow split my heart if ever I
Did hate thee, or thy father!
Edgar: Worthy prince, I know't.
Albany: Where have you hid yourself?
How have you known the miseries of your father? 180
Edgar: By nursing them, my lord. List a brief tale;

183-187 *The bloody . . . rags:* The necessity of escaping the death warrant that came near to claiming me taught me to dress in a madman's rags; *O, our . . . once:* Life is so sweet that we choose to suffer death every hour rather than die at once and have it over!

187 *semblance:* dress, appearance

188 *habit:* clothing

189 *rings:* eye sockets

190 *precious stones:* eyes

193 *past:* ago

194 *success:* victory over Edmund

196 *pilgrimage:* the path I took (after being declared an outlaw); *flawed:* broken

197 *conflict:* the conflicting emotions of sadness at the suffering he had inflicted upon Edgar and the joy of knowing him to be a loving, faithful son

198-199 *'Twixt two . . . smilingly:* Gloucester has died from excessive emotion. Grief broke his heart and the sudden surge of happiness was too much for him.

202-207 *This would . . . extremity:* To describe even one more sorrow in detail would be to go beyond any limit (to go too far).

203 *dissolve:* melt into tears

208 *big in clamour:* loud in my grief

209 *estate:* condition

210 *abhorred:* detestable

211 *endured:* suffered

213 *As:* as if; *him:* himself

215 *recounting:* telling

216-217 *puissant:* overwhelming, powerful, mighty; *strings of . . . crack:* threads of life which kept him alive, began to break. Kent has had a heart attack and is near to death.

217 *Twice then the trumpets sounded:* signalling the battle

218 *tranced:* in a trance, unconscious

And when 'tis told, O that my heart would burst!
The bloody proclamation to escape
That followed me so near (O, our lives' sweetness!
That we the pain of death would hourly die 185
Rather than die at once!) taught me to shift
Into a madman's rags, t' assume a semblance
That very dogs disdained; and in this habit
Met I my father with his bleeding rings,
Their precious stones new lost; became his guide, 190
Let him, begged for him, saved him from despair;
Never (O fault!) revealed myself unto him
Until some half hour past, when I was armed;
Not sure, though hoping of this good success,
I asked his blessing, and from first to last 195
Told him my pilgrimage. But his flawed heart
(Alack, too weak the conflict to support!)
'Twixt two extremes of passion, joy and grief,
Burst smilingly.

Edmund: This speech of yours hath moved me,
And shall perchance do good; but speak you on; 200
You look as you had something more to say.

Albany: If there be more, more woeful, hold it in;
For I am almost ready to dissolve,
Hearing of this.

Edgar: This would have seemed a period
To such as love not sorrow; but another, 205
To amplify too much, would make much more,
And top extremity.
Whilst I was big in clamour, came there a man,
Who, having seen me in my worst estate,
Shunned my abhorred society; but then, finding 210
Who 'twas that so endured, with his strong arms
He fastened on my neck, and bellowed out
As he'd burst heaven; threw him on my father;
Told the most piteous tale of Lear and him
That ever ear received; which in recounting 215
His grief grew puissant, and the strings of life
Began to crack. Twice then the trumpets sounded,
And there I left him tranced.

Albany: But who was this?

220-221 *enemy king:* hostile king, the king who declared him an enemy; *service/Improper for a slave:* the lowest and most menial duties, those necessary to care for an old and helpless man

Stage direction – *Gentleman:* member of the court circle, fit company for a king

228 *contracted:* engaged to be married; betrothed

229 *marry:* unite, are united

230 *be they alive or dead:* whether they are alive or dead

232 *Touches us not with pity:* does not cause us to feel pity; *is this he?:* Is it you, Kent?

233 *compliment:* ceremony

234 *very manners:* ordinary politeness

235 *aye:* forever

236 *Great thing of us forgot:* I forgot about this; *of us:* by us

238 *object:* spectacle, sight

239 *Yet Edmund was beloved:* Two women died for his love: a triumph of sorts.

245 *writ:* written order

246 *on the life of:* to take the life of

Edgar: Kent, sir, the banished Kent; who in disguise
Followed his enemy king and did him service 220
Improper for a slave.
[*Enter a Gentleman with a bloody knife.*]
Gentleman: Help, help! O, help!
Edgar: What kind of help?
Albany: Speak,
man.
Edgar: What means this bloody knife?
Gentleman: 'Tis hot, it smokes.
It came even from the heart of—O, she's dead!
Albany: Who dead? Speak, man. 225
Gentleman: Your lady, sir, your lady! And her sister
By her is poisoned; she hath confessed it.
Edmund: I was contracted to them both. All three
Now marry in an instant.
Edgar: Here comes Kent.
[*Enter Kent.*]
Albany: Produce the bodies, be they alive or dead. 230
[*Exit Gentleman.*]
This judgement of the heavens, that makes us tremble,
Touches us not with pity. [*To Kent.*] O, is this he?
The time will not allow the compliment
Which very manners urges.
Kent: I am come
To bid my king and master aye good night. 235
Is he not here?
Albany: Great thing of us forgot!
Speak, Edmund, where's the King? And where's Cordelia?
[*The bodies of Goneril and Regan are brought in.*]
Seest thou this object, Kent?
Kent: Alack, why thus?
Edmund: Yet Edmund was beloved.
The one the other poisoned for my sake, 240
And after slew herself.
Albany: Even so. Cover their faces.
Edmund: I pant for life. Some good I mean to do,
Despite of mine own nature. Quickly send
(Be brief in't) to the castle; for my writ 245
Is on the life of Lear and on Cordelia.

248 *office?:* duty, assignment

249 *token of reprieve:* sign of pardon

251 *for thy life:* as if your life depended on it

255 *fordid:* destroyed, killed

256 *hence:* away from this place

257 *men of stones:* men incapable of feeling

258 *eyes:* for seeing and for weeping

259 *vault:* wide arch of heaven, sky

261 *a looking glass:* a mirror

262 *stone:* the mirror (of crystal or polished stone)

263 *the promised end?:* the Last Judgment, the end of the world. Is it to this that all things lead?

264 *Or image of that horror?:* or the exact likeness of that day; *Fall and cease:* Let the heavens fall and let there be an end to everything.

268 *Prithee away:* Lear does not at first recognize Kent.

Nay, send in time.
Albany: Run, run, O, run!
Edgar: To who, my lord? Who has the office? Send
Thy token of reprieve.
Edmund: Well thought on. Take my sword; 250
Give it the Captain.
Edgar: Haste thee for thy life.
[*Exit an Officer.*]
Edmund: He hath commission from thy wife and me
To hang Cordelia in the prison and
To lay the blame upon her own despair
That she fordid herself. 255
Albany: The gods defend her! Bear him hence awhile.
[*Edmund is borne off.*]
[*Enter Lear, with the dead Cordelia in his arms, Captain and others following.*]
Lear: Howl, howl, howl! O, you are men of stones.
Had I your tongues and eyes, I'd use them so
That heaven's vault should crack. She's gone for ever!
I know when one is dead, and when one lives. 260
She's dead as earth. Lend me a looking glass.
If that her breath will mist or stain the stone,
Why, then she lives.
Kent: Is this the promised end?
Edgar: Or image of that horror?
Albany: Fall and cease!
Lear: This feather stirs; she lives! If it be so, 265
It is a chance which does redeem all sorrows
That ever I have felt.
Kent: O my good master!
Lear: Prithee away!
Edgar: 'Tis noble Kent, your friend.
Lear: A plague upon you, murderers, traitors all!
I might have saved her; now she's gone for ever! 270
Cordelia, Cordelia! Stay a little. Ha!
What is't thou sayest? Her voice was ever soft,
Gentle, and low—an excellent thing in woman.
I killed the slave that was a-hanging thee.
Captain: 'Tis true, my lords, he did.
Lear: Did I not, fellow? 275

276 *biting falchion:* sharp sword, light sword with point bent slightly inwards

278 *crosses:* troubles; *spoil me:* weaken me as a swordsman

279 *I'll tell you straight:* I'll recognize you in a moment.

280-281 *If fortune . . . behold:* If destiny ever had two men whom she raised to their heights of favour and dashed to the depths of misery, Lear is certainly one of them.

282 *This is a dull sight:* I can't see clearly; or, this is a sad spectacle.

283 *Caius?:* apparently the name used by Kent when he was disguised

285 *strike:* as in "a blow"

287 *I'll see that straight:* I'll understand that in a moment.

288 *from your . . . decay:* from the beginning of your change in fortunes and their decline

291 *fordone:* destroyed

292 *desperately:* in a state of despair

294 *bootless:* useless

295 *a trifle:* of no importance here, where the tragedy of Lear and Cordelia is greater

297 *decay:* the tragic decline of Lear

298-300 *applied:* used, employed; *For us . . . power:* Albany is ruler because Cornwall, Goneril, and Regan are dead. However, he resigns his office for the short time that Lear has to live so that Lear may die as king; *you to your rights:* The words "We will restore" are understood before "you."

301 *With boot, and such addition:* with such additional titles and rights; *honours:* brave deeds

305 *fool:* Cordelia. "Fool" was a term of endearment. Some scholars believe that, since the Fool made Lear face absolute truthfulness, and since Cordelia also stood for utter truthfulness, the two have become as one in Lear's mind.

I have seen the day, with my good biting falchion
I would have made 'em skip. I am old now,
And these same crosses spoil me. Who are you?
Mine eyes are not o' the best, I'll tell you straight.
Kent: If fortune brag of two she loved and hated, 280
One of them we behold.
Lear: This is a dull sight. Are you not Kent?
Kent: The same;
Your servant Kent. Where is your servant Caius?
Lear: He's a good fellow, I can tell you that.
He'll strike, and quickly too. He's dead and rotten. 285
Kent: No, my good lord; I am the very man—
Lear: I'll see that straight.
Kent: That from your first of difference and decay
Have followed your sad steps.
Lear: You are welcome hither.
Kent: Nor no man else! All's cheerless, dark, and deadly. 290
Your eldest daughters have fordone themselves,
And desperately are dead.
Lear: Ay, so I think.
Albany: He knows not what he says; and vain is it
That we present us to him.
Edgar: Very bootless.
[*Enter a Captain.*]
Captain: Edmund is dead, my lord.
Albany: That's but a trifle here. 295
You lords and noble friends, know our intent.
What comfort to this great decay may come
Shall be applied. For us, we will resign,
During the life of this old Majesty,
To him our absolute power; [*To Edgar and Kent.*] you
to your rights; 300
With boot, and such addition as your honours
Have more than merited. All friends shall taste
The wages of their virtue, and all foes
The cup of their deservings.—O, see, see!
Lear: And my poor fool is hanged! No, no, no life! 305
Why should a dog, a horse, a rat, have life,
And thou no breath at all? Thou'lt come no more,
Never, never, never, never, never!

309 *Pray you . . . sir:* Lear feels the suffocation preceding his death, but thinks that his clothing restricts his breathing.

310 *Do you . . . lips:* Some scholars suggest that Lear dies of joy, believing Cordelia to be alive. Lear is trying to believe that the terrible finality of Cordelia's death is impossible.

312 *Break, heart; I prithee break:* Kent may be speaking of his own heart, but more probably he is beginning a prayer, continued in his next speech for mercy on Lear; *prithee:* I pray, I beg you.

313 *ghost:* departing spirit

314 *rack:* instrument of torture that stretched a victim's joints until dislocation took place

315 *longer:* both for a longer time and with his body stretched further by the track

317 *usurped:* wrongly held possession of, lived beyond his rightful span of life

320 *gored:* wounded, war-ravanged; *sustain:* maintain, support

321-322 *I have . . . no:* Kent evidently feels that after Lear's death little is left in life, and that he must prepare for his own death; *calls me:* to follow him (Lear) into the darkness

323 *weight:* sorrow

323-326 *The weight . . . long:* In some versions of the play, these lines are given to Albany. Some critics believe it is right for the older man to speak the epilogue; others believe that the reference to "we that are young" indicates the lines were meant to be spoken by Edgar.

325 *oldest:* Lear and Gloucester

Pray you undo this button. Thank you, sir.
Do you see this? Look on her! Look! Her lips! 310
Look there, look there! [*He dies.*]
Edgar: He faints! My lord, my lord!
Kent: Break, heart; I prithee break!
Edgar: Look up, my lord.
Kent: Vex not his ghost. O, let him pass! He hates him
That would upon the rack of this tough world
Stretch him out longer.
Edgar: He is gone indeed. 315
Kent: The wonder is, he hath endured so long.
He but usurped his life.
Albany: Bear them from hence. Our present business
Is general woe. [*To Kent and Edgar.*] Friends of my soul, you twain
Rule in this realm, and the gored state sustain. 320
Kent: I have a journey, sir, shortly to go.
My master calls me; I must not say no.
Edgar: The weight of this sad time we must obey,
Speak what we feel, not what we ought to say.
The oldest hath borne most; we that are young 325
Shall never see so much, nor live so long.
[*Exeunt with a dead march.*]

Act 5, Scene 3: Activities

1. Suppose you are a reporter for a major newspaper. Write the report you would send back to your newspaper based on the events that occur in Act 5. Remember, you will probably be limited by space so you may have to be selective. Remember too that a good reporter attempts to be objective, relating facts without personal comment. Before you write, gather and select your facts. Share your article with others in the class.

2. Reread the lines Lear speaks when he enters with Cordelia's body (lines 257–263). In groups, discuss to what extent you believe these lines to be a commentary on the action of the play as a whole. Remember to consider Lear's comments at various places in the play. As an observer of a performance of the play for the first time, write a letter to a friend, or a note in your journal, recording your reactions to these lines.

3. Lear's final speech (lines 305–311) frequently puzzles directors because it is not clear whether Lear dies happily or in misery. In groups, discuss how you would interpret the speech in light of what has happened in the play. Prepare a careful reading of it and present it to a partner or to the class. You have succeeded when your audience clearly recognizes your intent.

4. Do you think it is necessary for both Lear and Cordelia to die? In groups, discuss what alternative endings might be possible and how they might affect the outcome of the play. Share your ideas with the members of other groups.

5. Throughout most of the play, Edmund seems to know exactly what he wants and how to get it. It is only in this final scene that he seems willing to accept a different kind of responsibility. What do you think causes this change in Edmund? Make a note of your ideas and share them with a partner or members of your group.

6. An epitaph is an inscription on a tombstone that usually tells something about the personality of the deceased. In groups, select one character from the following list and write an epitaph for him or her: Edmund, Kent, King Lear, Cordelia, Goneril, or Regan. You may wish to research several epitaphs before you begin this activity. Share your epitaphs with the class. If you wish, you can draw and label your monument for display.

7. Imagine you are Edgar about to take over as the ruler of England. In your notes or your journal make a list of the things you feel must be done in order to restore peace and stability to the land, as well as to gain the support of the people. Share your list with others in your group.

Consider the Whole Play

1. There are many puzzling moments, incredible moments, and unexpected moments in this play. In a group, find the location in the play of as many of these as you can recall. In each case, discuss the extent to which you can or cannot accept them and explain why.

2. Lear and Gloucester have grounds to accuse young adults of being selfish and cruel. Young people, on the other hand, see a disparity between what their elders say and what they do. Looking at the play as a whole, make a list of Lear's and Gloucester's individual complaints against their children. Respond to this list as an appropriate young person in the play, giving the other side of the issue. What suggestions can you offer to both sides that might have made them understand each other better? What applications do your suggestions have beyond the play?

3. The words "nature," "nothing," and "fool" are constantly repeated in *King Lear*. In your group, select one of these words and trace where and how it is used throughout the play. What do you think the repetition of the word you have selected adds to the play? Present your findings to the class.

4. *King Lear* raises many general questions of a philosophical nature. Some of these questions are, "Why do bad things happen to good people?", "Are human beings governed by fate?" and "Are some people naturally evil?" In your group, brainstorm and make a list of as many of general, philosphical questions as you can. Select one that seems particularly interesting and, as a group, explore all its possibilities. Before deciding on an answer, be sure to consider all possible objections, using *King Lear* as a resource, and reply carefully to those questions you have raised.

5. With your group, select one scene or a segment of a scene in the play and convey dramatically the important information it contains. You might do this in one of the following ways:
   - by telling the story in the role from one character's point of view;
   - by using movement only;
   - by creating a story theatre, using narration, dialogue, and movement;
   - by creating an improvisation;
   - by rewriting it and presenting it as reader's theatre (see Act 1, Scene 3, Activities, page 44.)

6. With the entire class, simulate a courtroom trial using lawyers for the defence and the prosecution, a judge, a jury, a court clerk, and witnesses. Try King Lear for tearing apart his kingdom and causing the death of his daughter.

   In order to keep your trial orderly and meaningful, keep the following guidelines in mind:
   - The court clerk is the person who makes all announcements and swears in all witnesses.
   - The accused is presumed innocent until proven guilty.
   - The prosecution must establish guilt beyond any shadow of doubt.
   - The jury acts on the facts presented, and members of the jury can ask for clarification on points at any time during the trial.
   - The judge sustains or overrules objections from the prosecuting and defence attorneys and generally keeps order in the proceedings.
   - The judge determines the sentence after the jury has reached a verdict.

7. With your group, create a tableau to show the relationships among all the characters in the play. Have each member of your group, in role, explain to the class who he or she is and why he or she chose this character.

Alternatively, retell the story of *King Lear* through five tableaux – one from each act. Imagine that these tableaux are to be used as actual illustrations for the text. Explain why you have made the selections that you have and why you think they are significant to an understanding of the play.

8. With your group, choose one character in the play who you all agree would make an interesting subject for a case study. Have each person assume a different relationship to that character, such as a father, brother, sister, social worker, psychiatrist, or doctor. Have each of these people prepare and present an individual report on the character. As a group, create a single case study that takes these differing perspectives into account.

9. Select a character from the play and assume that he or she had been given one last opportunity to comment on his or her life. In your journal, record your character's recollection of events. Remember that, with the pressure of events, the character's memory may hide, distort, or embellish the reality of what actually happened. You may wish to share the recollection with other members of your group.

10. In groups, plan a video that conveys your feelings about King Lear in the last scene of the play. You may decide to shoot one complete sequence of the scene, or several brief segments from different places in the scene.

    Before you shoot, decide how you wish to portray King Lear:
    - What qualities do you wish to highlight?
    - What mood do you wish to establish?
    - How do you want your audience to respond?

    Remember to prepare a video script describing the kind of camera shot you want to use for each frame of your segment. Make sure that your beginning and ending have dramatic impact.

Share your video with your classmates to see how they respond.

11. John Keats recorded his reponse to *King Lear* in the following sonnet:

On Sitting Down to Read *King Lear* Once Again

O golden-tongued Romance with serene lute!
Fair pluméd Siren! Queen of far away!
Leave melodizing on this wintry day,
Shut up thine olden pages, and be mute:
Adieu! for once again the fierce dispute 5
Betwixt damnation and impassioned clay
Must I burn through; once more humbly assay
The bitter-sweet of this Shakespearean fruit.
Chief Poet! and ye clouds of Albion,
Begetters of our deep eternal theme, 10
When through the old oak forest I am gone,
Let me not wander in a barren dream,
But when I am consuméd in the fire,
Give me new Phoenix wings to fly at my desire.

John Keats (1818)

Keats interprets the essence of *King Lear* to be a "fierce dispute/Betwixt damnation and impassioned clay" that he, as a reader, must "burn through." Do you think that King Lear, either consciously or unconsciously, chose to "wander in a barren dream"? Write a response to Keats in a poem in which you support his point of view, disagree with him, or hold an entirely different perspective.

12. As a class, create an overview graph for the play. To do this, write all the characters' names down the left side of a large sheet of paper. List the numbers of each act and its scenes across the top of the page. Now form five groups. Each group should concentrate on only one act. Your task is to check off the scenes where each character appears on stage. When all the groups are

finished, you will have a master graph. From your graph, determine:

- who is on stage the most;
- who is on stage the least;
- who appears in every act;
- who is off stage more than on;
- if there is a balance of any sort.

13. Students often complain that literature is often too morbid and tragic. Nineteenth-century directors must have felt that way also because they frequently altered the ending of *King Lear* to make Lear and Cordelia live happily ever after. If you could speak to one of these directors, how would you respond to such a practice? Write your response as a letter, a journal entry, or a magazine article for a drama publication.

14. Throughout the play, King Lear tries to make other people do what he wants. He devotes about the same amount of time to these attempts in each act. Set up five groups, with each group being responsible for one act. Determine the methods that Lear employs to manipulate people and whether his approach changes between acts. What conclusions do you draw about Lear from his different attempts to influence others?

15. Often, the body language we all use when we speak conveys as much as what we say. In fact, many of us exhibit a habitual or defining gesture. With a group, select the characters from the play who you think would have pronounced gestures. Select three of these characters and pair each one in a conversation with a character. Present a brief interchange between one pair of characters, emphasizing the body language and gestures of the chosen character. Rehearse the scene several times, emphasizing words to complement the body language and gesture. Perform the conversation for classmates.

In a group, note the effect that body language, gesture, and word emphasis can have on the presentation of a character.

16. In his final speech, King Lear makes the comment, "And my poor fool is hanged!" (line 305). Many people interpret this to mean that the dying king links Cordelia and the Fool together because he has always regarded them both in the same way. What do you think? What ultimately happened to the Fool? Express your own convictions in a journal entry. Then discuss your thoughts with your group.

17. With a group, read the illustrated children's book *Moss Gown* by William H. Hooks (Clarion Books, New York, 1987). What, if any, features of this story are similar to events in *King Lear*?

    On your own, draft a children's story or legend that you might create from any aspect of *King Lear*. You may prefer to create a group story. Illustrate it and present it to an elementary school class. After your presentation, decide what alterations you might make to your story if you were to present it to another group of young children.